The European Community in World Politics

The European Community in World Politics

Edited by

Ole Nørgaard, Thomas Pedersen
and Nikolaj Petersen

Pinter Publishers
London and New York

*Distributed in the United States and Canada
by St. Martin's Press*

Pinter Publishers Ltd.
25 Floral Street, Covent Garden
London WC2E 9DS, United Kingdom

First published in 1993

Distributed exclusively in the USA and Canada by St. Martin's Press Inc., Room 400, 175 Fifth Avenue, New York, NY 10010, USA

British Library Cataloguing in Publication Data
A CIP record for this book is available from the British Library

ISBN 1 85567 147 6

Library of Congress Cataloging-in-Publication Data
The European Community in world politics / edited by Ole Nørgaard,
    Thomas Pedersen and Nikolaj Petersen.
        p.   cm.
    Includes bibliographical references and index.
    ISBN 1-85567-147-6
    1. European federation. 2. European cooperation. 3. European
Economic Community countries—Foreign relations. 4. European
Economic Community countries—Foreign economic relations.
I. Nørgaard, Ole. II. Pedersen, Thomas. III. Petersen, Nikolaj.
JN15.E824 1993
321' . 04 ' 094–dc20   93-5588
                                                  CIP

Set in Monotype Plantin by Ewan Smith, 48 Shacklewell Lane, London E8 2EY
Printed and bound in Great Britain by Biddles Ltd, Guildford and King's Lynn

Contents

List of Figures

List of Tables

Contributors

Knud Erik Jørgensen is Assistant Professor at the Institute of Political Science at Aarhus University. He has published works on Western responses to Soviet Policy under Gorbachev, anti-politics in Central Europe and issues of European security. His main research interests are Western European multilateralism and international relation theory.

Peter Nedergaard, has a Ph.D. in political science and a Ph.D. in business administration and is Assistant Professor at the Copenhagen Business School, Institute of International Economics and Management. He has published several books on European integration, among others *EF's markedsintegration. En politisk økonomisk analyse* (The Political Economy of EC Market Integration) and *EF's landbrugspolitik under omstilling* (Restructuring the EC Agricultural Policy).

Ole Nørgaard is Associate Professor at the Institute of Political Science at Aarhus University. Specializing in Comparative Politics and Eastern Europe, he is the author of numerous books and articles on the politics, economy and foreign relations of communist and post-communist systems.

Morten Ougaard, Dr.scient.pol., is Associate Professor at the Copenhagen Business School. He has published books and articles on international political economy, US hegemony, and US foreign policy. Recent publications include 'Dimensions of Hegemony', *Cooperation and Conflict*, vol. 23, 1988, pp. 197–214; 'The US State in the New Global Context', *Cooperation and Conflict*, vol. 27, 1992, pp. 131–162; and 'USAs hegemoni og den ny verdensorden', *Politica*, vol. 24, no. 2, 1992, pp. 132–150.

Jørgen Dige Pedersen is Associate Professor at the Institute of Political Science, Aarhus University. His research area is development studies and he has worked on South–South relations and national development strategies with special focus on India and Brazil.

Thomas Pedersen is Associate and Jean Monnet Professor at the Institute of Political Science, Aarhus University. In 1988 he was visiting scholar at the Royal Institute of International Affairs, London. Recent publications include 'Political Change in the European Community: The SEA as a Case of System Transformation', *Cooperation and Conflict* (vol. 27, no. 1, March 1992), and 'Maastricht-traktaten i føderalistisk belysning'

(The Maastricht-treaty in a Federalist Perspective), in Jon Bingen (ed.), *Europa etter Maastricht*, Oslo: Cappelen, 1992.

Nikolaj Petersen is Professor of International Relations at the Institute of Political Science, Aarhus University. He is Co-chairman of the Danish Commission for Security and Disarmament Affairs and Deputy Chairman of the Danish Institute of International Affairs. He has written numerous books and articles on foreign and security policy and European affairs.

Mette Skak is Associate Professor at the Institute of Political Science at Aarhus University, specializing in peace and conflict research. She is a member of the Danish Commision for Security and Disarmament Affairs. She is the author of books and articles on Soviet–Eastern European relations, post-communist foreign policy and post-communist regionalism as well as on the new post-Cold War East–West relationship.

Clemens Stubbe Østergaard is Associate Professor of Political Science and Co-director of the Center for East Asian Studies at Aarhus University. He has published a number of books and articles on East Asian politics and society, as well as on foreign policy.

Glossary

ACP	African, Caribbean and Pacific countries
ALA	Asia and Latin America
ASEAN	Association of South-East Asia Nations
CAP	Common Agricultural Policy
CECs	Central and Eastern European Countries
CFSP	Common Foreign and Security Policy
CIS	Commonwealth of Independent States
CMEA	Council of Mutual Economic Assistance
COPA	Comité des Organisations Professionelles Agricoles de la CEE
COREPER	Comité des Représentants Permanents de la CEE
CSCE	Conference on Security and Cooperation in Europe
EDC	European Defence Community
EEA	European Economic Area
EFTA	European Free Trade Association
EIB	European Investment Bank
EMU	Economic and Monetary Union
EPC	European Political Cooperation
FDI	Foreign direct investment
GATT	General Agreement on Tariffs and Trade
GSP	Generalized System of Preferences
IGC	Intergovernmental Conference
IIP	International Investment Partner Programme
IMF	International Monetary Fund
INF	Intermediate-range nuclear forces
MFA	Multifibre Arrangement
MFN	Most Favoured Nation
NAFTA	North American Free Trade Agreement
NIC	Newly Industrialized Country
NIEO	New International Economic Order
NIS	Newly Independent States
OECD	Organization for Economic Cooperation and Development
OEEC	Organization for European Economic Cooperation
PHARE	Poland and Hungary Aid for Economic Restructuring

QMV	Qualified Majority Voting
SEA	Single European Act
TACIS	Technical Assistance to the Commonwealth of Independent States
UNCED	United Nations Conference on Environment and Development
UNCTAD	United Nations Conference on Trade and Development
WEU	Western European Union

Preface

In response to a call from the Danish Social Science Research Council for research on European integration, a research group was established in late 1989 at the Institute of Political Science, Aarhus University, to study the external relationships of the European Community. The group was composed of EC and area specialists and was subsequently joined by two colleagues from the Copenhagen Business School. The chapters presented in this book are part of the end-product of the project, which has resulted in numerous conference papers, articles and monographs.

The group would like to thank the Danish Social Science Research Council, which has provided valuable financial support for the project. The chapters of this book were presented and discussed at a conference at Ry, Jutland, in January 1993, and we wish to thank the following participants for their valuable and constructive critiques: Professor Finn Laursen, Maastricht; Dr Christian Lequesne, Paris; Dr Boris Pichugin, Moscow; Dr John Pinder, London; Dr Elfriede Regelsberger, Bonn; Dr Reinhard Rode, Halle; and Dr Albrecht Rothacher, Vienna. Their comments did much to improve the quality of the book, although the authors and editors are, of course, responsible for whatever weaknesses remain.

Finally, the book would not have been possible without the qualified assistance of our research assistants, Marie Frasez, Annet-Tine Kristensen, and Esben Egede Rasmussen and our secretaries, Anne-Grethe Gammelgaard, Helle Jørgensen, Lisbeth Widahl, and especially Anette Riber who was responsible for the final preparation of the text. Dr Steven Sampson carried out the final editing of the manuscript.

Ole Nørgaard
Thomas Pedersen
Nikolaj Petersen   *Aarhus, March 1, 1993*

1

Introduction

OLE NØRGAARD, THOMAS PEDERSEN
AND NIKOLAJ PETERSEN

The 1980s have seen the steady expansion of the international role of the European Community (EC), both as a partner to other major actors in international economics and politics, and as an actor in its own right. The Single European Act (SEA) of 1985 and the Internal Market increased perceptions of Europe as an economic power to be reckoned with, the SEA constituting an important step in the development of a higher profile in international politics as well. Outside Europe, the Single European Market or 'Europe 1992' was a turning point which effectively did away with lingering impressions of 'eurosclerosis' and replaced these with fears of 'Fortress Europe' – of a strong, self-contained and self-reliant European political and economic bloc. These fears subsequently proved exaggerated or plainly false, but the image of Europe as a major economic power, and therefore an important political power, has remained, both among the EC's major partner-rivals – the United States and Japan – and among the developing countries. In Eastern Europe, the relaunching of the Community contrasted starkly with the miserable and ever worsening performance of Eastern Europe's own economic and political systems, thus adding to popular frustration and the delegitimation of their governments.

The 1989 revolutions provided a tremendous boost to the attractiveness of the Community. In the wake of the disintegration of the Soviet Empire, the newly liberated East European countries sought both political models and economic support in the rich and stable Western Europe, presenting the Community with expectations which it was only partly equipped to live up to. German unification presented another challenge by reviving the spectre of a powerful, unbound Germany, ready to exploit the gaping power vacuum opening on its eastern borders. The result was the Maastricht Treaty of February 1992, which attempted to increase the external actor capability of the Community as well as its internal efficiency.

At the same time the Community was presented with a major challenge by the Yugoslav War, a challenge which it clearly failed to deal with adequately. During 1992 the Maastricht Treaty ran into unexpected troubles as a result of its rejection in the Danish referendum in June. At the time of this writing (February 1993), the Treaty is still in the balance, and its demise (which could happen in the case of a second rejection by the Danish electorate followed by a British renegement) is still a possibility, though not the most likely outcome. Irrespective of the fate of the Treaty, the international role of the Community can still be expected to grow due to external changes such as continuing chaos in the East, mounting pressures from the South, and American concentration on internal affairs in the West.

The political science literature on the Community's external relations, already considerable, has been expanding in recent years concurrently with the expansion in the Community's international role. Yet the available literature on the subject contains a number of lacunae. Broadly speaking, the external relations of the Community can be analysed from an internal or an external perspective. One can focus attention on foreign policy-formulation within the Community or on its actual external relations. The studies undertaken so far have mainly focused on the former aspect. Some of these have concentrated on describing the institutions and procedures of European Political Cooperation (EPC) (e.g. Pijpers et al., 1988; Froment-Meurice and Ludlow, 1990). Others have dealt mainly with the causes of foreign policy cooperation among the Twelve (e.g. Hill, 1983; Holland, 1991) or with the historical evolution in foreign policy cooperation (Ifestos, 1987; de Schoutheete, 1986; Nuttall, 1992).

The most interesting studies combine an internal and external perspective, focusing on the policy output of EPC or assessing the international impact of the Community's foreign policy activity. These include case studies of EPC activity in specific areas (e.g. Holland, 1988) and fruitful attempts to generalize about the foreign activity of the EC member states (Ginsberg, 1989; Allen and Smith, 1990, 1992). Allen and Smith deserve particular credit for their pioneering theoretical study (1990) of the impact of a politically more cohesive Europe on international politics.

Few studies have looked into the Community's complex network of external relations, and those which have done so have either had a specific focus or been highly empirical. The study by Regelsberger and Edwards (1990), though highly valuable, adopts an inter-regional perspective, leaving out relations with Japan and the United States. The recent book by Redmond (1992) is more comprehensive in terms of geographical reach but somewhat disappointing in its neglect of theoretical interpretation. This brings us to the final and perhaps most serious lacuna in political science writings on the external relations of the Community: the scarcity of theory. Holland (1991), himself one of the few analysts who have tried to elevate the theoretical level in EPC studies, rightly points out that '... EPC has been poorly served by theory'. Apart from Holland's work and the rather unwieldy study by Ifestos (1987), the one major theoretically based examination of foreign policy cooperation in the Community is Ginsberg's stimulating book *Foreign Policy Actions of the European Community* (1989).

The present volume combines an internal and external perspective, emphasizing the interface between external relations and internal developments in European integration. The major part of the book, however, is reserved for in-depth empirical analyses of the Community's relations with its European periphery, as well as with its global partners and rivals. Stressing the interplay between economics and politics, these studies examine the external effects of internal Community measures as well as the Community's responses to structural changes in the European and international system. One of the theoretical ambitions of the book is to assess the validity of Philippe Schmitter's theory of externalization (Schmitter, 1969) which is also applied by Ginsberg. Another objective is to shed light on the functioning of the Common Commercial Policy and the dynamics behind the creation of a Common Foreign and Security Policy and its potential in the light of geographical widening. The book also tries to assess briefly the extent to which the Community can be said to be evolving into an international actor, assuming that the Maastricht Treaty is approved.

This book is divided into three parts, each with specialized analyses. Part One focuses upon the Community as an international actor, both in foreign policy and trade policy. In Chapter 2, Nikolaj Petersen analyses the making of the Common Foreign and Security Policy element of the Maastricht Treaty in order to evaluate whether it represents a qualitative change in the European Political Cooperation (EPC) as codified in the Single European Act. He finds that by expanding the scope of the European Union's foreign and security policy, by increasing its depth of commitment, and by moving its model for decision-making towards the 'Community method', the Maastricht Treaty entails a qualitative change and provides the potential for a higher foreign and security policy profile for the Union. The chapter also analyses the background of this development, concluding that the national governments and their perceived interests were the main dynamics behind the change, together with changes in the EC's external environment.

In Chapter 3 on common foreign and security policy and enlargement, Thomas Pedersen examines how enlargement can be expected to affect the overall constitutional development of the European Union and particularly its 'actor capability' in world politics. The chapter focuses on the impact of enlargement on internal EC developments, and on the consequences of admitting the neutral EFTA countries as union members. Thomas Pedersen argues that there is growing pressure for the adoption of a more flexible integration model. The most likely scenario for most applicants remains full membership but a worst case scenario may push the EC towards a variable cooperation model in order to set up effective defence structures in the new Europe. Pedersen argues that in the foreign policy and security area cohesion can be safeguarded by means of a combination of pragmatic adjustment and system transformation. In the defence sphere, subsystem formation is a more realistic approach.

In Chapter 4, Peter Nedergaard discusses the trade policies of the Community from a political economy perspective. He raises the question of whether changes in the EC's trade policies in the 1990s stem from the influence of special interests or from overriding political concerns about the New World Order. His answer to this question is rather pessimistic, as he finds that the concern is expressed primarily at the rhetorical level, while genuine changes in foreign trade stem from the pressure of special interests. Nedergaard predicts that the impact of these interests will increase as integration proceeds and that it could therefore lead to higher levels of protectionism.

Part Two concentrates on relations between the Community and Central and Eastern Europe and the Ex-Soviet Union. In Chapter 5 Knud Erik Jørgensen summarizes the Community's new policy towards the East, concentrating on policy towards the Balkans, and in particular the case of the Yugoslav war. He suggests that Western European disagreement has hampered a successful involvement, but that the role of the EC has not been entirely negative. Jørgensen also focuses on the problem of conditionality and on the conflicting aims of successful economic and political reforms and stability. He argues that EC efforts to prevent further instability have led to the development of a somewhat restrained conditionality.

In Chapter 6 on relations between the EC and the ex-Soviet states, Ole Nørgaard argues that the present European orientation of Russia is solidly based in social and political structures. He examines the prospects for trade with, investment in and aid to the ex-Soviet states, basing his analysis on the foreign trade potentials of the individual states in conjunction with their prospects for a successful transition to a full market economy. Nørgaard's analysis indicates that Russia is the only ex-Soviet state which scores reasonably on all dimensions and which in the medium-term perspective can be seen as a significant economic partner for the EC. He argues that to prevent further economic decline and threats of military conflicts, CIS market access to Western Europe should be widened and the EC should use its political and institutional resources to mediate in conflicts between the ex-Soviet states. Economic aid should focus on institution building and provide access to the West for those elites which support the European orientation of the new states.

Mette Skak, in Chapter 7, explores the background of the EC policy of the so-called Visegrad countries: Hungary, Poland and the former Czecho-slovakia. Distinguishing between structural and political factors, she finds that amidst domestic political turmoil and economic recession factors such as the collapse of trade with the Soviet Union, the EC market as an export option and the attraction of community integration are major reasons for the attraction of the EC for these countries. At the political level, she finds a double quest for national pride and international integration. She also observes that the turmoil surrounding the Maastricht Treaty and the limi-tation on market access in the Europe Agreements has mobilized a critical reflection in the Visegrad countries, but so far without challenging the basic orientation towards the EC.

The chapters in Part Three move outside Europe, to the Community's relationship with the United States, Japan and the developing world.

In Chapter 8 Jørgen Dige Pedersen describes relations between the EC and the developing countries as an example of asymmetrical interdepend-ence. He asserts that this asymmetry will persist, but that the nature of interdependence will change. Using the cases of India and Brazil, Pedersen traces a growing globalization of the EC's policy towards the developing countries. The impetus for this development is the greater capacity of the Community stemming from its strengthened economic and political inte-gration. Pedersen concludes that Community policy is characterized by an increasing commercialisation of relations with the developing countries and that the winners and losers will be determined by the 'attractiveness' of the countries to the EC in economic and political terms.

Clemens Stubbe Østergaard's contribution (Chapter 9) focuses on the interplay between external Japan-related forces and the EC's internal integration process since 1989. Seeing integration as the result of elite bargaining, which is itself a reflection of structural changes in the international system, Østergaard argues that changes in the international system caused partially by Japanese behaviour have been an important impulse behind the drive towards European integration. Finally, Østergaard examines the EC's political links with Japan and concludes that the Japanese response to the Single Market Process has been a further catalyst behind EC–Japanese integration.

Chapter 10, written by Morten Ougaard, examines the response of the Bush Administration to the European integration process. He portrays the Bush Administration's policy as being a consistent pursuit of national interests in terms of wealth and power. The US has accepted the internal market and the prospect of the Economic and Monetary Union, while it has opposed protectionism and macro-economic policies that have been to the detriment of American interests. The Bush Administration has been opposed to a separate European military structure outside the NATO framework. Future conflicts between the US and the Community are most likely in the area of defence policy, where the US is troubled by the prospects of West European political decisions that might jeopardize the present institutional structures of the Atlantic relationship.

The book concludes with some theoretical remarks on the Community as an international actor.

References

Allen, D. and M. Smith (1990) 'Western Europe's Presence in the Contemporary International Arena', *Review of International Studies*, no. 16, pp. 19–37.

Froment-Meurice, H. and P. Ludlow (1990) 'Towards a European Foreign Policy', in *Governing Europe*, Brussels: CEPS Paper.

Ginsberg, Roy (1989) *Foreign Policy Actions of the European Community. The Politics of Scale*, Boulder: Lynne Rienner Publishers.

Hill, Christopher (ed.) (1983) *National Foreign Policies and European Political Cooperation*, London: George Allen & Unwin.

Holland, Martin (1988) *The European Community and Southern Africa*, London: Pinter.

Holland, Martin (1991) *The Future of European Political Cooperation*, London: Macmillan.

Ifestos, P. (1987) *European Political Cooperation. Towards a Framework of Supranational Diplomacy?*, Aldershot: Gower.

Nuttall, Simon (1992) *European Political Cooperation*, Oxford: Clarendon.

Pijpers A., E. Regelsberger, W. Wessels and G. Edwards (1988) *European Political Cooperation*, Dordrecht: Martinus Nijhoff Publishers.

Redmond, John (ed.) (1992) *The External Relations of the European Community*, London: Macmillan/St. Martin's Press.

Regelsberger, E. and G. Edwards (eds) (1990) *Europe's Global Links*, London: Pinter.

Schmitter, Philippe (1969) 'Three Neo-Functional Hypotheses about International Integration', *International Organization*, no. 23, pp. 161–66.

de Schoutheete, P. (1986) *La Cooperation Politique Européenne*, Brussels: Edition Labor.

PART ONE

The European Union and Foreign and Security Policy

NIKOLAJ PETERSEN

Introduction

From its inception, the European Community (EC) has been a polity *sui generis*, more easy to define in negative than in positive terms. It is more than an international organization and more than a regime, and despite important confederal traits it is also more than a confederation. On the other hand, the EC is less than a federation, though it has important federal features. And the concept of 'union', which is presently in vogue (Pinder, 1991) is both politically and analytically undefined.

This being so, the Community's external relationships are not easily covered by traditional notions of foreign policy (Rummel, 1982; Edwards and Regelsberger, 1990). The problem is compounded by the fact that the so-called external relations of the Community, e.g. tariff and trade policy, are regulated by the Rome Treaty and fully within the Community's competence, while foreign and security policy proper are dealt with in a predominantly intergovernmental mode. The latter policy areas are the focus of the present chapter, while the external relations are excluded from the analysis.

The foreign and security policy of the Community can be analysed from three perspectives: (1) as an extra dimension to the foreign policies of the twelve member states; (2) as a separate, discrete policy parallel to national foreign and security policies, i.e. as a thirteenth West European foreign policy, and (3) as an independent expression of the Community's foreign and security policy identity, which in some respects is superior to the national policies. The latter perspective is used for this analysis of the Common Foreign and Security Policy (CFSP) inscribed in the Maastricht Treaty on European Union. The question to be answered is whether the CFSP represents a qualitative change compared to European Political Cooperation (EPC). As a qualitative change in foreign and security policy is crucial to the development of European integration, the analysis focuses on an important element of what Lindberg and Scheingold term 'systems transformation':

> Systems transformation means an extension of specific or general obligations that are beyond the bounds of the original treaty commitments, either geographically

or functionally. It typically entails a major change in the scope of the Community or in its institutions, that often requires an entirely new constitutive bargaining process among the Member States, entailing substantial goal redefinition among national political actors (1970: 137).

The following section develops an analytical framework which defines the growth dimensions of a common foreign and security policy and the factors likely to promote or impede its development. Next, the evolution of European foreign policy cooperation is analysed with an emphasis on the Inter-Governmental Conference on Political Union of 1990–91 and the Maastricht Treaty. The final section discusses these forces, which condition qualitative change in foreign policy cooperation.

So far, most studies of European integration, especially those in the neo-functionalist tradition, have focused on the dynamics of integration, while inertia factors have largely been neglected, except by intergovernmentalists. A main point of this chapter is that dynamic and inertial factors are locked in an intricate interplay whose outcome depends not only on their relative potency, but also on factors in the Community's environment, both external and internal. That is, the development of a common foreign and security policy depends not only on the internal policy-making processes, but also on the interplay between the Community and its environment.

The dynamics and inertia of foreign policy cooperation

In this section, a simple analytical scheme is elaborated for the analysis of the constitutional aspects of foreign and security policy cooperation. The focus is limited to those factors which affect the overall level of joint decision-making in the foreign policy area, excluding factors which determine 'normal' everyday policies.

An operational definition of common policy

The formation of a common foreign and security policy involves three main parameters: scope, depth and decision-making mode (cf. Lindberg and Scheingold, 1970: Chapter 3). Scope concerns the number and character of functional policy areas covered by the common policy. The more areas, and especially the more core functions of the nation-state are included, the higher the level of integration. Historically, security and defence are core functions of the nation-state, and their inclusion is therefore a good litmus test of the scope of the Community's foreign and security policy at any given time.

The second parameter, depth, relates to the degree of commitment and the character of policy output. Degree of commitment refers to the obligation of member states to observe common decisions. Are they just to be taken into consideration in national foreign policy making, or are they of a more binding character? The more binding the decisions, the closer the situation is to a common policy. Policy output may vary, from information sharing and consultation to declarations, policy decisions and joint actions.

The closer policy output is to the action end of the continuum, the closer the situation is to a common policy.

Decision making in international fora is normally by consensus among governments, i.e. intergovernmental. Deviation from this norm may occur both in the way decisions are made, and in the form of participation by actors other than the governments. Steps towards majority voting indicate a higher level of common policy, as does the inclusion of supranational institutional actors such as the Commission or the Parliament. The more the latter are involved, the closer the situation is to one of a common foreign and security policy.

Actors and their environment

The above definition views Community institutions as potential actors on a par with member governments. While the European Parliament or the Commission hardly have genuine institutional interests in concrete foreign and security policy decisions, they certainly have interests in their constitutional aspects. At stake are influence and participation, attributes which both institutions have been sadly lacking so far. Hence, their ambition is to have the same level of control over foreign and security policy as over other policies. In contrast, the Council of Ministers and the European Council cannot be viewed as genuine actors in the constitutional process; they are mainly decision-making fora for the member governments.

This 'institutional interest' perspective differs from that of the neo-functionalists, who view the Commission as a source of supranational leadership. In foreign and security policy, however, the ground rules have been so different from those of communitarian politics as to leave little room for such leadership. Of course, the Commission is certainly interested in a decision-making set-up which would allow it to exercise supranational leadership.

Member governments have so far remained the main actors, both in day-to-day politics and in constitutional matters. The latter also follows from the fact that constitutional changes are the prerogative of member governments (Art. 236 in the Rome Treaty). As Lindberg and Scheingold (1970: 244) note, systems transformation involves the remaking of the 'grand bargains' between the Community's main players.

Up to now, most explanations of the development of political integration have centred upon the Community's internal policy-making process. And as we shall see, internal dynamics and inertia are important explanatory factors. However, they also interlock and interact with demands from and changes in the internal and external environments of the Community.

The environment presents actor-generated demands, expectations, etc., to which Community actors (must) react and which affect the level of joint decision making. Changes in the environment also provoke reactions on the part of the Community and affect the balance between dynamic and inertia forces. However, both demands and changes have to be perceived in order to generate a reaction. Member governments and EC institutions must view them as worth reacting to either because they create political opportunities which can be exploited, or because they pose challenges which cannot be avoided (Sandholz and Zysman, 1989).

Dynamics and inertia at the community level

As we have seen, the development of a common foreign and security policy proceeds from the interplay of governmental and institutional actors on the EC scene and their interaction with their external and internal environments. Factors of dynamism and inertia occur at each of these levels.

At the Community level, the relevant factors include both actor interests, national or institutional, and derivative effects from the integration process, such as spill-over and externalization.

It is difficult to predict the positions of national governments. Fundamentally, a certain reluctance to relinquish control over a national core function like foreign and security policy is to be expected. On the other hand, the willingness to pool sovereignty differs markedly between states and governments. Certain member states have consistently supported an expansion of the scope and level of integration, while others have invariably been opposed to it. Among the Twelve, Germany, Italy, Belgium, Luxembourg and – with certain reservations – France and the Netherlands have a record of support for expanding joint policy making, even though they may differ on the specifics; e.g. France's predilection for intergovernmentalism compared to the other countries' more communitarian approach. Relevant background factors are the actual or historical weakness of the nation-state (e.g. Italy, Belgium and Germany), limits to the national power base (France), or an ideological commitment to supranationalism (Netherlands, Belgium, Germany and Italy).

On the other hand, Britain, Denmark and Ireland have normally been status quo-oriented. The relevant background factors here are competing external orientations, such as Britain's Atlantic orientation and Denmark's mixed Atlantic–Nordic direction, specific security policy traditions (Ireland and Denmark), and a preference for intergovernmentalism among the political elites (Britain and Denmark).

The institutional actors, i.e. the Parliament and the Commission, see themselves as guardians of the Community's interest *vis-à-vis* the governments. These actors therefore have a clear interest in expanding and deepening foreign policy cooperation, because this will strengthen both the Community as such and their own roles in it. Specifically, the Parliament can be expected to opt for an expanded information and consultation process, while the Commission would want a right of initiative and a part in policy implementation. Parliament and Commission must therefore be considered dynamic, though often weak, actors in the foreign policy field.[1]

The neo-functional thesis of spill-over has been experiencing a renaissance of late, as recent developments in the EC seem to confirm some neo-functionalist tenets which appeared refuted at an earlier stage (Laursen, 1990; Kelstrup, 1992b). In this particular case, the thesis refers to dynamic effects on the scope and level of foreign and security policy making of developments in economic and monetary integration – e.g. the Internal Market or Economic and Monetary Union.

More generally, Lindberg and Scheingold note that 'incremental growth (forward linkages) is unlikely to occur in one area if it is not accompanied by some growth in other areas, too', and that qualitative, constitutional growth (i.e. systems transformation) tends to be 'system-wide' (1970: 138). However, the process may also have retarding or even retroactive ('spill-back') effects. Thomas Pedersen (1992) has recently pointed to system collapse as a relevant possibility. Finally, in a variant of the spill-over thesis Schmitter (1969: 165) has formulated an 'externalization' hypothesis, according to which participants in an integration scheme

> will find themselves compelled – regardless of their original intention – to adopt common policies vis-à-vis third parties. Members will be forced to hammer out a collective external position (and in the process are likely to rely increasingly on the new central institutions to do it).

For instance, common policies will often elicit a reaction from affected outsiders.

Factors of dynamism and inertia in the environment

Actors in the external environment may perform either role, depending on their degree of control over or dependency upon the Community. Politically or economically dependent states, such as the Central and East European countries, may want the Community's foreign policy role to expand, while actual or potential competitors for political power, such as the United States, will want to limit its role.

Change and stability in the external environment also influence the constitutional process. While a stable environment may at best produce an incremental expansion of foreign and security policy cooperation, environmental changes may provide the impetus for qualitative increases in scope and level. Radical changes in the environment may produce a 'quantum leap' in cooperation, but may also lead to paralysis by overloading the adaptive capacity of the Community.

Finally, changes in the domestic environment of the Community may affect foreign policy cooperation. Reduced support for integration will negatively affect possibilities for expansion, as occurred, for example in the Danish referendum on Maastricht on 2 June 1992. As emphasized by Thomas Pedersen (1992: 194–95) the costs of integration may become more visible for the public as integration proceeds. Therefore, 'as the EC reaches the later stages of its evolution, it will become more important to examine the level of support for the system ...'.

European political cooperation and the
Single European Act

Until 1970, when the European Political Cooperation (EPC) was created, a number of unsuccessful attempts were made to add a foreign and security dimension to European integration. The most ambitious attempt, the European Defence Community (EDC) of the early 1950s, foundered on the rocks of French nationalism, while the Fouchet Plan of 1961–62 was aborted in the face of resistance by Atlanticists and pro-integrationists.

The EPC was born at the Hague Summit of December 1969 in a linkage between widening (i.e. the admission of Britain and others) and deepening of the Community. Until formalized in the Single European Act (SEA) of 1986, the EPC was an informal cooperation network among the member states, based on the original Davignon (or Luxembourg) Report (1970), and the subsequent Copenhagen (1973) and London Reports (1981). Though its scope, depth and decision-making mode developed in this period, its basic intergovernmental features were retained.

This resulted in several abortive attempts outside the EPC to deepen and institutionalize foreign policy cooperation, such as the Tindemans Report of 1975, the Genscher-Colombo Plan of 1981, and the European Parliament's ambitious Draft Treaty Establishing the European Union (the Spinelli Plan) of 1984. By the mid-1980s these efforts had started to bear fruit.

In 1984 the long-dormant Western European Union was revitalized, and foreign policy cooperation was included in the negotiations leading to the Single European Act (SEA) of December 1985 (Pedersen, 1992).

In concrete terms, the SEA amounted mostly to a codification of previous practices and understandings. With respect to scope the SEA confirmed the importance of increased cooperation in the political and economic domains of security and also emphasized the importance of maintaining the technological and industrial conditions necessary for European security. Military security was referred to NATO and the Western European Union (WEU), however.[2]

The obligations of member states mostly concerned information and consultation. They undertook to inform and consult each other on foreign policy matters of general interest and were obliged to 'take full account' of other partners' positions and to 'give due consideration to the desirability of ... common European positions'. 'Common principles and objectives' were to be gradually defined and were to constitute a 'point of reference' for national policies.

The decision-making mode remained intergovernmental. The EPC continued to operate on the basis of quarterly meetings of foreign ministers (even though possible foreign policy discussions in conjunction with meetings of the EC Council were explicitly mentioned). Between meetings the Political Committee of Political Directors and the group of European Correspondents, both composed of national officials, were responsible for maintaining momentum and continuity together with the Presidency, which was specifically responsible for policy initiatives and coordination, representation *vis-à-vis* third parties and the general management of the EPC.

The Commission was to be fully 'involved' in the EPC's proceedings, but its role was not further defined, apart from its sharing of responsibility with the Presidency for the coordination of EC external relations and the EPC. Even though the European Parliament was assured of close association in the EPC, in practice this boiled down to an obligation for the Presidency to inform the Parliament regularly of foreign policy issues examined within the EPC and to ensure that its views be duly taken into consideration.

Finally, a small permanent Secretariat of the EPC was established in Brussels, but manned by officials seconded from national governments.

Negotiating the common foreign and security policy

Setting the agenda

In European post-war politics 1989 was the great watershed. The process of establishing the Internal Market had been launched and pressures released for expanded cooperation in adjacent areas. The Twelve (minus Britain) felt a growing need to add a social dimension to the EC, and there were both economic and political pressures for an Economic and Monetary Union (EMU). The Germans – who were supposed to pay for the EMU by sharing monetary responsibility and giving up the Deutschmark – demanded compensation in the political realm. Germany also argued that the Internal Market should lead to joint policies in the areas of cross-border crime and of immigration and asylum questions (Corbett, 1992: 272).

The dramatic upheavals in Central and Eastern Europe in 1989 gave an added impetus to foreign policy cooperation. Removing the traditional security threat, they strengthened expectations of a reduced American presence in Europe. The emerging democratic states of Central and East Europe looked to the EC for political and economic support, transforming the Community into Europe's 'anchor of stability'. Finally, the prospect of German unification revived a problem which Germany's neighbours had faced once before in the early 1950s. To France, the answer lay, now as then, in a reinforced foreign policy cooperation which could tie Germany to a joint European framework. From being opposed to a conference on political union, France became a leading proponent of institutional change in the foreign policy field.

The institutional actors were the first to react to the situation. Jacques Delors, President of the Commission, argued in the winter of 1990 for accelerating Europe's economic and political integration, calling for a major upgrading of foreign policy cooperation through the formation of a 'common strategy' and the inclusion of security policy (*Agence Europe*, 19 October 1989; 18 January and 23 February 1990).

In November 1989 the European Parliament had charged its Committee on Institutional Affairs to draw up specific proposals on political union. The first, interim report, the 'Martin I Report' of 14 March 1990, argued that the EPC should be integrated into the Community (Corbett, 1992: 274).

By this time governments had also started to move. A Belgian memorandum of 17 March 1990 (reprinted in Laursen and Vanhoonacker, 1992: 269–75) called for a 'truly joint foreign policy', and a few days later the Italian Parliament endorsed the Martin I Report. The most important initiative, though, was a joint proposal by French President Mitterrand and German Chancellor Kohl on 19 April to prepare an intergovernmental conference (IGC) on political union which, among other things, should 'define and implement a common foreign and security policy' (Laursen and

Vanhoonacker, 1992: 276). In June the European Council decided to convene such a conference for December 1990.

Prior to the start of the IGC, interested actors sought to influence the agenda. In July the European Parliament called for the abolition of the distinction between the EC's external relations and the EPC and proposed that the latter be integrated into the Community. The Council should have primary responsibility for foreign and security policy, but the Commission should have the right of initiative and a share in the external representation of the Community. The Community's foreign policy should also be subject to scrutiny in the European Parliament. The Community should aim at common policies on all matters in which member states share essential interests, including issues of security, peace and disarmament (Martin II Report, 11 July 1990; in Laursen and Vanhoonacker, 1992: 282–91).[3]

The Commission presented its opinion in October 1990 (*Agence Europe*, Document 1659, 31 October 1990). It emphasized the need for a unified Community with a single, though flexible, institutional structure, and suggested that a new treaty should 'point the way towards a common security policy, including defence'. Specifically the Commission proposed the inclusion in the union treaty of a mutual security guarantee akin to Art. 5 of the Brussels (WEU) Treaty. The Commission further envisioned a shared right of initiative for itself as well as a share in the preparation of decisions. It also proposed that common actions should be decided by a qualified majority, once the European Council had transferred an area from political cooperation (the EPC) to that of the new common policy.

The most significant inputs, however, came from member governments. Belgium and Greece published memoranda which strongly supported the notion of a common foreign policy within the Community framework (in Laursen and Vanhoonacker, 1992: 269–75 and 277–81), while Portugal and Denmark took a more cautious approach (ibid.: 193–303 and 304–12). The Danish memorandum of 4 October 1990 was status quo-oriented, rejecting majority voting and 'co-operation in defence policies, *inter alia* the setting-up of common military forces'.

More heavyweight proposals came from Italy, Germany and France. On 18 September 1990, the Italian Presidency presented a proposal on common foreign and security policy, which was termed 'the most visible objective' to be realized at the IGC (Laursen amd Vanhoonacker, 1992: 292). All aspects of security were to be included by transferring the competencies of the WEU to the Community, including the mutual security guarantee, consultation and coordination of defence and security matters, crisis management outside Europe, and common military–technological policies. These proposals were also supported by Spain (*Agence Europe*, 27 September 1990).

On 6 December, just before the Rome Summit, Kohl and Mitterrand addressed another letter to the EC Presidency (Laursen and Vanhoonacker, 1992: 313–14). Its delayed arrival was probably due to differences in views between the two leading proponents of European Union, France being more in favour of an independent European foreign and security policy than was Germany, which feared a weakening of NATO. Furthermore, France's general approach was intergovernmental, while Germany's was communitarian.

The Franco-German joint position was therefore not entirely clear. In accordance with the French view, it emphasized the role of the European Council in laying down essential guidelines for the Union, 'in particular in the area of common foreign and security policy'. Foreign policy was to encompass all areas, and the European Council was to decide the priority areas for common action.[4]

'Moreover, Political Union should include a true common security policy which would in turn lead to a common defence.' The latter was also a French idea. More concretely, the IGC was asked to establish an organic relationship between the WEU and the Political Union, and to review 'how ... the WEU, with increased operational capacities, might in time become part of Political Union and elaborate, on the latter's behalf, a common security policy'. Decision making in the foreign and security sphere should in principle be unanimous, but implementation decisions might be adopted by majority vote.

On the basis of a report from the personal representatives of the Foreign Ministers who had been preparing the IGC since May (*Political Union*, 1991) the European Council began its conference in December 1990. The Council welcomed the broad agreement on the basic 'vocation' of the Union in foreign and security policy (Laursen and Vanhoonacker, 1992: 318–21). Specifically, it mentioned the need for one decision-making centre, the Council, a unified secretariat, a reinforced role for the Commission, and adequate procedures for consulting and informing the Parliament. Consensus should be the rule in defining general guidelines, but there should also be a possibility of voting by qualified majority.

On security policy, the European Council was rather vague. The Union's role should in the first instance be considered in relation to issues like arms control, disarmament, CSCE, etc. Furthermore, the Union's role in defence matters should be 'considered', but without prejudicing existing obligations and bearing in mind the importance of maintaining and strengthening the Atlantic Alliance. This vagueness was probably in deference to the new British Prime Minister, John Major.

The IGC and the Maastricht Treaty

The Setting The Inter-Governmental Conference opened under the shadow of the Gulf War and the confused reaction to it by the EC countries. While the war constituted a serious question mark for EC ambitions of a common foreign and security policy, it also provided a rationale for strengthening cooperation. Similarly, the latter part of the IGC convened during the developing crisis in Yugoslavia, which evoked similar reactions (Hort, 1991).

The format of the conference naturally put governments at the helm. Besides monthly meetings of the foreign ministers, their personal representatives met on a weekly basis, with the Secretariat-General of the Council playing an important coordinating function. The Commission participated fully in the IGC, but did so rather ineffectively, especially in foreign and security policy (Christoffersen, 1992: 34).[5] The Parliament was consulted in monthly inter-institutional conferences (Corbett, 1992: 276). Besides the Secretariat-General, a major influence lay with the Presidencies, Luxembourg and the Netherlands. The major official documents produced for discussion included a Luxembourg 'non-paper' presented in April and a Draft Treaty presented in June. The Dutch Presidency produced a much criticized and subsequently withdrawn revision of the Luxembourg Draft in September, and two months later there appeared the final draft, which followed the Luxembourg model. The Maastricht Treaty was finalized at the European Council meeting in Maastricht on 11 December 1991, and signed there two months later, on 7 February 1992.

When the IGC on Political Union started in December 1990, most of the issues to be debated during the next year were already on the table, and most countries had shown their hands, with Britain a notable exception.[6] The following section describes the IGC negotiations and their results in terms of scope, depth and mode of decision making.

The scope of common foreign and security policy During 1990 a consensus was formed (with Denmark and Ireland as the main sceptics) that the European Union should encompass all aspects of foreign policy, including defence issues. The overall objectives of the Common Foreign and Security Policy, as defined in Art. J.1 of the Maastricht Treaty, were therefore largely uncontroversial.[7] The crucial question, though, was how to define 'defence' and how to solve its organizational aspects.

Before the IGC the defence issue had been raised by Italy, France and Germany as well as by the Commission. The Italian (and Commission) proposal for a mutual security guarantee was supported by Greece, but strongly opposed by Britain, Denmark, Portugal and the Netherlands. Other member governments, such as Germany, France and Belgium, were critical as well, arguing that as long as the Union had no military structure to underwrite such guarantees, they should not be adopted.

On the other hand, France and Germany viewed the building of a security component within the Union as vitally important. Basically, they proposed a long-term objective of common defence, combined with an intermediate-term objective of integrating the WEU into the Union. In the immediate future the WEU was to operate as a kind of security and defence entrepreneur for the Union.

While Denmark and Ireland expressed reservations,[8] most other countries accepted the linkage. Britain and the Netherlands, however, demanded that the WEU should be a genuine link between NATO and the Union rather than a part of the Union as such. Portugal took the same position.

The final formulation had to await the conclusion of the parallel debate over NATO's future. However, at the NATO meeting at Rome (November 1991) the United States recognized a European security identity and accepted the strengthening of the WEU, both as a European pillar in NATO and as a component of the European Union. As a *quid pro quo*, the Europeans, including the French, accepted the primacy of NATO.

The concluding IGC discussions focused on two initiatives, a British–Italian declaration of 5 October 1991, and another joint French–German initiative of 11 October (Laursen and Vanhoonacker, 1992: 413–14 and 415–18). Both initiatives related the WEU to the Union, and both laid out a long-term perspective for defence cooperation. There were also significant differences, however.

First, the British–Italian document stressed the complementarity between NATO and the Union and the WEU's equidistance between the two as the defence component of the Union and as a means of strengthening the European pillar of NATO. The Franco-German draft was more clearly focused on a European defence identity, as indicated by its announcing a joint military force which could serve as 'a core of a European corps, including the forces of other WEU Member States'.

The second difference was that the link between the WEU and the Union was considerably weaker in the British–Italian declaration than in the French–German initiative, which declared the WEU to be 'an integral part of the process of European Union'.

Third, the long-term perspectives differed. The British–Italian declaration called for 'a common defence policy' compatible with NATO defence policy, while the Franco-German document sought a 'common defence'. Even though the difference between defence policy and defence was never clearly spelled out, the Franco-German formulation foresaw the eventual establishment of defence forces under the European Union, while the British–Italian paper did not.

The final solution to the role of defence issues in the European Union was Art. J.4 of the Maastricht Treaty, accompanied by certain declarations by the WEU. Art. J.4,1 proclaims that 'common foreign and security policy shall include all questions related to the security of the European Union, including the framing of a common defence policy, which might in time lead to a common defence'.

In practice, however, the Union will 'request the Western European Union, which is an integral part of the development of the European Union, to elaborate and implement decisions and actions of the Union which have defence implications' (Art. J.4,2). The WEU thus appears as the defence entrepreneur of the Union, but is not put under its immediate control (Menon et al., 1992).

These formulations should be read in conjunction with a WEU declaration, appended to the Maastricht Treaty, according to which the WEU will be developed 'as the defence component of the European Union and as the means to strengthen the European pillar of the Atlantic Alliance'. 'While the WEU will act in conformity with the positions adopted in the Atlantic Alliance', its members will at the same time coordinate their NATO policies 'with the aim of introducing joint positions agreed in WEU'. The WEU also declared its willingness to elaborate and implement decisions and actions of the Union and to make the necessary practical arrangements for this, for example by moving the seats of the WEU Council and Secretariat to Brussels.

Delegating defence issues to the WEU was viewed as a temporary step.

If it is not prolonged, the WEU will expire in 1998, and the Maastricht Treaty therefore stipulates that another government conference shall be called in 1996 on the basis of a review of experiences up till then (Arts J.4,6 and N.2). Christoffersen (1992: 251) envisages three stages: a first phase in which all issues can be discussed in the Union, but where actions in the defence area are delegated to the WEU; a second phase involving the formulation of a common defence policy within the Union, and finally, a third long-term phase where common defence forces are established.

By including defence issues and by defining procedures for their handling within the European Union, the Maastricht Treaty represents a significant and important expansion of the functional scope of foreign policy coopera- tion; there no longer exist any taboo themes in this area (Wessels, 1992: 14). On the other hand, the scope of common security policies is so far circum- scribed by extensive deference to NATO. As Regelsberger points out, there is now a mutually agreed complementarity between NATO and the Euro- pean Union concerning functions and institutions in the security area (Regelsberger, 1992: 241).

The depth of commitment and cooperation At the IGC, most countries advo- cated strengthening cooperation by distinguishing between those issues in which important common interests were at stake and where cooperation should entail increased commitments, and other less vital issues for which existing EPC procedures might continue (Christoffersen, 1992: 228ff.). Such a differentiation would permit a gradualist approach in which issues could be transferred to more committing procedures, as they became ripe for it. Only Spain and Britain objected, Spain for fear that its foreign policy priorities in North Africa and Latin America might be relegated to the less ambitious category, Britain because it saw no need for strengthening the EPC.

The end result was the distinction within CFSP between 'systematic cooperation' or 'common positions' (Art. J.2) and 'joint action' (Art. J.3). Art. J.2 provides for a continuation of the EPC, while Art. J.3 stipulates a more ambitious and binding kind of cooperation in certain questions. Over time more and more policy areas will be gradually transferred from 'com- mon position' to 'joint action', but confined to areas 'in which the Member States have essential interests in common' (Art. J.1,3).[9]

EPC-type cooperation is strengthened as well. National policies must 'conform to the common positions', rather than take them as 'point[s] of reference' (SEA). Member states shall also 'refrain from any action which is contrary to the interests of the Union', while under the SEA they promise only to 'endeavour to avoid any action or position which impairs their effectiveness'.

With respect to 'joint action', the level of commitment is significantly higher. Christoffersen cites four differences compared to the EPC (1992: 230ff.):

1. The objective is common action, rather than coordination of national foreign policies. The Union will act in international politics as a unitary actor with one voice and one negotiating position.

2. Joint action aims at establishing more elaborate and deliberate policies than the EPC. As stipulated in Art. J.3,1, '[w]henever the Council decides on the principle of common action, it shall lay down the Union's general and specific objectives in carrying out such action, if necessary its duration, and the means, procedures and conditions for its implementation'.
3. Joint action involves a higher degree of commitment on the part of member states.
4. Joint action implies the possibility of majority voting.

The Maastricht Treaty thus entails a significant deepening of foreign policy cooperation compared to the SEA. The level of commitment is higher, and the range of policy instruments is wider through the addition of joint action and defence cooperation.

Decision-making mode Even though the SEA brought together the Community and the EPC under a joint framework, the EPC remained separate and intergovernmental. At the IGC, efforts were made to strengthen the institutional unity of the Union by integrating the Community and the CFSP, but because of the specific character of foreign policy its total inclusion in the Community was not envisaged. Both the institutional actors and several member states wanted to insert the CFSP into the EC Treaty as a special chapter containing its own decision-making rules. In the negotiating jargon of the IGC, the European Union was to have a 'tree structure' with the CFSP as one of the main branches. The alternative model, known as the 'Greek temple structure', envisaged three pillars, consisting of the EC, the CFSP, and cooperation in justice and home affairs.

In its first draft of April 1991, the Luxembourg Presidency opted for the temple structure, but giving the CFSP a more communitarian quality than the EPC. The proposal was criticized by a majority of member states who preferred the tree approach.[10] Key countries such as France and Britain were opposed though, and the Presidency, in its draft of June 1991, stuck to the temple structure. However, the draft was amended to stipulate that 'the Union shall be served by a single institutional framework', and that the Community would be its main pillar.

In an attempt to enforce its priorities, the Dutch Presidency reverted in September to the tree approach, but met with fierce opposition from almost every direction. Consequently, the Maastricht Treaty came very close to the Luxembourg Draft on this point. The European Union will thus rest on three pillars, one of them the CFSP, but within a single institutional framework, which means that the special EPC institutions will lose importance. Maastricht makes the Council, rather than the Meetings of Foreign Ministers, responsible for policy making within the CFSP; the EPC Secretariat will be merged with the Council's Secretariat-General; meetings will be prepared by the COREPER, replacing the Political Committee of Political Directors (who nevertheless retain a supervisory role), etc. These changes will allow for a higher degree of coordination between the external policies of the Community and the CFSP.

The Council has thus become the institutional 'victor' with respect to the CFSP. The European Council was strengthened as well. In the EPC it has no formalized role, even though it has gradually come to discuss and lay down principles and guidelines. In the CFSP the European Council 'shall define the principles and general guidelines' for the CFSP (Art. J.8) and decide which matters shall be included under joint action (Art. J.3,1).

The Commission's role has been strengthened somewhat. It shall be 'fully associated' with the CFSP, including implementation and external representation and is also accorded a non-exclusive right of initiative (Art. J.8,3). However, the Commission will be subordinate to the Presidency, which remains responsible for day-to-day management, including external representation and the implementation of decisions.

Finally, the Parliament's role has been slightly enhanced. The Presidency shall consult it on principal aspects of the CFSP and ensure that its views are taken into consideration. The Parliament shall also be kept regularly informed of the development of the CFSP.

Majority voting was one of the toughest issues concerning the CFSP. Broad agreement occurred on unanimity as the general voting procedure,[11] but with respect to joint actions (Art. J.3), important member countries wanted to open up for voting by qualified majority (QMV). Some countries, Belgium and Italy for example, preferred a general QMV rule; others, most notably France and Germany, argued that major decisions on guidelines, etc., should be taken unanimously, while the implementation would be decided by QMV. Britain, Denmark and Ireland opposed majority voting, arguing that distinctions between major and implementing decisions would be arbitrary.

Britain did not give way on the issue until Maastricht, and the end result hardly satisfied the proponents of majority voting. The Dutch Presidency came up with the formula which carried the day, namely that '[t]he Council shall, when adopting the joint action and at any stage during its development, define those matters on which decisions are to be taken by a qualified majority' (Art. J.4,2).[12] Such decisions on QMV shall be taken unanimously.

In all other matters, including 'common positions' (Art. J.2) and defence-related questions (Art. J.4) unanimity rule prevails. However, the Maastricht Summit also issued a Declaration on the CFSP, according to which '[m]ember States will, with regard to Council decisions requiring unanimity, to the extent possible, avoid to prevent a unanimous decision where a qualified majority exists in favour of that decision'. This obligation not to abuse the unanimity rule applies to all aspects of the CFSP, including defence matters. In the latter sphere, however, it is difficult to view the declaration as very binding. It is more likely to have some effect with respect to 'common positions' and 'common action'.

Even though majority voting only got 'a foot in the door' at Maastricht, recognition of the QMV principle constitutes a significant change. Together with the general rapprochement to the Community system and the modestly increased role of the Commission and the Parliament, the decision-making mode may be said to have been qualitatively changed.

A qualitative change in foreign and security policy? While it may be debated whether the SEA really amounted to a qualitative change in the foreign policy field, the picture is clearer with respect to the Maastricht Treaty. The scope of cooperation is widened; the depth of cooperation is increased, both in terms of commitment and with respect to policy instruments; and finally, the decision-making mode, though still mainly intergovernmental, approaches that of the Community proper. Foreign and security policy cannot be compared with the Community's external policies with respect to tariffs, fisheries and agriculture (Regelsberger, 1992: 237), but the two policy areas have been brought somewhat closer together, and their coordination made easier. All in all, changes in the foreign and security policy field must be considered an important element of the overall systems transformation inherent in the Maastricht Treaty. As a consequence, the role of the CFSP in the European Union has expanded compared to the SEA. If it is ratified, and if the member states so wish, the Maastricht Treaty will permit the Union to act increasingly as an international actor in its own right.

Why qualitative change?

Internal factors: interests and bargaining

The preceding analysis points clearly to the member governments as the major agents of systems transformation in the Community. This accords with the Community's constitution as well as with theoretical expectations. The Maastricht Treaty should therefore be seen primarily as the product of bargaining and coalition-building among the Twelve. As the analysis also shows, the outcome was primarily decided by the national interests of the member states as defined by their governments. Most countries had their special interests and pet projects, but most differences on the CFSP coalesced around two issues: 1) intergovernmentalism vs. the Community method, and 2) Atlanticism vs. Europeanism. Even though the precise position of individual countries on these issues may be debated, it is possible to single out four general positions: (1) intergovernmental/Atlanticist, (2) communitarian/Europeanist, (3) communitarian/Atlanticist, and (4) intergovernmental/Europeanist.

The most conservative, 'minimalist' position combined intergovernmentalism with Atlanticism. The basic outlook was therefore status quo-oriented: the EPC was in no need of improvement, and nothing must be done to damage the Atlantic Alliance. The paradigmatic spokesman of this position was Britain, which was sceptical towards joint action, opposed majority voting to the very last, and negotiated hard to place the WEU at equidistance between the Union and NATO. Portugal's views were close to Britain's, and for reasons of their own Ireland and Denmark also belonged to the status quo group (Nedergaard and Petersen, 1992).

The opposite position may be termed revisionist or 'maximalist'. Its adherents argued for a more communitarian approach to decision making and for the development of a European defence identity, though without impairing transatlantic bonds. The clearest exponents of this view were

Belgium, Luxembourg and the southern rim members, Italy, Spain, and Greece, the latter in a dramatic turnabout since the days of the Papandreou government. Germany also belonged to this group, although it was close to the middle on both issues. In most cases, though, Germany came down on the side of Europeanism and communitarianism, but it was hemmed in by important regards for its primary allies: the United States pulled in the direction of Atlanticism, while France pulled towards Europeanism and intergovernmentalism. The German positions were therefore often unclear.

Two countries fell outside the status quo and revisionist positions. The Netherlands was in a minority of one with its combination of Atlanticism and preference for the Community method. When the Netherlands tried to use the Presidency to further its views, it courted disaster, and even though it subsequently reverted to the mediating role of the Presidency, its impact in this role was hampered by its special position.

France was also a minority of one. It was the primary spokesman for a European security identity, but conservative with respect to decision making. The French priority was to give the intergovernmental European Council a primary role in defining the guidelines of the CFSP. In contrast to the Netherlands, however, France had an important ally in Germany, as well as considerable political clout of its own.

The Franco-German alliance provided important leadership for the Maastricht process. The two countries jointly proposed an IGC on Political Union in early 1990, and they continued to provide important inputs to the process during 1990 and 1991. At the same time, their will to cooperate – despite obvious differences of view – prevented stalemates which might otherwise have occurred at the IGC.

Italy aspired to a leadership role and was quite effective in agenda setting during its Presidency in 1990. During the IGC, Foreign Minister de Michelis played a mediating role, most conspicuously by the joint declaration with Britain, which probably paved the way for Britain's acceptance of a defence dimension within the Union.

The conference setting gave important roles to the two 1991 Presidencies. While Luxembourg played the straight mediator and coordinator and was successful in finding both the overall model and many important formulations of the later Maastricht Treaty, the Dutch suffered a humiliating defeat before accepting the mediator role. In the final phase, Dutch Prime Minister Ruud Lubbers acted as go-between and mediator between Chancellor Kohl and Prime Minister Major (Laursen, 1992).

Finally, the ground rule of the IGC, unanimity, gave the most status quo-oriented participant, Britain, considerable negotiating power. Britain's reservations on QMV, on an independent European defence identity, and on deepening commitments in the CFSP go a long way toward explaining the compromises struck at Maastricht.

Among the institutional actors, the Secretariat-General of the Council was centrally placed as the Secretariat of the Conference and was often responsible for transforming political ideas into treaty terms, especially concerning the Political Union (Christoffersen, 1992: 33). The specifics of its activities are not known, however.

The Commission's and the Parliament's influence was mostly in evidence before the IGC. Both contributed by calling attention to the need for stronger foreign policy cooperation in the winter of 1990, and both made important contributions to agenda setting. During the IGC the Parliament could only make its views heard in monthly inter-institutional meetings, but exerted at least some indirect influence through the pledge of the Italian Parliament not to ratify a treaty rejected by the Parliament.

The Commission was more closely associated with the IGC and was able to present its views in the negotiations, which it frequently did. The actual impact on the CFSP was limited, however, and the Commission and its President, Jacques Delors, grew increasingly critical of the conference. At one moment, Delors even threatened to denounce the Maastricht Treaty (*Financial Times*, 20 November 1991).

It is therefore difficult to assert that supranational leadership was very important for the Political Union, especially if one compares it with the making of the Economic and Monetary Union or the Internal Market. The agenda-setting activities in the early phase of the process should not be underestimated, but by and large, supranational leadership is at a disadvantage when it comes to constitutional changes because of government dominance.

To a large extent, the Maastricht Treaty and its formulations on CFSP can be explained by reference to national interests, to bargaining and coalitions between member states, and to the leadership provided by the Presidency, the Franco-German alliance and institutional actors. The decisive factors were probably Franco-German leadership on one hand and the veto-power which a reluctant Britain was able to wield on the other.

Internal factors: spill-over

Earlier it was hypothesized that institutional processes such as spill-over might also play a role. Direct spill-over effects are somewhat difficult to trace in the foreign policy field, even though the strains experienced in the 1980s between the Community's external relations and the EPC provided an incentive for the Union's institutional unity. Indirectly, there also existed an important political spill-over from the Internal Market via the Economic and Monetary Union to the Political Union, when Germany countered the French call for EMU with a demand for a political union, an important element of which was strengthening foreign policy cooperation (cf. Laursen, 1992: 238). Compared to the interaction of actor interests, however, spill-over processes can provide only a minor part of the explanation.

The interplay between actors and environment

The externalization hypothesis is one example of the possible impact of interplay between the Community and its environment. In a broad sense, it is possible to discern an externalization effect. The success of the Community, especially in the context of the break-down of the Cold War system, turned it into a magnet for the outside world. EFTA countries began to apply for membership; Central and East European countries directed their attention and expectations towards the Community; and the United States and Japan came to view Europe as an increasingly important economic and political partner and rival. This, in turn, became a powerful stimulus for the Community to intensify cooperation in the foreign and security field.

The main impact of the external environment was more direct, however. Governments and institutional actors simply reacted to demands from the environment and to relevant changes in it. The clearest example of external demands was the American warning against going too far in the direction of a common European security identity. NATO, said the US, should remain the primary security organization in Europe, and efforts to strengthen European defence cooperation should aim at strengthening, not weakening, the Alliance.

The American position reinforced the Atlanticist member states, and placed Germany in a situation of cross-pressure between Washington and Paris. And as we have seen, it was not possible to arrive at a compromise over CFSP until NATO had concluded its discussions. The American attitude was therefore a major inertia factor.

On the other hand, the break-up of the Cold War system gave an added stimulus to Europeanization by removing superpower 'overlap' and potentially reducing the US incentive to play a dominant role in Europe. Attempts to forge a European security identity were rooted in expectations of a gradual American withdrawal from Europe. At the same time, chaos and disruption on the Community's eastern and southern borders stimulated efforts towards according the EC a larger foreign policy capacity.

The most dynamic factor, though, was German unification. Among Germany's neighbours, most notably in France, but also in cautious Denmark, unification gave a boost to integrationist sentiments by presenting the spectre of a strong unbound Germany which might conceivably turn either hegemonistic or neutralist. In this situation, a reinforced *Einbindung* in a political union seemed the only feasible strategy. As it happened, this strategy dovetailed with the German preference for being part of a broader European framework, in order both to mollify its neighbours and to forge a convenient frame for implementing national foreign policy. The result was the creation of the Franco-German alliance at the IGC.

Of additional importance were other foreign policy developments, such as the Gulf War and the break-up of Yugoslavia. Their impact, though, probably served more to reinforce existing views than to change them. Those already convinced of the need for a stronger European foreign policy profile saw their view confirmed by Europe's weak performance in the Gulf and in the Balkans, while those who were sceptical from the beginning only saw their worst fears confirmed.

In most countries the internal environment played a minor role. A broad political consensus and a supportive or docile public opinion allowed European governments considerable leeway. In some countries the government had to take domestic factors into consideration, though. Public concern over EMU and the potential loss of the Deutschmark made the German government demand a *quid pro quo* with respect to political union.

The British government felt pressured by Mrs Thatcher and Euro-sceptic backbenchers, and the Danish government was forced to heed the views of a sceptical political opposition and to ensure that it could secure a popular mandate in a subsequent referendum.[13]

Conclusions

The Maastricht Treaty introduces an authentic qualitative change in the Community's handling of foreign and security policy questions. Compared to the SEA, the CFSP represents a significant expansion of both scope and depth and important changes in decision-making procedures in the direction of the Community method. These changes are significant elements in the overall systems transformation which Maastricht represents.

Changes in this field derived from the interests of national and institutional actors as they interpreted them in the light of changes in their environments. Explanation of this process involves both dynamic and inertia factors. At the actor level, the supranational institutional actors played a dynamic, though rather weak role, while national governments illustrated both dynamics and inertia. A majority of member countries were on the dynamic side, in that they sought to expand the EPC in significant ways, while four countries, of which Britain was by far the most important, opted for minimal changes in the status quo. On the dynamic side, the Franco-German alliance provided important, even essential, leadership.

Spill-over and externalization effects were dynamic, albeit rather weak forces in favour of an expanded CFSP, while the external environment had a mostly dynamizing effect. Changes in Eastern Europe and the break-down of the Cold War system were important stimuli, with German unification the main catalyst. On the inertia side, American admonitions and the Community's difficulties over the Gulf War and Yugoslavia were the most important factors inhibiting the CFSP. Finally, the domestic environment was an important factor of inertia in some countries.

Looking towards the future, events since the signing of the Maastricht Treaty suggest that domestic support will be a more crucial factor in European integration than it has been so far. The analysis also points to the importance of the external environment. In the Maastricht process, external influences were mainly of a dynamic nature, but there is no guarantee that they will remain so. The external challenges to the Union may reach a magnitude where its adaptive capacity is overburdened and turns into a disincentive, rather than a stimulus for further cooperation. Finally, the analysis points to the crucial role of Franco-German cooperation. While strong in the Maastricht process, it need not remain so, especially as the balance between the two partners has perceptively changed over the last few years due to German unification and the shift of the European centre of gravity to the east.

Notes

1. This analysis takes issue with Lindberg and Scheingold's statement that Community officials have a vested interest in the existing system and are therefore less likely to promote hazardous and unpredictable system transformation (p. 245). This may be true in some, or even most, issue areas. In foreign and security policy, however, community officials have no vested interests. On the contrary, they would like to have them!

2. As a matter of fact, informal dinners in the European Council were sometimes used for discussion of defence affairs, e.g. the deployment of short-range nuclear weapons in Europe (Christoffersen, 1992: 239).

3. The Parliament's views were further expressed in the 'Martin III Report' of 22 November 1990, and the Colombo Report of 12 December 1990 (in Petersen, 1991: 91–110).

4. This proposal was sharply criticized by the Dutch government in a letter to the Italian Presidency on 12 December 1990 (Laursen and Vanhoonacker, 1992: 315–17).

5. Christoffersen is *chef de cabinet* in the Secretariat-General of the Council and was intimately involved in the IGC negotiations.

6. The Belgian Permanent Representative to the EC, Philippe de Schouteete, noted that 'the final result cannot be correctly appreciated if one ignores the fact that one of the principal participants had no objectives and was seeking no results ...' (Quoted in Corbett, 1992: 277).

7. These objectives were 'to safeguard the common values, fundamental interests and independence of the European Union; to strengthen the security of the Union and its Member States in all ways; to preserve peace and strengthen international security ...; to promote international cooperation; to develop and consolidate democracy and the rule of law, and respect for human rights and fundamental freedoms'.

8. Ever since the revitalization of the WEU in 1984, Denmark's relationship with the organization had been a hotly contested issue in domestic politics. The bourgeois government parties were for Denmark's membership, but a parliamentary majority led by the Social Democratic Party was against.

9. In the Conclusions from the Maastricht Summit, four initial areas for common action were defined: the CSCE process, disarmament in Europe, non-proliferation and economic aspects of security policy, particularly the transfer of military technology to third countries and weapons exports. At the same time, the Foreign Ministers were requested to identify 'areas open to joint action *vis-à-vis* particular countries or groups of countries' for the June Summit in Lisbon. In their report, the Foreign Ministers discussed joint action *vis-à-vis* Central and Eastern Europe, Russia and the former Soviet republics, and the Balkans including former Yugoslavia, Maghreb and the Middle East (Report to the European Council in Lisbon).

10. According to Corbett (1992: 279) Belgium, Germany, Greece, Ireland, Italy, Spain and the Netherlands.

11. According to Christoffersen this agreement on unanimity represents an evolution from the EPC, which is based on consensus. Consensus in EC terminology requires positive votes from all member governments, while unanimity allows for abstentions (p. 234).

12. Qualified majority was further defined as the usual fifty-four votes in the Council with the added special requirement that these votes should be cast by at least eight members.

13. As it turned out, the government and other pro-Union forces had misread public opinion. With almost five-sixths of the votes in Parliament behind the Maastricht Treaty, the 50.7 per cent 'No' to Maastricht in June 1992 came as a great shock.

References

Agence Europe

Christoffersen, Poul Skytte (1992) *Traktaten om Den Europæiske Union. Baggrund – forhandling – resultat*, Copenhagen: Jurist- og Økonomforbundets Forlag.

Corbett, Richard (1992) 'The Intergovernmental Conference on Political Union', *Journal of Common Market Studies*, 30, pp. 271–98.

Edwards, Geoffrey and Elfriede Regelsberger (1990) *Europe's Global Links. The European Community and Inter-Regional Cooperation*, London: Pinter.

Hort, Peter (1991) 'Europas Aussenpolitik – ein Fernziel', *Europa-Archiv*, no 20, pp. 577–82.

Kelstrup, Morten (ed.) (1992a) *European Integration and Denmark's Participation*, Copenhagen: Copenhagen Political Studies Press.

Kelstrup, Morten (1992b) 'European Integration and Political Theory', in Kelstrup, 1992a, pp. 13–58.

Laursen, Finn (1990) 'Explaining the EC's New Momentum', in Finn Laursen, (ed.) *EFTA and the EC: Implications of 1992*, Maastricht: European Institute of Public Administration.

Laursen, Finn (1992) 'Explaining the Intergovernmental Conference on Political Union', in Laursen and Vanhoonacker, 1992, pp. 229–48.

Laursen, Finn and Sophie Vanhoonacker, (eds) (1992) *The Intergovernmental Conference on Political Union. Institutional Reforms, New Policies and International Identity of the European Community*, Maastricht: European Institute of Public Administration.

Lindberg, Leon N. and Stuart A. Scheingold (1970) *Europe's Would-Be Polity: Patterns of Change in the European Community*, Englewood Cliffs, N.J.: Prentice-Hall.

Menon, Anand, Anthony Forster and William Wallace (1992) 'A Common European Defence?', *Survival*, 34, pp. 98–118.

Nedergaard, Peter and Nikolaj Petersen (1992) *Det nye EF: Traktaten om Den Europæiske Union*, Copenhagen: CO Metal *et al.*

Nugent, Neil (1992) 'The Deepening and Widening of the European Community: Recent Evolution, Maastricht, and Beyond', *Journal of Common Market Studies*, 30, pp. 311–28.

Pedersen, Thomas (1992) 'Political Change in the European Community. The Single European Act as a Case of System Transformation', in Kelstrup, 1992, pp. 184–212.

Pentland, Charles (1970) *International Theory and European Integration*, London: Faber.

Petersen, Nikolaj (1991) *EF, den politiske union og Danmark. Analyse og dokumentation*, Copenhagen: SNU.

Pinder, John (1991) *European Community. The Building of a Union*, Oxford: Oxford University Press.

Political Union (1990) Outcome of the proceedings of the personal representatives of the Ministers for Foreign Affairs. European Communities, The Council, No. 10356/90, 30 November 1990.

Regelsberger, Elfriede (1992) 'Gemeinsame Aussen- und Sicherheitspolitik', *Jahrbuch der Europäischen Integration*, 1991/92, pp. 231–43.

Report to the European Council in Lisbon on the Likely Development of the Common Foreign and Security Policy (CFSP) with a View to Identifying Areas Open to Joint Action *vis-à-vis* Particular Countries or Groups of Countries. June 1992.

Rummel, Reinhardt (1982) *Zusammengesetzte Aussenpolitik. Westeuropa als internationaler Akteur*, Kehl: N.P. Engel Verlag.

Rummel, Reinhardt (1992) *Toward Political Union. Planning a Common Foreign and*

Security Policy in the European Community, Baden-Baden: Nomos.

Sandholz, Wayne and John Zysman (1989) '1992. Recasting the European Bargain', *World Politics*, 42, pp. 95–128.

Schmitter, Philippe C. (1969) 'Three Neo-Functional Hypotheses about International Integration', *International Organization*, 23, pp. 161–66.

Wessels, Wolfgang (1992) 'Maastricht: Ergebnisse, Bewertungen und Langzeittrends'. *Integration*, 15, pp. 2–16.

The Common Foreign and Security Policy and the Challenge of Enlargement

THOMAS PEDERSEN

Introduction

Though highly important to the development of European integration, the issue of enlargement has not received much scholarly attention. One explanation is undoubtedly that the bulk of the theoretical political science literature on regional integration dates back to the period before the first enlargement. Several empirical studies have examined the effects of EC membership on applicant states (e.g. Schneider, 1990; Hamilton, 1987; Barth Eide *et al.*, 1990). Less attention has been paid to the increasingly important question of the effects of enlargement on the internal constitutional development of the union.[1] This chapter examines the effects of enlargement on Common Foreign and Security Policy (CFSP) under different assumptions. Foreign policy and security cooperation is a high-priority area in the current European unification process. In a sense, therefore, CFSP constitutes a test-case for the validity of the Maastricht model in a wider Europe. If it can be convincingly argued that widening is compatible with deepening of integration in the field of foreign and security policy, then this would constitute a powerful argument in support of the Maastricht model.

This chapter first offers a brief survey of the countries which have applied for EC membership. It goes on to examine possible developments in the pattern of European cooperation, focusing on the impact of enlargement on internal EC developments. A number of scenarios for the future of European cooperation are sketched out, each based on different combinations of 'unification models' and 'affiliation models'. The chapter then discusses structural trends and the evolution of the European policy debate with a view to identifying the 'most-likely scenario'. A final section discusses the effects of enlargement on the CFSP in the 'most-likely scenario' focusing specifically on how the actor capability and cohesion of the union would be affected by the admission to the union of the neutral EFTA countries.[2] Actor capability is defined in Sjøstedt's terms as 'an autonomous (political) unit's capacity to behave actively and deliberately in relation to other actors in the international system' (Sjøstedt, 1976: 16).[3]

The membership candidates

The relationship between the Community and the rest of Europe can be described as a centre–periphery relationship characterized by asymmetrical interdependence. The internal market has had important external effects. Third countries in the European periphery have been affected economically as well as politically. The downfall of the Soviet Union has made the Community a new stabilizing force in Europe and a pole of political attraction for non-members. Not all outsiders find membership equally attractive, but they all face the problem of the high costs of staying outside the Community. The costs of marginalization are most acutely felt in the economic area, but at the level of political elites exclusion from the centre is also perceived as politically costly.

At present there are three groups of European countries seeking access to the centre through membership of the Community: the EFTA countries; the Central and Eastern European countries; and the Mediterranean countries (see Table 3.1).

Table 3.1 Statistics on countries seeking EC membership (figures from 1989)

Country	Population in millions	GNP per capita in Ecu	Exports to EC in per cent	Employment in agriculture
EFTA				
Austria	7.4	15,306	63.9	8.1
Switzerland	6.1	25,581	56.6	5.7
Norway	4.2	19,711	65.2	6.4
Sweden	8.2	20,869	53.5	3.8
Iceland	0.3	18,697	56.5	—
Finland	5.0	20,826	43.9	9.8
Central and Eastern Europe				
Poland	38.7	4,639	(28.9)	26.4
Hungary	10.8	6,166	(25.6)	20.0
Czechoslovakia	15.8	6,763	(18.2)	11.5
Romania	23.7	4,299	(17.6)	27.9
Bulgaria	9.0	5,500	(4.6)	19.2
Albania	3.3	—	—	—
Yugoslavia	23.7	2,156	(38.5)	—
Mediterranean neighbours				
Cyprus	0.7	5,846	47.0	—
Malta	0.4	5,134	69.6	—
Turkey	54.7	1,309	46.5	50.6

Source: Adapted from EUROSTAT. Figures for Central and Eastern Europe are now outdated, but give an indication of the relative importance of the EC market for individual economies in this area. Figures on agriculture are percentage figures.

The Mediterranean neighbours

The first group of countries to apply were the Mediterranean neighbours: Turkey, Malta and Cyprus. Turkey applied on 14 April 1987, having had an association agreement with the EC since 1963. The Commission opinion on Turkey's request for membership which was submitted to the Council in December 1989 argued that Turkish membership was not possible in the short term, mainly due to economic factors (SEC (89) 2290 final, 20 December 1989). Despite the high level of economic growth in Turkey, there remains a sizable gap between Turkey's and the Community's level of economic development. As can be seen from Table 3.1, around 50 per cent of the Turkish workforce is still employed in agriculture. Besides, industrial development has been achieved in part by means of a high level of external protection. The Commission therefore feared (and still fears) that Turkey would not be able to fulfil its obligations as an EC member. In particular, Turkish membership would put pressure on the structural funds and the Common Agricultural Policy (CAP). Turkey's poor record in the field of human rights was also used as an argument against its acceptance as a member of the Community.

The context of EC–Turkish relations is changing, however. The economic and political barriers to membership should be weighed against the growing importance of Turkey as a security ally of the EC. In geo-strategic terms Turkey is located in the midst of some of the most important new trouble spots: Turkey could play a decisive role in the Balkans, the Caucasus, Central Asia and the Middle East. Most importantly, Turkey was the first country to recognize the independence of the Caucasian and Central Asian republics and now serves as an example for the newly independent Turkish-speaking republics and indeed as an investor in their modernization. Turkey's growing strategic importance confronts the Community with a serious dilemma: as in the case of United Germany the Community needs to prevent Turkey from 'going it alone' in an attempt to exploit new opportunities; whereas Germany can probably be accommodated, it is difficult to see what the Community could offer Turkey in concrete terms – at least as long as the present integration model is maintained. As to Malta and Cyprus, both countries applied for membership in 1990. The Commission has not yet issued an opinion on these applications.

The EFTA countries

Given the fact that the EFTA countries are economically closer to the EC than the Southern European applicants, one might have expected the EFTA countries to have applied for EC membership immediately after the launching of the Internal Market. To most EFTA governments this indeed appeared an attractive option. There were several constraints, however. First, neutrality was generally held to be incompatible with membership of an international community with a political finality. Only after 1990 with the collapse of the bipolar system did membership seem a realistic option for the neutral EFTA countries. Secondly, in several EFTA countries, notably Norway and Switzerland, important internal constraints existed regarding European policy. In both countries domestic opinion was very sceptical about transfers of sovereignty to supranational organizations. Finally, the majority of EC members were wary of enlargement in the late 1980s, as the Community was in the midst of wide-ranging internal reforms. Therefore, there was a tacit agreement between the two sides that EC–EFTA cooperation in the 1980s should aim at partial (economic) membership instead of full membership while keeping open the option of full membership at a later stage.

After three years of often cumbersome negotiations, the EC and EFTA countries on 2 May 1992 concluded a treaty with the EC on the creation of the European Economic Area (EEA) (Pedersen, 1993). The Swiss 'No' in the referendum on the EEA treaty on 6 December 1992 has temporarily blocked the EEA taking effect, but it is not expected to stop the EEA process. The treaty gives the EFTA countries a sort of partial economic membership. EFTA countries obtain free access to the Internal Market and a right to take part in a number of sectoral cooperation arrangements. They are also allowed to remain outside a number of cooperation areas in the EC. Thus foreign policy and security policy are not a part of the EEA. However, the EFTA countries must contribute financially and through market-liberalizing measures to economic and social cohesion in the EEA and, most importantly, they have not been granted a genuine influence on the formulation of rules and regulations in the area despite the fact that EEA law – in most cases identical to EC law – will take primacy over national law in the EFTA countries. Indeed, the lack of influence over rules which they will in any case have to follow is the most important reason why almost all EFTA countries have subsequently decided to opt for EC membership (Schwok, 1992).

Austria was the first EFTA country to apply for membership. Given the realities of economic interdependence, this is not surprising. What is perhaps more surprising is the fact that even before the collapse of the Cold War system Austria considered its neutrality to be compatible with membership. Austria's application contained a neutrality clause stating that the policy of neutrality should not be compromised by membership. But the Austrian government received clear signals from EC capitals indicating that Austria had to adapt its neutrality policy if it wanted to become a member of the EC. The Austrian government appears to have based its optimism on three factors (Schneider, 1990; Luif, 1988). First, it viewed its important geopolitical location at the gateway to Eastern Europe as something with which it could negotiate. Secondly, Austria based its European policy on the prognosis – which was in fact mere guesswork – that the EC would scale down its political ambitions as a consequence of the opening towards the East. Moreover, although this is less clear, the Austrian government may have felt that it could count on very valuable support from the (West) German government in the negotiations with Brussels. To this should be added the image problem which haunted Austria in 1988–89. The Waldheim affair created the need for an initiative that would underline Austria's democratic respectability. The Commission delivered its opinion on Austrian EC membership on 31 July 1991 (*Europe Documents*, no. 1730, 3

August 1991). The opinion was on the whole favourable to Austrian membership, arguing that accession negotiations would involve few problems, the problem areas being neutrality, transit and agriculture. The Commission considered that these problems could be solved during the negotiations.

Sweden applied for EC membership on 1 July 1991 following a very brief membership debate (Stålvant, 1991). Unlike the Austrians the Swedes did not attach a neutrality clause to their application. There were two main reasons for the Swedish application. First – and most importantly – the Swedish economy was in great difficulty. A major factor behind the Swedish economic crisis was the fact that Swedish multinationals invested heavily in the EC in anticipation of the internal market, thus eroding the productive basis of the Swedish economy. Secondly, as already indicated, the collapse of the Cold War meant that Sweden suddenly had much more room to manoeuvre in its foreign policy. It also meant that 'neutrality' lost much of its meaning. The security structure in the new Europe was no longer based on bipolar confrontation, and the new European power structure increasingly looked like a centre-periphery structure with Sweden squarely located in the periphery (Nordlöf-Lagerkranz, 1990). On 31 July 1992 the Commission delivered its opinion on Swedish EC membership (SEC (92) 1582 final). It was broadly positive, welcoming Sweden as an advanced economy able to make valuable contributions to the EC in areas such as environmental protection, monetary policy and social affairs. However, it was adamant in demanding that Sweden abandon its traditional neutrality and asked for 'specific and binding commitments' on this point. Other obstacles to EC membership were said to be found in the area of regional policy and competition policy, a concrete problem being the state monopoly over alcohol.

In March 1992, five months after the official conclusion of the EEA negotiations, Finland applied for EC membership. Finnish motives for applying resembled those of Sweden. Like Sweden, Finland's neutrality was losing its meaning and like Sweden Finland also chose not to attach a neutrality clause to its application. Yet Finland took more time than Sweden in adjusting its foreign policy. Only after the abortive military coup in the USSR in August 1991 did the Finnish Government feel that external security parameters permitted a Finnish reorientation towards the Community. To an even greater extent than in Sweden, economic interests were the fundamental driving force behind the reorientation in EC policy. Finland's economy was – and still is – in deep crisis, partly because of the collapse of the Soviet economy, partly because of heavy direct investments in the EC. There are also indirect effects of the Swedish crisis and fears of further negative economic consequences if Sweden joins the EC and Finland remains outside.

New security considerations add to Finland's determination to join the Community. Unlike the other EFTA applicants, Finland shares a long border with a large unstable neighbour. Finland fears negative 'spill-over' from the difficult transition in Russia. The welfare gap between Russia and the West is acutely felt at the border between Finland and Russia and, if the

Russian situation deteriorates, could lead to massive emigration to Finland. This is why Finland has recently signalled a clear wish to become a member of NATO and the WEU. Finland's special security situation and the potential need for outside protection could explain why the Finns are apparently less critical of the Maastricht Treaty than are the Swedes. In early November 1992, the Commission issued its stamp of approval regarding Finnish EC membership to the Council of Ministers (SEC (92) 2048 final). While its response was broadly positive, the Commission recommended that member states seek guarantees from the Finnish government that it would remain committed to the goal of creating a Common Foreign and Security Policy (CFSP).

Switzerland decided to apply for EC membership on 18 May 1992. EC membership poses a number of problems for Switzerland relating to its federal system; direct democracy; its policy towards foreigners (especially the sale of real estate to foreigners) and agriculture (Schwok, 1992: 71). Swiss federalism would have to be reformed, if Switzerland joins the Community, although the new emphasis on subsidiarity may reduce Switzerland's problems in this regard. To take but one example, Swiss cantons presently exercise autonomy in the area of public procurement. Direct democracy is also considered to be difficult to fit into a European Union. It has been estimated that the EEA Treaty alone would imply a Swiss withdrawal of about one-fifth of all federal laws from the control of direct democracy (Germann, 1992: 227). Switzerland would have to reshape its political institutions if it became a member of the Community. For instance, there would be a need for a genuine head of state. At present Switzerland has a Federal President who is but a *primus inter pares* within a collegiate governing body and who is replaced once a year. The Swiss debate about EC membership focuses on the risk of political satellization in the European Economic Area as well as on the risk of Swiss isolation if all important members of EFTA join the EC. Some of the Swiss elite feel that perhaps their country is not yet prepared for EC membership. At the same time they realize that if Switzerland does not apply now, it will probably not be able to join the EC until the second round of enlargement expected in the late 1990s or later. This entails a risk of having to negotiate with the European Union from a very weak bargaining position (Meier, 1991).

For the neutral applicants the greatest difficulty lies with the requirement that they accept the long-term goal of creating a common defence policy and perhaps even a common defence force. In all neutral EFTA states, but notably in Sweden and Austria, neutrality is currently being redefined. European neutrality now has a narrower meaning: it appears to signal a wish to remain militarily non-aligned. Despite assurances from Swedish and Austrian government sources that these countries accept the *finalité politique* of the union, doubts remain as to their willingness to live up to the Union's ambitions in the defence area. As defined by the WEU, common defence implies a willingness on the part of any member state to defend by military and other means another member state at its borders in case of attack. Members of the European Union are not obliged to adhere to the WEU. The neutral applicants stress that they cannot be formally committed to something to which the EC member states themselves are not committed. Yet they also realize that some EC member states will ask for 'proof' that the applicants subscribe to the *finalité politique* of the Union (Wallace and Michalski, 1992).

Norway applied for EC membership in November 1992. Among the EFTA applicants Norway is special in several respects. The major arguments in favour of Norwegian EC membership relate to foreign policy and security as much as to economics (Sæter and Knudsen, 1991: 179–94). Norway, a NATO member, fears being isolated in a new constellation where the main foreign policy and security debates will be conducted between the United States and a European pillar organized in the WEU or the European Union. Moreover, Norway is special because of the strength of EC resistance from its general public, due mainly to a profound distrust of the pro-EC elite in Norway's peripheral districts. Norwegians have already once rejected EC membership in the 1972 referendum. The outcome of the current Norwegian debate on EC membership, though still very uncertain, will in part depend on developments in the European policy of the UK, Denmark, Sweden and Finland.

Central and Eastern Europe

Whereas most Central and Eastern European countries (CECs) face severe economic problems in trying to adapt to the new EC, politically they do not have the same problems as do the EFTA countries. In contrast to the neutral EFTA countries the Central and Eastern Europeans have a very positive view of the CFSP (see Chapter 7). Especially since the abortive coup in Moscow in August 1991 these countries have put pressure on the EC, the WEU and NATO to grant them security guarantees. So far they have failed to obtain anything approaching direct guarantees, but they have at least obtained a loose affiliation with the western defence organizations. In a report to the Edinburgh Summit, the Commission suggests *inter alia* a deepening of the political dialogue with the countries of Central and Eastern Europe (SEC (92) 2301 final).

In discussing the enlargement of the EC, a distinction must be made between current and potential candidates. As we have seen, there are some eleven current candidate countries if we include the three 'front runners' in Central Europe, who have already concluded association agreements within a perspective of future EC membership. To these countries could, however, be added a number of potential applicants such as Bulgaria, Rumania, Albania, Lithuania, Latvia, Estonia, and possibly even Moldova, Slovenia and Croatia.[4] Altogether, one can envisage more than twenty potential applicants seeking access to the new centre in European politics. Most of these states are small or 'micro' states making Turkey (and to some extent also Poland) stand out as a special case.

The various applicants compete for influence in Brussels, and this tends to further reduce whatever leverage they have. The risk of being 'overtaken' by the CECs in the foreign policy and security area in terms of access to the power centre in the new Europe thus exerts a certain pressure on the neutral

EFTA countries to accommodate the EC. Similarly, Turkey is jealous of any moves to offer the CECs a political partnership that is more privileged than that currently enjoyed by Turkey.

Enlargement and the future of European cooperation

In trying to understand the linkages between geographical enlargement and the constitutional development of the EC/Union we need concepts describing the possible evolution of the European Union. Moreover, we need concepts which can help us understand the status of non-member countries in relation to the union. Constructing various scenarios is one means of developing such concepts.

When analysing the evolution of the Union we may distinguish between three unification models: a) *Centralized federation*, b) *decentralized federation*, and c) *confederation*. The concept of confederation is notoriously vague. Following Hague, Harrop and Breslin we define a confederation as a relatively weak form of political union between sovereign states in which decisions are generally taken by unanimity and the supranational centre lacks its own means of taxation, law-making and enforcement. The difference between a federation and a confederation has been studied by, *inter alia*, Duchacek, who relies mainly on the American experience. Duchacek's main point is that apart from a number of decentralizing guarantees, a federation must have full control over foreign policy, an independent central government and a perpetual political community embodied in the union treaty (Duchacek, 1970; Pedersen, 1992). The difference between a centralized and a decentralized federation can then be defined in terms of the strength of the supranational centre. A centralized federation will have a strong executive (or for our purposes a strong Commission), whereas the powers of the supranational executive will be more limited in a decentralized federation.

Turning to the issue of the status of the European periphery, it must be stressed that EC membership is only one of several possible models of affiliation with a prospective European Union. Given the new scepticism about EC membership evident in the electorates of some EFTA countries, the membership model ought not to monopolize our debate about the relations between the European Union and the rest of Europe. Enlargement is only one of several EC foreign policy actions taken in response to outside pressure for some form of accommodation (Ginsberg, 1989). I suggest we distinguish between three models of affiliation: a) *full membership* of the Union, b) *partial membership*, here defined as an arrangement whereby a state takes part in some, but not all of the Union's cooperation areas and enjoys the status of full member in the areas in which it takes part, and finally c) *association*, where a state is attached to an integration system without enjoying (full) membership rights in any area. If we combine these concepts with the concepts of unification outlined above, we get a number of different scenarios defined in terms of ideal-type combinations of unification models and models of affiliation between the union and its European periphery (see Table 3.2).

Some scenarios

The matrix does not allow us to take into account the fact that individual states within the 'European periphery' may have a different status in relation to the Community. As a point of departure, we merely try to identify *dominant trends* as regards the future status of the non-member states. The first scenario could be called *tight continental federation*. This would come about if the European Union were to be transformed into a more centralized state-like union having many member states. Integration theory and common sense suggest that to the extent that such a scenario is at all feasible, it would come about as a result of very severe external threats (Pinder, 1991; Riker, 1964). Centralization of the Union could, however, also be prompted by a large-scale enlargement. Sheer force of number could strengthen the power of the centre (Maclay, 1992: 14).

Table 3.2 Scenarios for the future of European cooperation

| Nature of Union | Status of European periphery | | |
	Membership	Partial membership	Association
Centralized federation	1) Tight continental federation	4) Semi-hegemonic Europe	7) Hegemonic Europe
Decentralized federation	2) Loose continental federation	5) Europe of variable co-operation areas	8) Two-tier Europe
Confederation	3) Continental confederation	6) Functionalist Europe	9) Europe of concentric circles

The second scenario still foresees a comprehensive enlargement of the European Union, but assumes that the union takes a more decentralized form. We could call this a *loose continental federation*. Decentralization could take the form of a relatively weak centre, but a loose federation could also mean that federal structures were 'segmented'. Thus, the Maastricht Treaty introduces a kind of segmented federalism, in which supranational institutions have federal-style competencies, but only in certain carefully defined sectors. At the same time, the provisions for revision and the fact that all three pillars have a common institutional framework make it reasonable to describe the union as a form of incremental federalism.[5]

The third scenario assumes that the union expands radically in terms of membership, while at the same time contracting in its functional scope and institutional capacity. We could call this a *continental confederation*. This scenario might come about if rapid and massive enlargement were not accompanied by institutional deepening. The result would be unmanageable diversity. In concrete terms, the Union could find itself bogged down in endless haggles about the distribution of the sector-economic costs of enlargement or about the foreign policy line of the union. The enlarged union might also be confronted with increasing problems of implementation of rules. In a continental-wide Union with weak administrative structures, existing implementation problems which already tend to undermine the legitimacy of the EC system would be compounded. Ultimately, the Union might decide to 'build-down', handing back some important powers to the national level.

In the fourth scenario, the creation of a centralized federation is combined with partial membership arrangements for the European periphery. Theoretically, it is difficult to see how this scenario could become a reality. It would imply a *semi-hegemonic relationship* between a federation and its local dependencies. A centralized union would imply such legal homogeneity and involve such stringent obligations for members that partial membership would be technically very complicated to organize. Yet it is possible to point to an empirical example of partial membership of a centralized federation. Under the US Federal Relations Act, Puerto Rico has a rather special affiliation with the USA: it shares a common market and a common currency with the US, but although subject to federal laws, Puerto Ricans do not pay federal taxes and do not vote in federal elections. They take part in US presidential conventions but have no representation in Congress! (Duchacek, 1970: 184ff.) One notes that Puerto Rico has no (Congressional) representation and consequently no taxation! However, Puerto Ricans are integrated in important parts of the American union and have limited political influence. The Puerto Rican relationship with the USA can be characterized as a mixture of association and partial membership.

Theoretically, partial membership would be more practicable if the European Union took a decentralized form. A decentralized Union would allow some scope for intermediate solutions. The Union itself – although having a common institutional roof – could have quite loose commitments in some sectors which would facilitate differentiation in policy towards European neighbours. In this scenario, the Union would thus be open towards differentiated models of cooperation, allowing individual European third countries – or groups of countries – a specific status at the fringe of the union. This we might call a *Europe of variable cooperation areas*.

A sixth scenario foresees a reduction in the present level of integration in Western Europe, with the Union gradually acquiring the features of a pure confederation. At the same time the scenario foresees partial membership of the new Union for the European periphery. This model we may call *functionalist Europe*, because it permits a plethora of cooperation arrangements structured according to the nature of the tasks. A functionalist Europe could come about, if the EC were to fail to implement the Maastricht Treaty and public opinion in the applicant states became more hostile to supranationalism.

Now let us assume that association along the lines of the EEA becomes the typical form of affiliation for the European periphery. Association with a highly developed centralized federation would create a *hegemonic Europe*, in which the states outside the Union would be confronted with a new regional entity having a global status as a new superpower. These peripheral states would have to adapt to the economic and social regime of the centre if they wanted to avoid a serious loss of welfare.

Association with a decentralized federation would also create a centre–periphery relationship, but a less clear-cut one. A decentralized federation would allow outsiders more scope for exploiting internal differences than would a centralized federation. We could call this a *two-tier Europe*. It could be argued that this roughly corresponds to what, in the debate, is called the Europe of Concentric Circles. The concept of 'two tiers', whatever the number of formal frameworks, is preferable because this arrangement places non-members in a secondary position in terms of political influence on the most important decisions in Europe.

Finally, let us consider the scenario of a confederalist development combined with association as the dominant form of affiliation for the European periphery. This is not a very realistic scenario. If the central integration structure in Europe were to abandon or move away from federal-style supranationalism, there would be little reason for the present non-members to remain on the sidelines. However, the European architecture might still differ in the political and economic area. Assuming a shift towards less ambitious integration models in the whole of Europe, it is possible to envisage a continental free trade area with a smaller circle of states cooperating on foreign policy and security matters, the rest of Europe being associated to this political core. This is 'concentric circles' *senso strictu*.

The most likely scenario

The Maastricht Treaty takes the EC to the threshold of a federation as recognized by the German federalist and chairman of the European Parliament, Egon Klepsch (Quoted in *Integration*, 15 April 1992: 104). But clearly what we are dealing with is a decentralized federation in the sense that the administrative centre (the Commission) is rather weak. The new emphasis on subsidiarity looks set to reinforce the trend towards a decentralized version of federalism more compatible with German thinking.

At the same time, we can point to the existence of various 'association structures' in Europe, of which the EEA is the most important. Some would interpret this as confirmation of the thesis that 'concentric circles' (or Two-Tier Europe) is the most fitting description of the emerging European architecture. Yet, the model of concentric circles (or Two-Tier Europe) suggests a geometrical clarity which does not quite correspond to current patterns of cooperation (Mertes and Prill, 1992).

There are signs that, following the British opt-outs and the Danish 'No' to the Maastricht Treaty, European cooperation is moving in the direction of the model of 'variable cooperation areas'. These arrangements mark the end of an epoch in which all members had to move ahead together at the

same pace (Landau, 1992). The European Union appears set to be characterized by a certain amount of institutional pluralism and various kinds of
membership (Nugent, 1992). The EC has always applied different types of
variable geometry, but only in the form of temporary exceptions. Now this
may be changing. New precedents are being set. It could also be argued that
the EEA contains elements of partial membership. After all, the EFTA
countries are, in a sense, allowed to participate in the EC à la carte, though
without being granted full membership rights in those areas in which they
take part in integration.

The move towards variable cooperation reflects a search for flexibility
on the part of EC member states. In a Union constructed according to the
variable integration model, the non-EC states would be able to take part
in selected EC ventures. Not all the present EC member states would have
to take part in all cooperation areas. Several factors are pushing the
Community towards variable cooperation. The EC needs flexible arrangements, when the number of actors in constitutional decision making
increases and the level of ambition is simultaneously raised. In these
circumstances, the search for rapid progress in integration leads to more
complex negotiation outcomes, which may reduce the legitimacy of the
integration system. Given the underlying socio-cultural diversity between
member states, which will increase with enlargement rapid institutional
integration can be obtained only at the cost of high complexity. In an elite-
oriented Community, socio-cultural diversity can be accommodated.
However, with the increasing participation of the European electorate in
EC constitutional politics – inevitable once integration moves into the
sovereignty-sensitive areas – diversity becomes a more serious problem
that cannot easily be ignored.

A second factor pushing the EC in the direction of variable cooperation
areas is outside pressure for more efficient European foreign policy and
security structures capable of acting quickly and efficiently. In these circumstances it is a problem that in the security and defence area the distinction
between members and non-members does not correspond to the patterns
of interests and attitudes. This state of affairs could become untenable, were
the Clinton administration to accelerate military disengagement from Europe at a time of growing security problems on Europe's Eastern or Southern borders. A Europe of variable cooperation areas would permit Turkey,
Norway and possibly even some Central and Eastern European countries to
take a fuller part in the emerging common European defence structure,
although Greek resistance to a stronger Turkish role would remain a
problem. A third factor favouring the Europe of variable cooperation areas
is the widely perceived need to stabilize Central and Eastern Europe. This
consideration translates itself into a search for ways of accelerating political
enlargement towards the East.

In a Europe of variable cooperation areas the Union's actor capability
vis-à-vis the international environment is likely to be higher than in a loose
continental federation, although differentiation may create problems of
coordination which weaken actor capability. One of the advantages of the
model of variable cooperation areas is precisely that it will allow parts of the

union to be organized according to patterns of interest convergence and ideological affinity rather than according to territorial location.

The variable cooperation model has its drawbacks, however. It may have negative consequences for the overall integration process. The main problem with the notion of variable cooperation areas is that a reduction in the number of cooperation areas in which all member states take part may make it more difficult to negotiate package deals. The range of common rights and obligations becomes dangerously narrow, thus threatening the unity of the community. To this should be added that most applicant governments are sceptical about partial membership arrangements.

While partial membership could be seen as part of an entirely new integration strategy it could also be fashioned as a transitional strategy – a way of inserting a measure of gradualism into the enlargement process by providing alternatives to the options of either membership or non-membership, while at the same time retaining the long-term goal of full membership. But clearly there is a risk of a 'domino effect', if partial membership arrangements prove impossible to encapsulate.

The EC policy debate has in recent years toyed with the idea of a more systematic differentiation in European integration. In 1991, the Dutch EC Commissioner for external economic relations, Frans Andriessen, proposed the model of 'affiliate membership' (Andriessen, 1991). Andriessen appeared to be looking for ways of accelerating the enlargement process, while at the same time maintaining the internal momentum of EC integration. Andriessen later made clear that the idea of affiliated membership was primarily directed at the CECs (*Neue Zürcher Zeitung*, 29–30 November 1992). The Andriessen model resembles the EEA model, but is different in one important respect: it suggests that affiliate members should in principle be granted full membership rights in the integration areas in which they take part.

German scholars have suggested other models of partial membership. Heinz Kramer from the *Stiftung Wissenschaft und Politik*, which has close ties with German decision makers, proposes a shift towards a 'European system of varying integrated circles or areas' (Kramer, 1992). There is also concrete evidence of a more widespread use of the variable integration method. Thus in 1992 the CECs were offered a kind of affiliation with EPC and other sectoral cooperation arrangements.

At present, Europe thus finds itself somewhere between a Two-Tier Europe and a Europe of Variable Cooperation Areas. Yet judging from official statements, the two leading member states in the EC clearly regard some kind of loose continental federation as the longer-term goal of the union (*Financial Times*, 9 December 1992, 1 January 1993). In discussing the effects of enlargement on CFSP, it therefore seems most relevant to examine the effects of full membership within a loose continental federation, the specific forms of which remain unclear. It should be stressed, however, that pressure for a more general application of variable geometry is considerable and that if Europe moves in the direction of *variable cooperation areas* widening will cease to be a major problem for the CFSP.

Enlargement and the CFSP

Enlargement would have a number of effects on the actor capability of a European Union organized as a loose continental federation. As pointed out by Ginsberg, enlargement is not only a consequence of foreign policy activity – in part it is a cause of (new) foreign policy activity (Ginsberg, 1989: 151ff.). One effect of enlargement is to broaden the Community's already extensive range of foreign policy activities. Each new member state brings to the Community special links. The accession of the UK was a major factor behind the setting up of the Lomé cooperation. In the case of Spain and Portugal, enlargement has led to a better understanding of Latin America. One consequence of the accession of the neutral EFTA countries will probably be to push the European Union's foreign policy in the direction of a more activist and 'radical' Third World policy, although it will take time to change established norms and practices.

At the same time, enlargement also has adverse economic effects for third countries, which can lead to trade conflicts. Costs are incurred by nearby non-members, if they lose EC market shares as a result of new members moving into markets in which they traditionally have a strong position. Thus the Iberian accession had negative effects on Turkish, Israeli and North African producers of textiles and horticultural products. The Moroccan application for EC membership in 1987 should perhaps be seen in this perspective. Enlargement therefore exerted pressure on the EC to open talks with these Mediterranean countries on more favourable trade and economic arrangements as a follow-up to Spanish and Portuguese accession. But enlargement may also offer opportunities to third countries to modify existing preferential trade accords.

Finally, and perhaps most important, enlargement adds to the EC's international economic and political clout. The accession of the EFTA countries will add to the Community's voting power in multilateral organizations such as the CSCE and the IMF. And the accession of the three Nordic applicants alone would add 7 per cent to the Community's GNP (Stålvant, 1991: 168). Moreover, enlargement gives the EC a higher self-sufficiency rate, which makes it easier for the EC to act independently in the international system. Thus, the accession of some EFTA countries, notably Norway, Sweden and Finland with their extensive natural resources, would be strategically important to the EC. Energy is of particular importance. As the percentage of wealth creation which originates from intra-Union trade increases, it will become less costly for the Union to pursue a protectionist policy towards outsiders. In Philippe Schmitter's terms externalization effects will become bigger (Schmitter, 1969: 161–66). At some point, a partly self-reinforcing pattern of (Union) action and (third country) reaction could develop which would force the Union to acquire more state-like features in foreign policy in order to defend itself. In terms of actor capability, this dynamic would be positive. Yet at the same time it raises new questions as to the possibility of preventing the emergence of a 'Fortress Europe' in the medium and longer terms.

Effects on cohesion

The general view among analysts is that during the last few years the distance between the foreign policy positions of the EC member states and the applicant states has narrowed considerably. Yet empirical evidence is still rather scarce. One way of trying to assess the magnitude of the problem is to compare the voting record of the EFTA neutrals and the EC member states in the UN General Assembly. An analysis of the evolution in EPC cohesion as reflected in UN voting patterns from 1973 to 1987 suggested that the foreign policy integration system is able to successfully absorb enlargements without permanently weakening political cohesion. Regelsberger's study showed that the percentage of unanimous votes was 46.8 per cent in 1973 and 46.7 per cent in 1987 (Regelsberger, 1988). Obviously this is a very aggregate measure, but it at least serves as a warning not to exaggerate the negative political effects of enlargement.

I shall confine myself to examining the voting on resolutions from the First Committee in the UN in 1991–92 dealing with disarmament and related international security issues, as this is an area where the EFTA neutrals can a priori be expected to adopt positions diverging from the EC core. My simple calculus is based on a definition of 'voting divergence' as cases where the neutral EFTA countries vote differently from both of the two dominant original EC member states, i.e. France and Germany. We assume that cases where the EFTA neutrals are in agreement with at least one of those states cannot be considered as cases of 'divergence' from the Community position.

At the Plenary Meeting of the 47th General Assembly on 9 December 1992, a total of nineteen resolutions were subjected to voting. Of these only two were cases of 'neutral divergence': 1) the resolution on a nuclear arms freeze, and 2) the convention on prohibition of use of nuclear weapons.[6] In the case of the resolution on a nuclear arms freeze, the EFTA neutrals were joined by Denmark, Ireland and Greece in abstaining.

Can one register a change in the voting pattern of the EFTA neutrals during the last few years following the breakdown of the bipolar system? The voting in the First Committee in November 1992 reveals one such case: on the issue of the importance of scientific and technological development for disarmament and international security, Sweden and Finland voted in favour in 1991, whereas in 1992 all Nordic countries and all EC member states except the UK abstained.

Although in quantitative terms our evidence is rather scarce, it does warrant some optimism as to the possibility of creating an effective CFSP in an enlarged Union. The normative rapprochement between EPC and the EFTA countries in foreign policy should not be seen purely as a response to a new international setting. There are clear indications that the rapprochement started earlier – for Sweden in 1987 (Stålvant in Hamilton, 1987: 220). The gradual rapprochement of foreign policy positions can partly be explained as an incremental political spill-over from economic cooperation, but it might also be seen in terms of a political price to be paid for gaining economic access to the centre.[7]

Institutional responses to enlargement

While enlargement entails structural changes which alter the parameters of European cooperation, decision makers are far from powerless. They can devise adaptive strategies aimed at protecting the cohesiveness of the integration system. What kinds of institutional and procedural strategies are available to the Community, if perceived as a unitary actor? At present, the Community relies on the principle that existing members determine the conditions of accession. New members not only have to accept the *acquis*: they also have to accept the *acquis politique* and the *finalité politique* (Wallace and Michalski, 1992: 4). Apart from this negotiating device, the effectiveness of which has been weakened by the British and Danish opt-outs, various institutional strategies can be envisaged: one solution might be *pragmatic adjustment*. Such adjustments are well known in the history of EPC. Member states can submit written reservations on texts setting out the Community's general policy. A member state can also choose not to take part in discussions on sensitive issues that it considers should not fall within the Community's competence (de Schoutheete, 1990: 212). Ireland chose this solution in the early 1980s, whenever its partners in EPC wanted to discuss sensitive security matters. Another way of facilitating foreign policy integration is to involve future member states in foreign policy consultations prior to their formal entry into the EC, the purpose being to soften the transition and start the socialization of officials from the acceding countries as early as possible. This procedure has been applied in all previous processes of enlargement. The Norwegian government, for example, managed to take part in EPC for several months in 1972 before being called back after the majority of Norwegians voted to reject EC membership.

Michael Maclay has proposed to go further down this road: he proposes that the EC call an international conference to bring together both the present Community members and the potential applicants from all sides (Maclay, 1992: 13). Finally, there is the possibility of opting out of the concrete actions or withdrawing from structures implementing a given policy. In the special agreement on Denmark's relationship to the Union concluded in Edinburgh, opting out is given a broader meaning. It is now in principle possible to opt out of the presidency role in individual policy areas.

At this point, however, pragmatic adjustments begin to add up to a qualitative change in the integration model. In a federal-style structure, even a rather loose one, pragmatic differentiation cannot be allowed to go too far or to be used very often. By definition, a federation has exclusive control over foreign policy (de Schoutheete, 1990: 221). Put in simple terms: a European federation must have the cohesiveness necessary to ensure that third countries regard it as a valuable and legitimate interlocutor in the international arena. In a loose continental federation, pragmatic differentiation can play a role in maintaining actor capability, but only provided there is a high degree of a priori commonality of attitudes and interests among constituent states.

Another, more effective approach would thus be to radically transform the institutional system and decision-making procedures in the foreign policy area, as suggested by a majority in the Commission. *System transformation*, as defined by the integration theorists Lindberg and Scheingold, implies a 'major change in the scope of the Community or in its institutions that often requires an entirely new constitutive bargaining process among the member states' (Lindberg and Scheingold, 1970: 137; Pedersen, 1992).[8] The EC has always tried to ensure that geographical enlargement did not lead to a dilution of the Community. In the late 1970s, as Greece and the Iberian countries moved closer to membership, suggestions were made by one of the larger member states to the effect that the bigger EC members ought to create substructures in order to safeguard the Community's political cohesion and efficiency (Tsoukalis, 1981). The adhesion of Greece caused a number of problems, some of which were of a short-term ideological nature. But at the same time the experience with Greek accession taught the EC the lesson that enlargement required accompanying measures in order to maintain the dynamism of the EC. In the debate on EC reform leading to the Single European Act, one of the arguments used dwelt on the need to prepare the EC for the admission of Spain and Portugal (Wallace, 1989). Indeed, the provisions of the Single European Act – notably the introduction of qualified majority voting – made the EC more efficient and thus capable of functioning with a larger membership. The reactivation of the WEU in 1984 may also in part have been inspired by fear, lest the entry of socialist Spain into the EC create problems for foreign policy integration.

One area where enlargement creates a need for institutional reforms is the institution of the Presidency. With, say, twenty member states, a big member state like France would hold the presidency only once every ten years. This is not likely to be acceptable to France nor to any other big member state in the Union. What adds to the problem of leadership in CFSP is the fact that most new member states will be small states. That the big member states – Germany, France, the UK, Italy, now also Spain – look askance at small member states holding the Presidency is not a new phenomenon. Former Commission President Roy Jenkins makes the following rather telling entry in his *European Diary* for 3 October 1977: 'Crispin back from Washington with the news that the next [world economic] summit is not to be until after the Danish presidency is out of the way' (Jenkins, 1989: 149) Ideology adds an extra twist to the problem. Even granting a radical overhaul of the foreign and security policy of the neutral EFTA countries, it remains difficult to envisage a country like Finland or Sweden acting on France's or the UK's behalf. There are several ways of overcoming this problem. The Commission task force on enlargement, in a report published in November 1991, suggested the introduction of collective 'troika presidencies' instead of individual presidencies, or alternatively, making a distinction between big and small member states so that only the big members hold full presidencies (*A Strategy for Enlargement*, 14 November 1991). Large-scale enlargement could also over time pave the way for the idea of direct election of a European president with specific foreign policy competencies.

There will also be pressure for a streamlining of decision making. Yet majority voting in foreign policy cooperation remains a sensitive issue. An ingenious solution to the problem of paralysis caused by large-scale enlargement would be to divide the Union into five or more 'subregions', each having one vote in an executive council which would make decisions by unanimity. Within each region, decisions would then be made by qualified majority voting (Verheijen, 1992: 31ff.).

Whereas system transformation might be a valid and realistic response to enlargement in the foreign policy area, it is questionable whether it is a realistic response in the defence area, particularly given the strong tradition for national defence in the neutral EFTA countries and some EC member states. The decision at the Maastricht summit to set up the defence component of the union as a subsystem reflects this problem. *Subsystem formation* in the field of defence is thus likely to be the most realistic response to enlargement in the field of defence. The creation of subsystems refers to a strategy that tries to maintain or enhance the cohesion and actor capability of the system via the creation of a dominant subsystem within the wider system (de Schoutheete, 1990). In this way, growth in the heterogeneity of the system caused by the admission of new members is counterbalanced by differentiation in the decision-making system between core members and non-core members. A variation on the theme of subsystem formation would be to organize European defence as a structure with a political centre coordinating a number of sub-regional military structures each having their own operative tasks. This model might imply, amongst other things, a revival of the old idea of Nordic defence cooperation.

Subsystem formation is probably compatible with a federal-style system, provided the subsystem formation remains a sector-specific and temporary solution (Wallace, 1985). The emergence of a more permanent *directoire* within a continental federation might, however, endanger the overall cohesion of the system.

Conclusions

It has been argued in this chapter that the effects of enlargement on the evolution of the CFSP will depend on the overall evolution in European cooperation. While there is strong and growing pressure for the introduction of a more flexible integration model which is here called 'Europe of variable cooperation areas', judged from statements by political leaders in the core countries, the official longer-term goal of the union is a loose continental federation. The second part of the chapter has therefore concentrated on examining effects of enlargement – notably enlargement with neutral EFTA countries – on CFSP in a loose continental federation and on strategies for reconciling enlargement with the setting up of an effective CFSP.

We first examined the existing degree of attitudinal similarity between the applicant neutrals and the EC member states. The results warranted some optimism as regards the possibility of setting up an effective, declaratory CFSP within a future loose continental federation. The fact that even in the sensitive area of security and disarmament there now exists a high degree of attitudinal similarity between the neutrals and the EC, when judged by voting patterns in the UN, suggests that the problems of political cohesion posed by enlargement may be rather modest in the near future. However, more thorough empirical research is needed before firm conclusions can be drawn. It should be kept in mind that the external parameters of a CFSP are rather unstable. A transformation in the security situation of Western Europe leading to a shift of focus towards the South could thus be expected to create tensions in an enlarged European Union.

We then examined the institutional strategies available to EC decision makers as they try to preserve political cohesion in the face of geographical enlargement. Apart from the take-it-or-leave-it strategy which is now coming under some pressure, three adaptive strategies were identified: i) pragmatic adjustments, ii) system transformation, and iii) subsystem formation. Whereas in the foreign and security policy areas system transformation is possible, in the defence area a more viable solution is likely to be subsystem formation. Finally, we argued that in the case of a worsened security situation in South-eastern or Eastern Europe and continuing American military disengagement, a security logic may prevail over the traditional integration logic: the Union may in the course of the 1990s move towards the variable cooperation model in order to be able to make rapid progress in setting up effective defence structures that include strategically important countries which at present are not members of the Union and which cannot easily become full members in the near future. The decision to allow associates of the WEU to be more closely attached to the WEU than the observers – who, after all, are members of the Community – could be seen as a first sign that such a move towards variable cooperation has already begun to take place.

Notes

1. An exception being the excellent study by Helen Wallace and Anna Michalski (1992) for Chatham House.

2. The concept of 'actor capability' was coined by the Swedish political scientist Gunnar Sjøstedt in his path-breaking but somewhat neglected study *The External Role of the European Community* (1976).

3. According to Sjøstedt the structural prerequisites of 'actor capability' are: a) A community of interests, b) a decision-making system, c) a system for crisis management, d) a system for the management of interdependence, e) a system for steering and control of actor behaviour, f) a network of external agents and external channels of communication and g) community resources and a mobilization system.

4. There could be a case for placing Slovenia in the category of current candidates.

5. Cf. Martin Sæter, *Det Politiske Europa* (1971), in which Sæter introduces the concepts of 'sector-specific federalism' and 'sector-specific confederalism'.

6. UN voting records have been provided by the Danish Ministry of Foreign Affairs. I thank them for their generous assistance.

7. This theoretical problem of adaptation to EC membership cannot be dealt with here, but clearly merits closer attention.

8. It should be noted that here the concept of 'system transformation' is used in a slightly unconventional way as referring to 'constitutional' changes affecting but one cooperation area.

References

Andriessen, Frans (1991) *Towards a Community of Twenty-Four*, speech to the 69th Plenary Assembly of Euro-Chambers, Brussels, 19 April 1991.

Duchacek, Ivo (1970) *Comparative Federalism*, New York: Rinehart & Winston.

Eide, Espen Barth, Andreas Gaarder, Ivar B. Neumann, Johan Vibe and Jan Dietz (1990) *EF, EFTA, Norge – tilpasning eller mistilpasning?*, Oslo: Norsk Utenrikspolitisk Institut.

Germann, Raimund E. (1992) 'Switzerland's Future in Europe: Isolation or Constitutional Change', *Governance*, vol. 5, no. 2.

Ginsberg, Roy (1989) *Foreign Policy Actions of the European Community*, Boulder: Lynne Rienner Publishers.

Hague, A., M. Harrop and S. Breslin (1992) *Comparative Government and Politics*, London: Macmillan.

Hamilton, Carl B. (ed.) (1987) *Europa och Sverige*, Stockholm: SNS Förlag.

Hosli, Madeleine (1992) *Voting Powers in the EC Council of Ministers after an Adhesion of EFTA States: An Analysis Based on the Banzhaf Power Index*, paper prepared for the ISA convention in Atlanta, GA, March 31–April 4, 1992.

Jenkins, Roy (1989) *European Diary*, London: Collins.

Kramer, Heinz (1988) *Die Europäische Gemeinschaft und die Türkei*, Baden-Baden: Nomos Verlagsgesellschaft.

Kramer, Heinz (1992) 'The EC and the Stabilisation of Eastern Europe', *Aussenpolitik*, no. 1.

Landau, Alice (1992). *La Communauté européenne et les théories de l'integration: Nouvelles épreuves, nouvelles approches*, Paper presented to the Association Suisse de Science Politique, Balsthal, 13–14 November.

Laursen Finn (1991-92) 'The EC and Its European Neighbours: Special Relationship or Widened Membership?', *International Journal*, XLVII, Winter.

Lindberg, Leon N. and Stuart Scheingold (1970) *Europe's Would-Be Polity*, Englewood Cliffs, New Jersey: Prentice-Hall.

Luif, Paul (1989) *Neutrale in der EG?* Wien: Wilhelm Braunmüller.

Maclay, Michael (1992) *Multi-Speed Europe. The Community beyond Maastricht*, London: Royal Institute of International Affairs.

Meier, Alfred (1991) 'Schweizerische Optionen im Europäischen Integrationsprozess', in *Herausvorderung Europa. Vereinigung für freies Unternehmentum*, Schaffhausen.

Mertes, Michael and Norbert Prill (1992) 'Europäische Strukturen: Ein Plädoyer für institutionelle Ökonomie', *Europaarchiv*, no. 6.

Norden i det nye Europa (1991) (The Nordic Countries in the New Europe), En rapport fra de udenrikspolitiske institutter i Norden (Report from the Foreign Policy Institutes in the Nordic countries), København, Stockholm, Oslo, Helsinki, Reykjavik.

Nordlöf-Lagerkranz, Ulla (1990) *Svensk Neutralitet, Europa och EG*, Stockholm: MH Publishing.

Nugent, Neill (1992) 'The Deepening and Widening of the European Community: Recent Evolution, Maastricht and Beyond', *Journal of Common Market Studies*, vol. XXX, no. 3, September.

Pedersen, Thomas (1994) *European Union and the EFTA Countries. Enlargement and integration*, London: Pinter.

Pedersen, Thomas (1992) 'Maastricht traktaten i føderalistisk belysning' (The Maastricht Treaty in a Federalist Perspective), *Økonomi & Politik*, no. 4.

Pedersen, Thomas (1992) 'Political Change in the EC: The Single European Act as a Case of System Transformation', *Cooperation & Conflict*, vol. 27, no. 1.

Pedersen, Thomas (1988) *The Wider Western Europe: EC Policy towards the EFTA*

Countries, London: Chatham House.

Pinder, John (1991) *European Community. The Building of a Union*, Oxford: Oxford University Press.

Regelsberger, Elfriede (1988) 'EPC in the 1980s: Reaching another Plateau?', in Regelsberger *et al.* (eds), *European Political Cooperation in the 1980s*, Dordrecht: Martinus Nijhoff/TEPSA.

Riker, William H. (1964) *Federalism. Origin. Operation. Significance*, Boston: Little Brown & Company.

Sæter, Martin (1971) *Det Politiske Europa*, Oslo: Universitetsforlaget.

Sæter, Martin and Olav F. Knudsen (1991) 'Norway', in Helen Wallace (ed.), *The Wider Western Europe*, London: Pinter.

Schneider, Heinrich (1990) *Alleingang nach Brüssel*, Bonn: Europa Union Verlag.

Schoutheete, Philippe de (1990) 'The EC and Its Subsystems', in William Wallace (ed.), *The Dynamics of European Integration*, London: Pinter.

Sjøstedt, Gunnar (1976) *The External Role of the European Community*, Westmead: Saxon House.

Schwok, Rene (1992) 'The European Free Trade Association', in John Redmond (ed.), *The External Relations of The European Community*, New York: St. Martin's Press.

Stålvant, Carl-Einar (1990) 'Sweden and the European Community in 1990', in *CEPS Yearbook 1990*, Bruxelles.

Tsoukalis, Loukas (1981) *The European Community and Its Mediterranean Enlargement*, London: Pinter.

Verheijen, Tony (1992) *Towards a United Nations of Europe: Possible Scenarios for Incorporating Central and Eastern Europe in the EC*, Maastricht: EIPA.

Wallace, Helen and Anna Michalski (1992) *The European Community: The Challenge of Enlargement*, European Programme Special Paper, London: Royal Institute of International Affairs.

Wallace, Helen (1989) *Widening and Deepening: The European Community and the New European Agenda*, London: Royal Institute of International Affairs.

Wallace, William (1985) 'Relaunching the WEU: Variable Geometry, Institutional Duplication or Policy Drift?', in P. Tsakaloyannis, *The Reactivation of the Western European Union*, Maastricht: EIPA.

Other sources

Commission Opinion on Turkey's Request for Accession to the Community. SEC (89) 2290 final.

Commission Opinion on Austria's Request for Accession to the Community. SEC (91) 1590 final.

Commission Opinion on Sweden's Request for Accession to the Community. SEC (92) 1582 final.

Commission Opinion on Finland's Request for Accession to the Community. SEC (92) 2048 final.

A Strategy for Enlargement, Brussels: European Commission, November 14, 1991.

European Commission Report on the Criteria and Conditions for Accession of New Members to the Community, *Agence Europe*, July 3, 1992.

Relations with the Central and Eastern European Countries, SEC (92) 2301 final.

Danish Ministry of Foreign Affairs.

4

The End of Special Interests? The Political Economy of EC Trade Policy Changes in the 1990s

PETER NEDERGAARD

EC trade policy in the 1990s is changing due to both internal and external factors: notably the European economic integration and a possible restructuring of the traditional hierarchy of EC trade relations.

This chapter discusses the extent to which the resulting changes in EC trade policy in the 1990s stem from the influence of special interests or whether the concerns of the new world order have now become more important.

The conclusions are rather pessimistic, despite an increasing awareness, at least at the level of EC Commission rhetoric, of several overriding concerns which must be taken into account when analysing how EC trade policy is formulated. However, accelerated economic integration will probably lead to increased protectionism, and the hierarchy of trade relations will change, though mostly due to international agreements and because certain countries find themselves in an extremely disadvantageous trade position. This chapter hypothesizes that the theory of special interests resulting in protectionism would be invalidated by a new era in the world scene. In fact, the conclusions of this chapter lend unexpected additional support to the theory. Hence, through the 1990s special interests will continue to be a persistent feature of the liberalized trade regime of the EC.

Introduction

The European Community's trade policy is changing in the 1990s due to both internal and external factors. Internally there is an accelerated European economic integration, while on the external front there is the spectre of a break-up of the traditional hierarchy of the Community's trade relations.

The purpose of this chapter is to discuss the extent to which the resulting changes of Community trade policy in the 1990s stem from the influence of special interests, or whether overriding concerns such as migration, security, environmental protection or extreme poverty are more important than before. Trade policy changes are thus the dependent variable, whereas special interests and overriding concerns are the independent variables in the analysis. At the same time, due to the nature of the EC, the national as well as the EC levels have to be considered.

It is often claimed that normative international issues will gain the upper hand over more individualistic and short-sighted interests in the new world order. As a parallel with the institutional strengthening of the United Nations, it is forecast that values and norms will become increasingly important in maintaining order among states. This position has been stated in the strongest possible way in Francis Fukuyama's famous essay, 'The End of History?', which points that the ideal of liberalism 'will govern the world in the long run' (Fukuyama, 1989). I will therefore discuss the validity of this neo-Grotian normative, liberal theory. I will use as an example EC trade policy, to the extent that an emerging theoretical framework, based on the dominance of special interests, can be tested against an already existing, strong, liberal free-trade norm and thereby serve as an effective test of the theory.

Future trade policy should therefore provide one of the strongest cases for the thesis about the victory of liberalism. In reality, liberal trade policy has already played a central role in the decisions of the G7 summit in July 1991, when the new world order was placed for the first time on the agenda. The political declaration of the meeting was entitled 'Strengthening of the World Order', and has been summarized by Damgaard Petersen (1992) as 1) open market economies, 2) a liberal trade policy, 3) democracy and human rights, 4) coordination of economic policy through symmetry, 5) assistance to ease the Third World's debt crisis and 6) increased access for Third World countries to the protected markets of the great industrial powers, provided they introduce market economies, accept democratic rules and promote human rights.

The political economy of trade policy

The fundamental questions asked in the theory of the political economy of trade policy are, 'Why does protectionism appear?', and 'Why is protectionism maintained or strengthened when free trade according to traditional theory[1] represents the optimal solution?'. In other words, according to this theory, the free trade imperative is taken as read. At the same time, the theory does not consider ignorance of the free trade imperative to be the sole explanation of the maintenance or rise of protectionism.

Instead, the explanation for the rise of protectionism is sought in the political process.[2] By including political decision making in the theory, the aim is to find the political factors which are decisive for the rise and maintenance of protectionism (Krueger, 1990). Implicitly, the traditional free trade theory is criticized for assuming that governments mainly act as some kind of benevolent dictators whose only aim is to secure for their respective populations the greatest possible welfare.

In other words, the answer to the question as to why protectionism arises and is maintained must be found among the actors in the political system involved. At the same time, the theory makes certain assumptions about the political actors and the political system.

Actors in the political system are assumed to be just as rational in maximizing their own interests as are economic actors. This assumption conflicts with the widespread conviction that politicians and bureaucrats make decisions in the public interest. Instead, it is assumed that politicians have re-election and government posts on their minds when making decisions, and that bureaucrats often try to further their own careers when they make administrative or semi-political decisions.

On the other hand, this assumption is less surprising in view of the popular belief that interest groups in society promote what they see as their own interests. Hence, organized economic interests must be expected to be nourished by their representatives when they carry out lobbying activities aimed at political decision makers.

Several reasons may cause business and trade unions to limit free trade and imports. Domestic unemployment, trade deficits, recession and 'overvalued' national exchange rates are used as arguments by organized interests in their efforts to influence political decision makers. Nevertheless, no analysis has shown that these factors alone can explain the rise of trade barriers (Ruigrok, 1991).

In addition to the assumption about political actors, the political economy of trade policy assumes the political system to be asymmetrical in the sense that many political or collective decisions benefit only limited groups of individuals while the costs (in terms of payments or lost incomes) are dispersed among a great number of individuals.

The asymmetrical character of the political system is another reason why there are many more interest groups lobbying in favour of protection than there are interest groups lobbying against it. The first type of interest group achieves some immediate benefits if it succeeds in limiting the import of goods that threaten profit and employment in domestic firms within the same sectors. The result of this kind of lobbying is higher prices for customers, though it is often difficult for consumers with an average level of information to link higher prices with the relevant political decisions.

Even if it were possible to link higher prices and political decisions, it would often be too costly to lobby against higher prices compared to the possible benefits. This is because the costs of lobbying against higher prices will be paid for by individual consumers while the benefits will be enjoyed by all. Therefore, most consumers tend to be 'free-riders'.

A classical illustration of the theory of the political economy of trade policy is the EC's Common Agricultural Policy (CAP). The strong interest organization and articulation of agricultural producers, as well as the consumers' incentive to continue to free-ride in the political decision-making process on agricultural prices, is a key explanation for the protectionist market in EC agricultural policy (Nedergaard, 1988). Another illustrative example of the political economy of trade policy is the EC barriers to textile imports.

In theory then, one can say that the level of protectionism is determined in a so-called political market where protectionist interest groups tend to exert the most weight. On the demand side of the political market, the voters can be separated into 'winners' or 'losers' depending on the effect of protectionist trade policy. The aggregate demand for protection from winners and losers consists, respectively, of the marginal propensity to pay for more protection and the marginal propensity to pay for opposition to it.

Because the political system is asymmetrical, those who see themselves gaining from protection possess more incentive to pay for the organization of interests. This is true of any political system. However, it could be argued that the EC political system is excessively asymmetrical, being a result of the establishment of numerous Euro-organizations, partly sponsored by the Commission, who are often given access to the EC decision-making process (sometimes even officially, such as COPA, the European agricultural organization).

The supply function in the political market for protection is predominantly determined by the interaction between voters and political decision makers. In a completely competitive political system, where political decision makers on every political subject must match the attitudes of the voters, the optimal political strategy is short-term vote maximizing. Political decision makers will therefore have to compare the number of potential votes from protectionist groups, and the resultant organizational and economic support, with the potential loss of votes from free trade-oriented voters if protectionist policies are followed. At the same time, the supply function is expected to increase as it becomes increasingly difficult to implement protectionist initiatives in the face of the majority of voters, as their protectionist content becomes more visible (Weck-Hannemann, 1990). This is shown by the supply function S_0 in Figure 4.1. The supply of protection is smaller where more voters directly influence the political decision-making process and where participation and information costs are reduced. At equilibrium in the political market, the degree of protection (T_0) and the corresponding price (P_0) in the form of lobbying costs are determined.

At market equilibrium, it is assumed that vote maximizing by politicians is solely a result of trade policy considerations. If it is more realistically assumed that decisions made by policy makers and/or voter preferences are influenced by issues other than trade policy, the political decision makers will possess a corresponding discretionary (i.e., autonomous and non-voter determined) power to practice a more free trade-oriented or more protectionist policy than at market equilibrium. If political decision makers want to supply more free trade-oriented decisions than at equilibrium, the supply function is removed from S_0 to S_1 in Figure 4.1. The reason for this removal could be that free trade is a strong international norm, and that the behaviour of other international trade policy actors has to be considered.

One might also imagine that the discretionary power of the policy makers is used to supply more protectionist decisions than at market equilibrium, i.e., the supply function is removed from S_0 to S_2 in Figure 4.1. One reason for this removal could be that the interaction between voters and political decision makers is fragile and indirect. Alternatively, political decision

makers' policy preferences may differ from those of the articulate population because other political issues push trade policy decisions in a specific
direction.

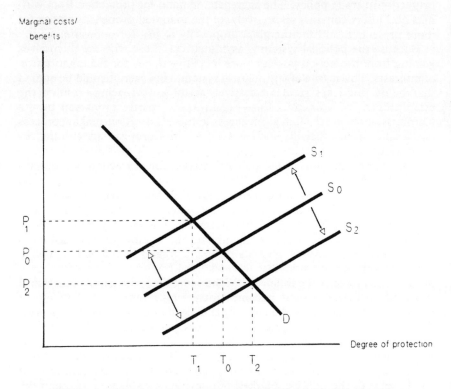

Figure 4.1 Supply and demand in the political market for protection

In the case of EC trade policy, it is possible to imagine a removal of the
supply function away from market equilibrium in both a free trade and a
protectionist direction. In any case EC decision makers exert considerable
discretionary power in trade policy issues. As far as trade policy is concerned, particular provisions were laid down in the EEC Treaty, whose
majority voting provisions have undoubtedly contributed to more rapid and
effective decision making (Commission, 1991b). Moreover, the EC Commission has the right to take initiatives on and negotiate about trade policy
matters without being in any direct way subject to voter approval (although
an EC Council decision is required to enter into negotiations with third
countries, usually on the basis of a specific negotiating directive). Finally,
the reason behind the considerable discretionary power of the EC decision
makers is that the media and voters generally took very little interest in
decisions made by the EC Council.[3]

At the same time, traditionally, there were indications that the discretionary powers of EC decision makers on trade policy matters meant that the supply function S_0 in Figure 4.1 was moved to S_2 rather than to S_1 reflecting the EC decision makers' more protectionist tendencies as compared to their national counterparts. One reason was that trade policy was to a certain extent used to create an external identity for the EC vis-à-vis other actors in the world. Frey and Buhofer (1986) reached the conclusion that the EC was generally more protectionist than member countries would have been individually.

However, there are now increasing indications that the discretionary power of EC decision makers means that the supply function S_0 in Figure 4.1 is moved to S_1 rather than to S_2. Increasingly different overriding concerns are used, for example by the EC Commission, as arguments for more free trade with certain groups of third countries.

The theory of the political economy of trade policy thus seems to explain the trade barriers which currently exist in the EC. Since the beginning of the 1970s, all member countries have experienced a sharp increase in unemployment and have sought to promote high employment by trying to protect their non-competitive and geographically concentrated sectors.

Nevertheless, the political economy-oriented trade theory has been criticized for its difficulties in trying to explain why trade liberalization is possible after all. The theory predicts that the political system contains so many interest groups who want to limit trade, and that politicians are so eager to listen to these groups, that it is difficult to identify where the pressure in favour of trade liberalization should derive.

One reason why it is difficult to explain trade liberalization within the framework of the political economy of trade policy is that the theory evolved as a means of explaining the growth in the public sector. In these cases, the theory is often called 'public choice theory'.

When the assumptions and concepts of public choice are applied to trade, the problem remains that it is much more difficult to claim that a growing public sector is welfare-decreasing than to claim that protectionism is welfare-decreasing. In other words, through its long history the free trade theory has been able to contribute to the creations of norms and a perception of reality that have an independent impact on the behaviour of political decision makers.[4] This is not yet the case with the theory of public choice.

A modern factor pulling in the direction of better fulfilment of the free trade norm is, of course, the ongoing GATT (General Agreement on Tariffs and Trade) negotiations. The Uruguay Round of multilateral GATT negotiations became the focal point for world trade policy in the late 1980s and early 1990s. As the successor to the Kennedy Round of the 1960s and the Tokyo Round of the 1970s, the outcome of the Uruguay Round will have a decisive effect on the global trading system. The present GATT negotiations officially began in Uruguay in 1986. The negotiations were scheduled to end by December 1990, but they are still deadlocked. One explanation for this is the difficulty of the EC in playing the role of an actively negotiating counterpart vis-à-vis the United States. Another explanation is that the present GATT Round is more ambitious than earlier rounds.

European economic integration

A significant step since the mid-1980s towards accelerated economic integration in the EC was the adoption of the Internal Market programme.

In 1985, a comprehensive programme was launched to revitalize the EC integration process. Following a Commission initiative, the EC Council in March 1985 identified as a first priority 'action to achieve a single market by 1992' and asked the Commission to submit a detailed programme. In response, on 15 July 1985 the Commission presented its 'White Paper on Completing the Internal Market'.

The purpose of the Internal Market programme was to eliminate all barriers to trade within the EC before the end of 1992. Therefore, cost-increasing barriers (border controls, different standards, etc.) and restrictions to market entry (public procurement, national market regulations, etc.) are the main targets of the Internal Market programme. As a consequence of the removal of border controls, however, a number of national quantitative restrictions and quotas will have to be eliminated when the EC trade policy becomes harmonized in the integration process.

The EC Commission has stated that 'after the completion of the Internal Market it will no longer be possible to use border controls at internal frontiers' to protect national markets (Commission, 1990a). Therefore, the White Paper points to a need to find substitutes for internal frontier controls when ideally, after 1992, all import restrictions would have to be applied on an EC-wide basis.

The removal of quantitative restrictions touches upon a traditional problem with the EC. From the very beginning, certain member countries (particularly France) insisted on prolonging their quantitative restrictions especially on agricultural goods, despite their incompatibility with the EEC Treaty. These quantitative restrictions were allowed to continue 'temporarily', although they entailed restrictions on the free circulation of goods within the EC. A new set of 'transitional' restrictions was established after the entry of Spain and Portugal.

The removal of quantitative restrictions will have implications for third countries, but it is difficult to determine how important these will be. The reason is partly lack of information, as it is difficult to identify all the quantitative restrictions currently being applied. For example, inclusion on the national lists of quantitative restrictions does not mean that restrictions are being enforced. On the other hand, a number of quantitative restrictions are being applied selectively; i.e., imports from certain countries are restricted while those from others are not. The complex nature of quantitative restrictions stems from the fact that some were originally intended to protect domestic producers while others were aimed at helping producers in certain exporting countries that the EC member countries wanted to safeguard from competition (Davenport, 1990: 36–38).

In order to demonstrate the impact on third countries of the removal of quantitative restrictions in the EC, one thus has to rely on examples and theoretical arguments. One of the most important examples of a product category not yet covered by a common import regime is automobiles. Car importers from Japan into the EC are subject to formal and informal restrictions or equivalent measures at the individual member level, the EC level, or both. At the national level, various EC countries have their own individual quota systems. Japanese imports account for 2 per cent of the Italian market, 3 per cent of the French market, 11 per cent of the British market, 14 per cent of the Portuguese market and below 1 per cent of the Spanish market. Overall, 60 to 65 per cent of the EC market operates under quota restraints at the national level.

At the Community level, surveillance has been the only policy applied to imports of cars from Japan. As part of the process to complete the Internal Market by 1992, however, the EC aims to create a single market for automobiles. In this process, the elimination of national import restrictions has encountered strong resistance from producers and might be difficult to achieve, given disparities in national levels of protection and in competitiveness among EC members.

According to the EC Commission, its objective is to ensure that national restrictions are gradually phased out. Nevertheless, given the degree of trade imbalance with Japan and the high dependence of their domestic manufactures on the five protected markets, certain EC countries are opposed to a rapid relaxation of quotas, and are calling for a long transitional period after 1993. The EC Commission favours a shorter transitional period which would be based on an agreement of voluntary export restraint by Japan. The objective is to avoid a situation similar to that of the United States, where Japanese self-restraint has been renewed annually for over ten years.

Resistance to elimination of national restrictions has raised concerns that they might be replaced by tighter EC-wide restrictions. In this context, car producers in several EC member countries have stated that the lifting of restrictions was dependent on both a reduction of Japanese car share to about 10 per cent of the European market (from 11 to 12 per cent in 1993), and increased access for the EC car industry to 5 per cent of the Japanese market, compared with about 3 per cent presently (Commission, 1991c; European Motor Business, 1993).

In general, non-European competitors fear that the liberalization of markets within the EC will lead to greater protectionism *vis-à-vis* third countries. There are two major sources of such increased protectionism (Teutemann, 1990: 29). First, there will be a need for changes in rules in cases where the EC countries have different bilateral trade regimes within various member countries, as in the case of car imports and import quotas under Article 115 in the EEC Treaty. Second, the exposure to more intra-EC competition provides incentives for interest groups to struggle for higher extra-EC protection.

As regards the first source of increased protection, for example, some EC countries have only a very few of their products affected by import restrictions under Article 115 of the EEC Treaty (e.g., Germany and Denmark), whereas other EC countries (France and Italy) have a whole range of products affected by these restrictions. The question thus arises as to whether a uniform trade regime for the EC will tend towards higher or lower levels of protectionism. Import restrictions under Article 115 are normally implemented on the initiative of well-organized national interest groups who seek protection against competitors from third countries, and it is unlikely that the power of these groups will be weakened by the Internal Market programme. A weakening of national interest groups can only be expected in those cases where, on the one hand, protectionist measures on the European level require concerted action by interest groups of different countries while, on the other hand, the implementation of such measures is resisted either within the group or by a third group.

Replacing bilateral import restrictions with EC-wide restrictions may demand internationally concerted action. However, there exist no countervailing conflicts between interest groups of different countries. For instance, although French car producers are the most active in reducing competition from outside the EC, German car producers are also interested in such action. Consequently, it is likely that the overall pressure for protectionism will increase as a result of the Internal Market. Foreign competitors who are negatively affected by intra-EC demands for protection are not clients of European political decision makers, and the role of European consumers in the decision-making process is negligible. Only in cases where producers in non-member countries obtain strong support from their governments could bargaining between powerful non-member governments and the EC Council temper the tendency of rising EC protectionism.

A second source of increase in EC protectionism stems from another element of the Internal Market programme. The liberalization of markets will expose certain services in some countries to greater competition; e.g. banking, insurance or transport services. The affected groups may request compensation in the form of extra-EC protection, as was discussed under the 'reciprocity' headline for banking and insurance sectors. Since such efforts are directed against third country competitors, they may be supported by pressure groups from all EC countries and thus may be more easily accepted by politicians and bureaucrats.

Ceteris paribus, we must conclude that the Internal Market programme is likely to reinforce protectionist pressures in the EC.[5] Furthermore, politically, the EC countries are a long way from forming a single action unit, a European state power. Even after the implementation of the Maastricht Treaty, the EC will only be able to conduct a low-profile and fragmented foreign policy and security policy. Such a structure favours a reactive and defensive, rather than an active and strategic, policy. Economic weight will translate only slowly into political power. The economic power of the individual EC countries will only gradually come to represent an aggregate political entity and even then it will be more a protective unit than a source of strategic influence on a global level (Weiner, 1992). However, it has been argued that protectionism is a necessary price to pay for more European political unity. Using the concepts of trade division and trade creation,[6] Hirschman (1981: 271) notes that:

> [t]he larger the trade-creating effects, ... the greater will be the resistance to the union among various concentrated and vocal producer interests of the member countries ... On the contrary, trade diversion implies that concentrated producer

groups of member countries will be able to capture business away from their competitors in non-member countries. These effects will therefore endear the customs union to concerned interest groups and will provide some badly needed group-support for a union.

The conclusion is that it might be necessary to balance economically desirable trade creation with some politically vital trade creation.

Protectionist trade measures on the part of the EC which are accompanied by parallel measures in the United States and Japan place severe strains on the international management of economic interdependence. Ideally, such a management would take over the organizational and control functions formerly exercised by the United States due to its hegemonic position. Previously, hegemonic powers, due to their superior economic position, would have a stake in free trade and would be willing and able to supply free trade as an international public good. From this viewpoint, the post-war hegemonic position of the United States explains why post-war trade was relatively liberal until the end of American hegemony around 1973.

However, according to the neo-Grotian idealistic view on international relations, it is now possible to replace former hegemonies by hegemonic liberal norms and values.

The hierarchy of EC trade relations

Alongside accelerated internal EC integration, a fundamental change in EC trade relations *vis-à-vis* third countries is likely to take place in the 1990s. In the present hierarchy of trade relations, those countries at the top of the hierarchy are subject to preferential treatment. However, this is no guarantee for growing exports to the EC (see Table 4.1).

Table 4.1 EC-12 imports from preferential sources, 1977–79 and 1991 (per cent)

	1977–79	1991	Change
Preferential sources:			
EFTA countries	17.3	23.1	+5.8
Mediterranean countries[a]	5.3	4.9	-0.4
Lomé countries	7.1	3.9	-3.2
Other GSP beneficiaries[b]	33.6	19.7	-13.9
Other sources	36.8	48.4	+11.6
Total imports	100	100	

Notes:
a Algeria, Cyprus, Egypt, Israel, Jordan, the Lebanon, Malta, Morocco, Syria, Tunisia, Turkey, Yugoslavia.
b 1990 definition.

Source: EC Commission

Table 4.2 shows the traditional hierarchy of EC trade relations.

Table 4.2 The traditional hierarchy of EC trade relations

Trade relationship	Countries involved	Trade conditions for export to the EC countries
Customs union	EC	All products and services
Free trade area	EFTA	All products except agricultural goods
Mixed	Mediterranean countries	All products except some agricultural goods, textiles etc.
One way preferences –Lomé Convention	ACP countries	All manufactured products, some agricultural goods
One way preferences –GSP	Other Third World countries	Manufactured products within quotas
Most favoured nation clause	Non-European developed countries	GATT rules
Ad hoc	State trading countries	Quotas

At the top of the hierarchy are the EFTA (European Free Trade Association) countries and the Mediterranean countries. They enjoy industrial free trade and concessions for processed agricultural products and industrial and agricultural trade concessions, respectively.

The EC and the EFTA countries have recently redefined their relationship in a treaty document of almost one thousand pages entitled The European Economic Area (EEA). The EEA, excluding only Switzerland among the EFTA countries, will probably be formed simultaneously with the implementation of the Maastricht Treaty on 1 January 1994.[7] About 80 per cent of the regulations in force in the EC will thereafter apply within all participating EFTA countries. However, instead of putting relations between the EC and EFTA on a new and lasting basis, the EEA has instead already become a kind of 'waiting room'. The goal of several EFTA countries is membership in the EC, not the EEA. Austria, Sweden, Greece, Finland, and Norway have already applied for membership.

Gradually, almost all Mediterranean countries have obtained preferential status in their trade relations with the EC. The EC has concluded association agreements with Turkey (1963), Malta (1970) and Cyprus (1972).

In 1975 and 1976, cooperation agreements were signed with Algeria, Egypt, Jordan, the Lebanon, Morocco, Syria and Tunisia, granting these countries free access to the EC market for all raw materials and industrial products. However, the agricultural exports from these countries are more restricted. Following its southern enlargement, the EC renegotiated conditions of market access with the Mediterranean countries whose traditional agricultural exports had been the subject of sizeable trade restrictions.

Lately, the EC has been urged to offer the Maghreb countries of North Africa more free trade as a means of encouraging stability and limiting migration. The EC Commission is already holding exploratory talks on Morocco's proposal for free trade with the EC and is planning to do the same with Tunisia. The other potential beneficiary is Algeria. The EC Commission has increasingly regarded a liberalization of exports as necessary in order to limit migration caused by demographic pressure in the North African countries. Trade liberalization between the EC and the North African countries is mainly a result of pressure from the Southern European EC countries seeking to prevent mass migration to Europe. These measures have been implemented even though producers in these countries will suffer most when the EC liberalizes imports of fruit, wine and textiles. Hence, in relation to Mediterranean countries, traditional interest groups seem to be counterbalanced by other overriding political concerns. Yet the EC will still have only a relatively moderate import trade with the Mediterranean countries compared with other groups of countries after a possible import liberalization.

Such a trade liberalization is a possibility in the near future, especially due to the fact that the EC Commission, at least at the conceptual level, has realized that serious overriding political concerns are at stake in the Community's relations with North African countries. Assuming unchanged economic conditions and extrapolating from the experience of migration between Latin America and the United States, it is estimated that the African migration potential will double over the next twenty years. Taking into account the demographic and economic imbalances on the European side of the Atlantic, this assumption seems quite modest. The current ratio of fertility rates between Latin America and North America is 2 to 1 and the ratio of purchasing power is 4 to 1. However, the ratio of fertility rates between North African/Middle Eastern countries on the one hand and Europe on the other hand is 4 to 1 and the ratio of purchasing power is 7 to 1. The Commission concludes that if 'present economic trends continue, for many urbanized young people, propping up walls in towns of the Maghreb, emigration will eventually represent their hope of social advancement, and clandestine migration, whatever its risks, will strike them as preferable to poverty' (Commission, 1990b: 52). 'The most important way to improve economies of the North African countries is to increase economic cooperation, i.e. aid, investments and, especially, to radically reduce restrictions on imports of goods' (Commission, 1990b: 66).

Even though it can be argued that the 'special relationship' between the EC and some developing countries is basically a result of overriding political concerns (e.g. colonial bonds, a guilt feeling because of former exploitation, etc.), and therefore already outside the realm of special interests, these special interests nevertheless have a stake in the EC relationship towards these developing countries. In general, however, the relations between the

Community and the developing countries beyond the Mediterranean area are likely to change, according to the EC Commission. In a recent policy paper to the EC Council and the European Parliament, the Commission concludes:

> Traditional forms of interdependence, which have prevailed in the North–South relations for many years and on which the claims of the 'New International Economic Order' were based, have been substantially altered or weakened in the last few years. With the end of the Cold War, the countries of the South have lost their role as 'relay stations' in the super powers' confrontation, and with it, the massive economic and military aid which was poured into them. In supplying the North with raw materials (leaving aside oil) the South no longer plays the same strategic role it did in the past. As trade outlets for industrial products, too, the developing world's markets, especially in Africa, are no longer as important to the North. Progress in recent years in dealing with Third World debt has, to a large degree, reduced the risk of a collapse (which appeared a possibility in the beginning of the eighties) of the international banking system. But the interdependence of the industrialized and the developing world has revealed itself in new and striking forms in the last few years, making clearer what is at stake for the international community (Commission, 1992: 38).

Among the developing countries, the Lomé countries are today, in principle, granted unrestricted and duty-free access to the EC market. This includes agricultural products outside the framework of the Common Agricultural Policy (CAP). As regards the bulk of agricultural products under CAP, the ACP (African, Caribbean and Pacific) countries are being ensured more favourable treatment than other suppliers under the MFN (Most Favoured Nation) clause.

Since 1975, successive Lomé Conventions have been negotiated with a view to maintaining and developing economic and commercial relations between the EC and developing countries. The first Lomé Convention was concluded shortly after the entry of the United Kingdom into the EC. It substantially widened the scope of beneficiary countries as compared with its predecessors, the two Yaoundé Conventions, which were confined mainly to French-speaking African countries.

Compared to Lomé III, Lomé IV (1990) reduced EC import restrictions on agricultural products not formerly exportable under duty-free conditions.

Regarding the effects of the various Lomé Conventions, it is possible to conclude, not surprisingly, that the basic economic relationship between the EC and the ACP countries has not changed. The EC continues to absorb about 50 per cent of the total exports from the Lomé countries while the latter represent only 5–10 per cent of total EC imports. Furthermore, the ACP countries have been disappointed at times by the Lomé Convention: their trade balances are in continued deficit, their share of the EC market has declined, and they have failed to diversify their exports. In spite of these disappointments, the ACP countries would probably have been worse off without the Lomé Convention.

The possibility of exporting agricultural products from non-ACP countries reflects the partnership priorities of the EC. Although the empirical evidence does not suggest that the Lomé Convention has been a significant source of trade diversion for agricultural products, certain features of the agreement discriminate against other developing countries. Since the Lomé signatories are at the top of the EC's hierarchy of trade relations, they are able to influence the level of concessions given to all other EC partners. This includes the majority of the countries of Latin America and Asia; i.e. countries covered by the GSP (Generalized System of Preferences) (McMahon, 1988: 200).

However, for the EC producers, the impact of these priorities is of only minor importance. The EC political decision makers have therefore had few problems in upholding the present set of trade priorities. Again it is possible that overriding concerns will alter EC trade policy *vis-à-vis* the Lomé countries and other developing countries. Environmental concerns have increasingly been introduced in the trade debate; however, these concerns are discussed in a manner other than is usual for trade negotiations between the EC and developing countries. Arguments have been made by several environmental groups that whatever the starting point, protection of the environment is incompatible with trade liberalization. It is suggested that trade liberalization, in so far as it entails expanding production, is associated with world contribution to environmental degradation. While trade policies can certainly have environmental implications, the resolution of environmental problems rests basically on the development of effective environmental policies. For developing countries, environmental problems tend to be the result of domestic policy failures or poverty-related factors or to both of these. Their resolution demands growth, which is facilitated by trade, as well as by international assistance. On the other hand, it is likely that environmental concerns will be used as a cover for interest groups trying to find new, legitimate protectionist arguments, as has been seen in the American debate about the inclusion of Mexico into NAFTA. As pointed out by OECD (1992: 17): 'In industrialised countries, producers have allied with the increasing powerful environmental lobbies to frustrate liberalisation. This has negative implications for developing countries, as their environmental problems are essentially poverty related; the eradication of poverty is facilitated by growth and access to industrialised markets'.

The GSP, first introduced in 1971 under the auspices of the United Nations Conference on Trade and Development (UNCTAD), provides for countries to reduce or waive restrictions on Third World exports. During the 1970s, all Western countries joined this 'generalized scheme of preferences', which originated in a European initiative of 1963. Since its introduction, the EC preference scheme has been extended, especially as regards processed agricultural products.

The starting point for establishing a hierarchy of trade relations between the EC and the developing countries outside ACP, i.e. in Latin America and Asia, is the most favoured nation tariff. The EC version of GSP has the following characteristics: 1) the EC accords tariff preferences for semi-manufactured and manufactured goods plus tariff-free access within certain limits; 2) textiles are excluded from the GSP, 3) agricultural products included in the Common Agricultural Policy are excluded from GSP; and 4) the EC demands no reciprocity.

The GSP does not change the fact, however, that the Common Agricultural Policy poses a serious problem for Latin American producers, since agricultural goods constitute over 50 per cent of the Community's imports from the region. One particular aspect of the policy, the variable levy, has been criticized by Latin American exporters as unduly protectionist.

In sum, the trade effects of the GSP have been modest (Laursen, 1986: 98). The most plausible explanations are as follows: 1) GSP in itself has been unambitious, 2) the EC version has so many exceptions, 3) protectionist pressures from producers within the EC are responsible for under-utilization of the GSP, 4) GSP deals with tariff reductions, whereas it is non-tariff barriers which are often more important and 5) the interests of other partners, such as the Lomé countries and the Mediterranean countries, are considered more important than those of the GSP countries in Asia and Latin America.

Hence, despite preferential treatment of developing countries by the EC (and by other groups of industrialized countries), 'developing countries have in practice been most exposed to discriminatory export restraint agreements and other trade distorting measures, with the incidence of this discrimination falling heaviest in those sectors in which they have a comparative advantage, such as agriculture, and textiles' (OECD, 1992: 19).

Until the revolutions in Eastern Europe, the final two stages of the traditional hierarchy of EC trade relations were occupied by the developed countries (most importantly United States and Japan) and state-trading countries (former members of the Council of Mutual Economic Assistance (CMEA). Since 1989–90, the Central and Eastern European countries have been gradually moving to the top of the hierarchy, but the EC trade relationships *vis-à-vis* the other former state trading countries for Soviet plus non-European CMEA are also undergoing a rapid change in the 1990s.

Obviously, the changing economic relations between the EC and countries from the former European CMEA countries stem from a desire by the EC to safeguard the democratic and economic revolutions in the East. These overriding political concerns are not new as far as relations between the EC and CMEA countries are concerned. From the beginning the EC was characterized in the Soviet literature as the 'economic arm of NATO' and 'an organ of Western European monopoly capitalism doomed to inevitable destruction because of its internal contradictions' (Nello, 1990). At the same time, imports from the CMEA countries were kept at an absolute minimum by the EC authorities for political reasons. Consequently, the traditional close trade links before the First and Second World Wars, particularly between Poland, Czechoslovakia, and Hungary on the one hand and between several Western European countries on the other, were broken.

Since the 1989 revolutions, most Central and Eastern European countries have expressed their interest in membership of the EC. As an alternative to the rapid expansion of the EC to include nine additional members from the former CMEA, especially Poland, Hungary, and Czechoslovakia, it has been made clear by the EC that full membership be made contingent on a prior phase of subregional, economic and political cooperation. As compensation, those Central and Eastern European countries which have made the most decisive progress in economic and political reform were offered the possibility of 'second generation association agreements', which later became known as Europe Agreements. The conditions for a future EC membership were spelled out and related to the rule of law, their human rights record (including respect for religious and ethnic minorities), political pluralism, free elections, and the liberalization of the economy (Nello, 1991: 204–6).

The Europe agreements are aimed at encouraging both wider economic integration and political and cultural cooperation. It is expected that in the first five years the EC will remove all specific quantitative restrictions and will then gradually reduce non-specific ones. At the same time, the Central and Eastern European countries will attempt to gradually eliminate their tariffs on non-sensitive products, and reduce tariffs on sensitive products to bring them in line with GSP.

During a second five-year period, the EC will dismantle all remaining tariffs and quotas. The Central and Eastern European countries will gradually reduce customs duties and restrictive taxes during this period, and although quotas will be allowed, there will be preferential treatment for EC products.

Textiles, coal and steel products and agricultural products would be treated in separate protocols attached to the agreements. At the same time, the Central and Eastern European countries have a known comparative advantage in these product areas (Junz, 1991). Therefore, it is no surprise that protection against imports of these products into the EC has given rise to debate, with the Central and Eastern European countries accusing the EC of *de facto* protectionism when they are attempting to liberalize their trade.[8]

However, the EC does seem prepared to make concessions. Tariffs on textiles will be eliminated over a ten-year period, but reduction of non-tariff barriers will depend on the outcome of the Uruguay Round GATT negotiations. Tariffs on iron and steel products will be eliminated over a five-year period. Certain agricultural concessions are also expected on fruit, vegetables and possibly pork and poultry. Mutton and beef are still subjects of contention, as the fall in EC beef prices in 1990–91 is partly due to a rise in imports from these countries following the agricultural arrangements which permitted limited quotas of cattle imports (Nello, 1991: 207–8).[9]

It is clear, however, that these steps are far from sufficient if the economic situation in Central and Eastern Europe is to improve. In this case, EC trade policy ought to be changed so that in the long term the Central and Eastern European countries might become, for example, substantial net food exporters. There are, at least, three reasons for this. First, they have a comparative cost advantage. Favourable natural conditions (such as the Ukraine's fertile soil) and the prospect of long-term low wages seem to make the former CMEA countries ideal agricultural producers. Given these advantages, the logical response would be to restore a European division of labour similar to that in place prior to the Second World War, when the

Central and Eastern European countries supplied raw or semi-finished materials and labour-intensive products to Western Europe.

Second, the Central and Eastern European countries have structural overcapacities. The planned economies of Central and Eastern Europe were characterized by waste at all levels of production, distribution and consumption. Therefore, in order to guarantee at least a reasonable supply of food to their populations, the agricultural sector was expanded. Output per capita frequently surpassed even that of the EC, and at the end of the 1980s, roughly 20 per cent of the work force in the Central and Eastern European countries was employed in agriculture and forestry.

Third, they have productivity reserves in agriculture itself. As in all sectors, low agricultural productivity stems from inefficient organization, lack of incentives or antiquated equipment. As the Central and Eastern European countries adopt a business mentality and start using modern technology, it will be possible to mobilize considerable productivity reserves.

On the other hand, it is difficult to see how it would be politically possible to reform the Common Agricultural Policy in order to allow for expanded imports from the Central and Eastern European countries. At the same time, precisely the same arguments could have been put forward regarding exports from the Central and European countries in the sectors of textiles, steel products and machines.

In principle, at the bottom of traditional hierarchy of EC trade relations are non-European developed countries, of which the most important are the United States and Japan. The United States supported Western European integration from the very beginning in the 1950s. The decision to support the EC was taken despite its potentially adverse impact on American competitiveness, despite the implicit discrimination against American exports that it entailed, and despite the threat that it would develop into a protectionist bloc (Zupnick, 1992). Overriding political concerns, which seemed to prevail over special interests, emerged because an economically strong Europe was necessary in order for the newly formed NATO to contain the perceived aggressive intentions of the Soviet Union. The motive of strengthening NATO continued to play a role until recently. At the same time, however, the United States took advantage of its hegemonic position in NATO to induce the Western European countries to make trade concessions. Consequently, the overriding concerns of the United States were more or less compensated for by forceful attempts to open up EC markets to American products.

The United States also used expanded deterrence as a means of pressure in the Uruguay Round of GATT to force the EC into making concessions on other points of disagreement such as agriculture, intellectual property rights and financial services. All in all, trade relations between the United States and the EC have been plagued by tensions ever since the EC was founded. Initially confined primarily to agricultural matters, the areas of conflict broadened in the 1970s and 1980s to include the steel, machine tools, and advanced technology sectors. The United States criticized the EC subsidy and procurement policies especially in aviation and telecommunications as American firms suffered discrimination in these areas. The United States' high balance of trade deficit accelerated American efforts to halt so-called unfair trading practices (Weiner, 1992). The deficit not only demonstrated the declining competitiveness of the American economy in world markets, but also triggered a wave of American protectionism which has not subsided. The EC considers American trade law, in particular Section 301 and its amendment by the Omnibus Trade Act of 1988, as signs of growing protectionism.

However, US economic power is still regarded as a challenge to European integration, especially by the EC Commission bureaucrats who are much influenced by French administrative culture and thinking. As a matter of fact, one of the most important explanatory factors behind the accelerated market integration process in the 1980s was external pressure from the United States and Japan. In particular, the (then) strong economic performance of the United States was used to legitimize the Internal Market programme, although it can be shown that economic pressure from Japan is much stronger and of a more fundamental nature (Nedergaard, 1990a: 94–9).

The EC trade policy approach *vis-à-vis* Japan has been aptly characterized by Taylor (1990: 88): '[s]ince the early 1980s EC national leaders have increasingly seen the need to act in concert at both Community and international levels to protect themselves against what they regard as a Japanese threat to their prosperity'. This approach is reflected in a trade policy paper from the EC Commission: 'Japan maintains a larger surplus with its developed partners while the USA and EEC are currently in deficit: this says something about the openness of markets' (Commission, 1991b).

Specifically, EC authorities claim that 'the main difficulties encountered by the Community in securing market access to Japan continue to be that of a structural character. In particular can be mentioned the distribution system, the interactions among industrial groups ("keiretsu"), the difficulties for foreign firms to participate in mergers and acquisitions' (Commission, 1991b).

However, even if the Commission's conclusions are valid, the EC trade policy approach towards Japan is far from being in correspondence with free trade norms where even unilateral trade openings are beneficial, and trade deficits say nothing about the openness of the Japanese market.

Conclusions

The beginning of this chapter raised the question of whether normative international issues will gain the upper hand over more short-sighted interests. The conclusion is pessimistic. The so-called new world order does not mean an end to special interests. In an area such as EC trade policy, it is unlikely that we will see substantial policy change, even though it can be strongly argued that such a change is needed if a number of severe problems facing the EC, Europe and Europe's neighbours are to be solved.

The new neo-Grotian-based normative liberal approach to international relations promoted as part of the new world order is not apparent in actual behaviour among states, even in an area like trade policy where liberal norms are historically very strong.

On the other hand, it is possible to discern an increasing awareness, at least at the rhetorical level, of a number of overriding political concerns that must be taken into account in the EC trade policy formulation process. In various policy papers, the EC Commission has argued in favour of increased trade liberalization *vis-à-vis* the Mediterranean countries, Central and Eastern Europe and the developing countries. However, the EC Council has taken only a few steps in the direction proposed by the EC Commission. Substantial progress towards trade liberalization has been made concerning the Central and Eastern European countries, but even these steps seem unsatisfactory in view of the difficulties in transforming the former CMEA countries into market economies. The proposed liberalization regarding the Mediterranean countries has difficulties in becoming a genuine EC trade policy even though some improvements have taken (and will take) place.

The traditional hierarchy of trade relations is certainly changing, but only because some countries (Central and Eastern Europe) have previously been in an extremely disadvantageous position. The gradual restructuring of the hierarchy of trade relations will mainly take place as a result of international agreements (EEA and GATT).

At the theoretical level, the political economy of trade policy helps to explain why EC protectionism is maintained at the present level or is even on the rise due to the implementation of the Internal Market programme. This chapter has attempted to falsify that theory in a situation where its theoretical assumptions were assumed to be invalidated by the new world economic order. Paradoxically, our analysis has revealed that the value of the theory has increased rather than decreased.

As a matter of fact, the theory has shown itself to be able to incorporate, for instance, environmental concerns into its framework, thereby strengthening its explanatory power. It is probable that the norms which will eventually gain ground in international trade policy will be those that maintain rather than conflict with special interests. On the other hand, where a broad perspective on world affairs or the general interest is necessary, free trade norms will have great difficulties in being implemented in actual trade policy.

Notes

1. The roots of the traditional free trade theory go back to Adam Smith and David Ricardo. In this century the theory has found its definite shape in the so-called Heckscher-Ohlin model which was finally formalized in the 1950s. According to the traditional free trade theory, when two countries trade with each other, both countries benefit from this trade. These benefits are assumed to be created due to the fact that different countries have different costs for different kinds of production. In this way, the individual countries have different comparative advantages in the production of certain kinds of goods and services. Therefore, gains are created when countries specialize.

2. The theorem of optimum tariff and the theory of strategic trade policy are competing economic explanations. In some circumstances a large country or group

of countries could earn a welfare gain by affecting prices on imported goods through a so-called *optimum tariff* (possible result: depressed prices for imported goods) and through limitations in export (possible result: increased prices for exported goods as in the case of OPEC). However, it is difficult to trace any kind of consciously established optimum tariff in the present customs union of the EC. On the other hand, it is possible that, solely because of its economic size, the EC customs union has contributed to an improvement of the EC terms-of-trade in some categories of import.

Discussing the theory of strategic trade policy, Haberler (1990) claims that the only novelty is the focus on the possibility of attracting sectors with an above-average profit. However, the strategic trade policy with the aim of securing sectors with above-average profit for a specific country (or groups of countries) presupposes a government or a state bureaucracy that is playing the role of an almost objective, benevolent, and omniscient dictator (Stegemann, 1989).

However, one must also separate the issue of whether or not strategic gains exist and whether the political decision makers (for example, the EC Commission) perceive that strategic gains exist. The first issue has been the subject of debate, but no matter the result, the EC Commission sometimes operates as if the strategic gains existed. For example, a group of experts from the EC Commission, the European computer industry, and independent European consultants published a report in 1991 on the need for a new EC programme aimed at the development of super-computers: 'Demand for high-performance computing is constantly rising. Europe does not get any benefit from this, rather it experiences *an economic loss*. This will become more and more serious as markets expand, and as the need reaches wider and wider sectors of society. The negative effects on the trade balance will also increase. The lack of an industrial infrastructure in the field causes the loss of *spinoffs*, both in the information technology at all levels and in other related industries' (Commission, 1991a).

3. If media have great interest in specific policy areas, the information costs for the general public are lowered.

4. The traditional free trade regime also owes some of its strength to a widespread conviction that free trade reduces the number of international conflicts; i.e. that more trade means a safer world.

5. This does not mean that the EC will eventually become a Fortress Europe any more than the United States and Japan are fortresses today. As a matter of fact, fewer barriers between EC member countries will tend to benefit non-EC firms, in spite of a somewhat more protectionist policy *vis-à-vis* third countries. American and Japanese multinationals are prime candidates for reaping great benefits from the implementation of the Internal Market because their business strategy is already pan-European.

6. Establishment of a customs union leads to more effective allocations and welfare benefits through trade creation if there is a shift in consumption from expensive, domestically produced goods to more cheaply produced goods from other parts of the customs union. On the contrary, customs union results in trade diversion if a shift occurs from consumption of low-cost goods produced outside the customs union to relatively high-cost goods produced in one of the member countries of the customs union.

7. Switzerland rejected the EEA in a referendum on 6 December 1992.

8. Polish president Lech Walesa, for example, accused the EC of replacing the old political iron curtain with a new economic silver curtain.

9. This price fall resulted in attacks by French and other farmers on trucks transporting the imported farm products into Western Europe.

References

Commission of the European Communities (1989) *International Trade of the European Community*, European Economy, Report No. 39.

Commission of the European Communities (1990a) *Industrial Policy in an Open and Competitive Environment*.

Commission of the European Communities (1990b) *Forward Unit Studies. Population Trends and Europe*, SEC (90) 8657.

Commission of the European Communities (1991a) *Report of the EEC Working Group on High-Performance Computing*.

Commission of European Communities (1991b) *Trade Policy Review Mechanism: The European Communities*.

Commission of European Communities (1991c) *Panorama of EC Industries, 1991–1992*.

Commission of the European Communities (1992) *Development Cooperation Policy in the Run-up to 2000*, SEC (92) 915.

Corden, W. Max (1990) *Strategic Trade Policy: How New? How Sensible?*, Washington: World Bank Working Papers, no. 396.

Davenport, Michael (1990) 'The External Policy of the Community and Its Effects Upon the Manufactured Export of the Developing Countries', *Journal of Common Market Studies*, vol. 24, no. 2.

Davenport, Michael and Sheila Page (1991) *Europe: 1992 and the Developing World*, London: Overseas Development Institute.

European Motor Business (1993) Research Report Examining the European Automotive industry, 2nd Quarter, The European Intelligence Unit.

Frey, Bruno S. and Heinz Buhofer (1986) 'Integration and Protectionism: A Comparative Institutional Analysis', *Aussenwirtschaft*, vol. 41, nos. 2–3.

Fukuyama, Francis (1989) 'The End of History?', *The National Interest*, no. 16.

Gilpin, Robert (1981) *War and Change in World Politics*, Cambridge: Cambridge University Press.

Gilpin, Robert (1987) *The Political Economy of International Relations*, Princeton: Princeton University Press.

Habeler, Gottfried (1990) 'Strategic Trade Policy and the New International Economics: A Critical Analysis', in Barry R.J. Jones and P. Krueger (1990) (eds), *The Political Economy of International Trade*, Cambridge, Mass.: Basil Blackwell, pp. 25-30.

Hirschman, Albert O. (1981) *Essays in Trespassing Economics to Politics and Beyond*, Cambridge: Cambridge University Press.

Junz, Helen B. (1991) 'Integration of Eastern Europe into the World Trading System', *American Economic Review*, vol. 81, no. 2.

Keohane, Robert O. and Joseph S. Nye (1989) *Power and Interdependence*, Glenview, Illinois: Scott, Foresman and Company.

Krasner, Stephen (1979) 'The Tokyo Round, Particularistic Interests and Prospects for Stability in the Global Trading System', *International Studies Quarterly*, vol. 23, no. 4.

Krueger, Anne O. (1990) 'Asymmetries in Policy between Exportables and Import Competing Goods', in R.J. Jones and B. Krueger (1990) (eds), *The Political Economy of International Trade*, Cambridge, Mass.: Basil Blackwell, pp. 161–78.

Krugman, Paul R. (1986) (ed.) *Strategic Trade Policy and the New International Economics*, Cambridge, Mass.: MIT Press.

Laursen, Finn (1991a) 'The EC, GATT, and The Uruguay Round', in Leon Hurwitz and Christian Lequesne (eds), *The State of the European Community: Policies, Institutions and Debates in the Transition Years*, Boulder, Colorado: Lynne Rienner Publishers.

Laursen, Finn (1991c) 'The EC in the World Context – Civilian Power or Super Power?', *Futures*, vol. 23, no. 7.

Laursen, Karsten (1986) *Udviklingslandenes Økonomi*, Working Paper, Institute of International Economics and Management, Copenhagen Business School.

McMahon, Joseph A. (1988) *European Trade Policy in Agricultural Products*, Dordrecht: Martinus Nijhoff Publishers.

Milner, Helen V. and David B. Yoffie (1989) 'Between Free Trade and Protectionism: Strategic Trade Policy and a Theory of Corporate Trade Demands', *International Organization*, vol. 43, no. 2.

Nedergaard, Peter (1988) *EF's landbrugspolitik under omstilling*, København: Jurist- og Økonomforbundets Forlag.

Nedergaard, Peter (1990a) *EF's markedsintegration. En politisk økonomisk analyse*, København: Jurist- og Økonomforbundets Forlag.

Nello, Susan Senior (1990) 'Some Recent Developments in EC-East European Economic Relations', *Journal of World Trade*, vol. 24, no. 1.

Nello, Susan Senior (1991) *The New Europe. Changing Economic Relations between East and West*, New York: Harvester Wheatsheaf.

OECD (1992) 'Trade Liberalization: What's at Stake?', *Policy Brief*, no. 5.

Petersen, Ib Damgaard (1992) 'The Role of the EC in an Emerging New World Order', in Morten Kelstrup (ed.), *European Integration and Denmark's Participation*, Copenhagen: Copenhagen Political Studies Press.

Richardson, J. David (1986) 'The New Political Economy of Trade Policy', in Krugman (1986) (ed.), Cambridge, Mass.: MIT Press, pp. 257–82.

Ruigrok, W. (1991) 'Paradigm Crisis in International Trade Theory', *Journal of World Trade*, vol. 25, no. 1.

Stegemann, Klaus (1989) 'Policy Rivalry among Industrial States: What Can We Learn from Models of Strategic Trade Policy', *International Organization*, vol. 43, no. 1.

Taylor, Robert (1990) *China, Japan and the European Community*, The Athlone Press: London.

Teutemann, Manfred (1990) 'Completion of the Internal Market: An Application of Public Choice Theory', Kommissionen, *Economic Papers*, no. 83.

Venables, Anthony J. (1990) *Trade Policy Under Imperfect Competition: A Numerical Assessment*, London: Centre of Economic Policy Research, Discussion Paper no. 412.

Viner, Jacob (1950) *The Customs Union Issue*, London: Carnagie Endowment for International Peace.

Weck-Hannemann, Hannelore (1990) *Institutional Analysis of Protectionism*, Paper, University of Konstanz.

Weiner Klaus-Peter (1992) 'Between Political Regionalization and Economic Globalization. Problems and Prospects of European Integration', *International Journal of Political Economy*, Spring 1992, pp. 41–62.

Zupnick, Elliot (1992) 'EC-US and the 1992: A Prelude to Trade Wars?', *European Affairs*, No. 2.

PART TWO

PART TWO

5

The European Community and Eastern Europe

KNUD ERIK JØRGENSEN

When the spy came in from the cold he could choose between Glienecke-Brücke and Checkpoint Charlie. Both border points were in Berlin, representative of the division of Germany, of Europe, and of the world. The spy would arrive in a disputed area. Was it part of the EC or part of Europe outside the EC? He did not care, but both EC and Soviet officials did. The status of West Berlin was among many issues which for decades hampered any rapprochement between the two halves of Europe. Other, and more important, issues included the German question and the status of what was then called Eastern Europe. This made EC *Ostpolitik* different in essence from Community foreign policy directed to other areas.

Although *Ostpolitik* was among the first policy issues to be dealt with within the framework of European Political Cooperation (EPC), the scope remained limited until a comprehensive policy was developed in the late 1980s. The policy issue has gradually gained in importance as a new area of concentration in the coordinated foreign policy of Community members. The new assertiveness in Western European multilateral foreign policy corresponded neatly with the simultaneous disappearance of declarations on what was euphemistically called 'East–West relations', but which was actually superpower relations. Detente made possible the EC–CMEA joint declaration of June 1988, and this declaration was among the first clear indications that the general policy review in the EPC, begun in 1987, had been transformed into substantive measures. The joint declaration was significant in at least two respects. It was a precondition for official relations between the Community and individual CMEA members, as well as a precondition for the introduction of more powerful conditionality in EC policy. In this perspective, it is obvious that subsequent EPC declarations contained the first contours of the future policy. The principle of conditionality was gradually employed as a general guideline and materialized in the trade and cooperation agreements, negotiated with the reform-minded countries only. Variation in timing, scope and speed well illustrates the principle operated in practice (Jørgensen, 1991; Lippert, 1991; Pinder, 1991).

This chapter deals with the eastern policy of the Community since 1988.

A distinction is made between the EC's approach to three regions: East Central Europe, the Balkans, and the former Soviet Union. Relations with the first region were poorly developed before the mid-1980s, being limited to a few sector agreements. Over a few years, however, relations rapidly evolved into the most intensive of all EC–East Europe relations. From 1986, links were developed at the unofficial levels and both parties of the relationship went through a learning process invaluable for the subsequent 'opening of Europe'. Yet the revolutions in East Central Europe made obsolete the just-concluded trade and cooperation agreements almost before their implementation. Subsequently a new type of intensive relations was outlined, termed 'Europe Agreements'.

Community relations with the former Communist Balkan states have undergone dramatic changes as well, although in a different direction. Before 1988 both Yugoslavia and Romania had played the role of mavericks within the Soviet dominion and were rewarded for their behaviour. The cooperation agreement with Yugoslavia dates back to 1980, when it supplemented a pre-existing trade agreement from 1970. Yet in the crucial years after 1989 the Balkans was somehow neglected. In the heady days following the 1989 revolutions, the power of the Community was fatally (mis)perceived by policy makers and the principle of conditionality was employed in a rather rigid way. With the beginning of the Yugoslavian warfare and especially after the acknowledged failure to influence events in Yugoslavia, this attitude changed rapidly. It was realized that strict conditionality could backfire. Yet the failure was not followed by a reduced presence of the Community in the Balkans. Instead the powerful economic means at the disposal of the Community were used, but now guided by considerations of stability as well as by the speed of reforms.

Third, relations with the Soviet Union and the successor states are of a different nature. The policy of the EC has been more symbolic than substantive. In fact, changes in the ex-Soviet Union have been so profound as to make consistent comprehensive foreign policy making almost impossible. Instead EC 'policy' has been limited to *ad hoc* responses and minor programmes. In order to put the EC Eastern policy into perspective, we can cite the 1992 capital flow to the former German Democratic Republic, which amounts to some Ecu 50 milliards. The EC 1992 budget amounts to Ecu 1.025 million for Central and Eastern Europe and Ecu 400 million for the entire region of the CIS. The EC budget, being some 60 per cent of the total, is not the whole story, and additional capital from G24 countries does not change the relative levels.

In general, the development of the Eastern policy of the EC has been a continuous learning process. In the mid-1980s the EC had only a minor staff with expertise concerning Eastern Europe. Yet from being almost non-existent less than a decade ago, the policy issue has been elevated to one of the most important places on the EC foreign policy agenda. This implies that policy making has been pursued under difficult conditions with limited resources, under the influence of strong lobbies, under time pressure, and often constrained by differing positions on the part of the EC members. In the following, a balanced approach to the dynamics of relations between the two Europes will be attempted. It requires a narrow analysis of EC policy as well as a broader analysis of intra-European relations.

The EC Central European policy

The internal development of the EC has profound external effects. The commencement of the Internal Market in 1987 entailed intense reconsideration of foreign economic policy in the European countries with strong economic links to the EC. Both EFTA and CMEA countries showed interest in being as close to the Internal Market as possible. Among the CMEA countries, the Central European members showed a particular interest in opening relations with the Community. It was widely recognized that the gap between levels of economic development had widened during the 1980s. In a Hungarian policy white paper it was predicted that the Internal Market would widen the gap even further (Balasz, 1989). In order to avoid this kind of marginalization, the economic side of the 'Return to Europe' metaphor was further developed. The advantage of this kind of reasoning was the high compatibility with the political discourse of former opposition movements, all of which were now governing (Jørgensen, 1992).

From the perspective of the Community, the Central European states were obvious candidates for a new conditional policy, made possible by the highly asymmetrical interdependence between Western and Eastern Europe. The previous unofficial contacts made it relatively easy to conclude trade and cooperation agreements with Hungary (September 1988) and Poland (September 1989). With regard to Czechoslovakia the lack of political reform resulted in a somewhat limited trade agreement (December 1988) and later in a trade and cooperation agreement (May 1990). The revolutions of 1989, however, required a new formula, the so-called Europe Agreements (Lippert, 1991: 133–6; Kuschel, 1992). In December 1990 the Council reached an agreement on negotiating Europe Agreements with Poland, Hungary and Czechoslovakia (CPR 10871/90). Yet it proved more difficult to reach agreement than expected. Contradictions in the Community between EC interests as a trade organization and the broader aims of a European anchor of stability delayed the process. The blocking behaviour of some member states, in particular France and Portugal, resulted in a virtual deadlock of the negotiations.

The coup in Moscow in August 1991 caused an acceleration of the rapprochement between the EC and the east of Europe. All EC member states emphasized their political intention to allow the Commission greater scope for manoeuvre. In early October, the Council agreed to some adjustments, covering areas such as agricultural trade, trade in textile products, financial cooperation, movement of workers, coal and transit (CPR 8400/91). The Europe Agreements were eventually signed with the so-called Visegrad countries (Poland, Hungary and Czechoslovakia) in mid-December 1991.

The political dialogue envisaged in the Europe Agreements was further developed during 1992. A joint meeting of foreign ministers in October marked 'a significant development in the process of strengthening dialogue and co-operation'. The Visegrad memorandum was 'recalled and welcomed' as preparation for the European Council meeting in December 1992. The Visegrad countries 'looked forward to considered response'. In the meantime, the meeting 'agreed upon a series of positions reflecting the present stage in their relations'. In general, the meeting was a forerunner to a meeting of Heads of State or Government in London on October 28, 1992.

In addition to the long-term Europe Agreements, the Community also engaged in short-term measures. In February 1991, the European Investment Bank (EIB) operations were extended to Czechoslovakia. The Council invited the EIB to grant loans (up to Ecu 700 million) and also provided medium-term financial assistance (Ecu 375 million) to ensure a sustainable balance of payment (CPR 4835/91). In June, the Council agreed to grant Ecu 180 million to Hungary. In these operations, the Community carefully watched the contributions from the other G24 countries, normally making an equal share a precondition for Community commitment. The important PHARE programme, launched in 1989, continued to be implemented in East Central Europe.[1]

Table 5.1 Institutional links between the EC and East Central Europe

1988	Joint EC–CMEA Declaration
	Trade and Cooperation Agreement between the EC and Hungary
	Trade Agreement between the EC and Czechoslovakia
	1st meeting of Joint EC–Hungarian Commission (December)
1989	Trade and Cooperation Agreement between the EC and Poland
	Launch of PHARE Programme
	1st meeting of Joint EC–Czech Consultative Group (June)
	2nd meeting of Joint EC–Hungarian Commission (November)
	1st meeting of Joint EC–Polish Commission (December)
1990	EC Commission Delegations established in Budapest and Warsaw
	Establishment of EBRD decided
	Trade and Cooperation Agreement between the EC and Czechoslovakia (May)
	PHARE Programme extended (July)
	2nd meeting of Joint EC–Polish Commission (September)
	3rd meeting of Joint EC–Hungarian Commission (November)
1991	1st meeting of EC-Czechoslovakia Joint Commission (May)
	Europe Agreement between the EC and Poland, Hungary and Czechoslovakia (December)
1992	1st 'political dialogue' meeting between the EC and Visegrad countries; i.e. Poland, Hungary and Czechoslovakia (October)
1993	EC recognition of the Czech Republic and Slovakia (January)

Sources: Various issues of *Bulletin of the European Communities*, *Agence Europe*, and *General Report on the Activities of the European Communities*

While the trade and cooperation agreements between the EC and East European countries reflected the status of relationship during the East–West detente, the Europe Agreements concern bilateral relations of the Community in Europe beyond the East–West division. The agreements have spurred two major debates on the Community's Eastern policy: the first whether the agreements are the appropriate response to a region in search of market economy, democracy and stability, and second, whether the agreements in time ought to be replaced by membership of the Community and/or complemented by other arrangements. A Commission report to the EC Summit in December indicated that the options might be viewed as complementary: that is, the Europe Agreements might be assessed appropriate if given a broad interpretation and if supplemented by additional measures.[2] The debate is linked to larger visions of Europe, i.e. whether the 'concentric circles' formula chosen in 1989 is still appropriate or whether it ought to be replaced or complemented. It is noteworthy that the originators of the concentric circles have made pleas for a new approach (Mertes and Prill, 1992).

Maastricht and Sarajevo: The EC and the Balkans

During the 1980s the Community developed institutional links with only two Balkan states. Romania was rewarded with a relatively limited trade agreement in 1980 for her relatively independent behaviour *vis-à-vis* the Warsaw Pact. In the same year, the Community and Yugoslavia extended an existing trade agreement from 1970, making the new agreement somewhat broader than the EC–Romanian agreement. It has generally been interpreted as a response to expected instability in Yugoslavia after the death of President Tito in 1979. The agreement was intended as a means to prevent Yugoslavia from sliding eastward. In this way, Community policy *vis-à-vis* Yugoslavia contained some aspects of crisis management (Rummel, 1982: 107).

During the so-called Second Cold War, considerations concerning human rights and political reform were not regarded as preconditions for improved relations between the Community and selected East European countries. The principle of conditionality materialized in a classic policy of *raison d'état*. The gradual 'opening of Europe' after the joint EC–CMEA declaration entailed the possibility of developing a different type of bilateral relations. The revolutions in Eastern Europe consolidated the U-turn in Community policy, and Community links with Eastern Europe were changed radically.

The principle of conditionality, presented in a laudably nuanced way by Laux (1991: 23–4), was interpreted in a new way and the 'trilemma' between political reform (democracy), economic reform (market economy), and stability emerged as a problem to the Community. Previous beneficiaries such as Romania and Yugoslavia were unable to fulfil the new conditions, since economic and political reforms had been slow or non-existent. With respect to Yugoslavia it was a rather mixed performance as the economy, with few important exceptions, was largely reformed, whereas political reforms were slow and further complicated by the federal structure of the Yugoslav state. In the words of an Italian diplomat, 'European diplomacy during this transitional period, therefore, tackled the gestation period of the Yugoslavian crisis presumptuously if not with indifference between 1988 and mid-1991, underestimating Italy's signals and warnings, which were, moreover, constantly repeated' (Vento, 1992: 36).

In the Balkans, no alternative candidates existed, as developments in Bulgaria and Albania were rather similar to Romania's. Hence no Balkan state was considered ripe for closer relations with the Community, and the Balkans were somewhat neglected.

The new conditional approach was indicated during 1989 through numerous statements on the violation of human rights in Romania. Symbolic policy was added, as diplomatic representatives of the Community member countries changed their practice by not attending the opening of the Congress of the Communist Party in November. The Community also decided to suspend negotiations on a new trade agreement. During the chaotic violence following the fall of Ceausescu in December 1989, the EC issued a brief statement reaffirming its readiness to offer immediate aid and cooperation 'as Romania takes control of her destiny' (EPC, 1989: 212). Yet until October 1990, relations with Romania were frozen. Shortly thereafter, the new trade agreement was signed. In January 1991 relations were 'placed on the same footing as Bulgaria' (Pinder, 1991: 77).

In Yugoslavia, federal Prime Minister Ante Markovic's reform programme met the Community criteria. In fact, the programme functioned well, bringing down inflation, increasing currency reserves, etc. In spite of this, the Community did not support Markovic during the most crucial phases of the reform programme. Apparently, it was not realized that demands for economic reform stimulated the fragmenting forces in Yugoslavia more than statements emphasizing the 'preservation of the unity and territorial integrity of Yugoslavia' (Vento, 1992: 33–4). The consequence of economic reform differed in the different republics of Yugoslavia. In Slovenia and Croatia, economic reforms were promulgated by the newly elected power elites whereas similar reforms in Serbia and Montenegro would undermine the power elites.

The Community had to balance the reality of fragmentation and the wish for unity, by meeting representatives of the break-away republics while demanding a continuation of federal unity. Problems with the political reforms, however, caused the Community to abstain from support for Markovic. This prompted some observers to characterize the policy as marked by arrogance, if not indifference (Vento, 1992: 35). The background for this attitude is clearly the happy days of the new world order, when the Community thought it possible to influence developments in the Balkans through the application of strict conditionality. The civilian power of the EC was celebrated and at the same time vastly over-estimated. Yet the differing views among Community members also contributed to the approach chosen. France was clearly preoccupied with the success of the Maastricht process, thereby downgrading policies towards Eastern Europe. Germany focused attention on developments in Central Europe and the

Soviet Union, whereas Great Britain was pre-occupied with problems outside Europe.

The European Community and the Yugoslav war

From the beginning of the Yugoslav war (June–November 1991), the main objectives of the EC were clearly to preserve Yugoslavia as a federal state, and to de-escalate the conflict.[3] The measures included diplomatic intervention, economic carrots and sticks, discussion of military intervention, and civilian EC observers being sent to Yugoslavia. In September 1991 the Dutch Presidency asked the Western European Union (WEU) to prepare plans for an eventual deployment of peace-keeping forces. Four alternatives, ranging from limited intervention to large-scale operations, were outlined. Yet two political preconditions for intervention of peace-keeping forces were added: a cease-fire existed, and a guarantee of the security of deployed forces. Neither the Croatian forces nor the Yugoslav People's Army (JNA) were ready to give such guarantees and this effectively shifted the initiative back to the political sphere, that is, to the Community (and later also the UN).

The Community policy of the autumn of 1991, with its emphasis on unity, should have reduced the insecurity of Serbian minorities in Croatia, thus modifying the security dilemma. As one observer notes:

> Western policy, by inflexibly insisting on a single Yugoslav state, wittingly or unwittingly backed Serbia, reinforced its intransigence and contributed to the diplomatic deadlock. Because the West wanted what Serbia wanted, Serbia and the federal army had little incentive to be flexible (Gow, 1991: 300).

Croatia's and Slovenia's moratorium on their declaration of independence ended in early October, and non-Serbian members of the collegial presidency of the Yugoslav Federation were at the same time forced to resign (WEU Doc. 1293: 335). As the preservation of a federal Yugoslav state became more and more unrealistic, the Community adapted to the new realities by suggesting a confederation as an alternative. The idea of a confederation was presented at the EC Peace Conference in the Hague, established at French initiative (Stark, 1992; Carrington, 1992).[4]

The negative response from Yugoslav participants was probably a minor surprise, since the plan was discussed during the shelling of Vukovar and Dubrovnik. A Yugoslav confederation had been for one year the objective of Slovenia and Croatia, backed by Macedonia and Bosnia-Herzegovina. But the idea was not backed by the Community before it was too late and in the autumn of 1991 it was an obsolete perspective (Gow, 1991). After the failure of plans for federation and confederation, the 'recognition issue' became the new panacea. The debate on recognition was a precursor to a major change in Community policy, and on the surface it represented a movement of the French and British positions towards that of Germany. Yet positions no longer reflected preferences for the different parts of the conflict, but rather views on how deeply the Community should involve itself (Guéhenno, 1992: 124).

Until the summer of 1991 the German attitude to Yugoslavia followed the general Western European view. Yet German foreign policy was in contradiction to the dominant domestic political discourse, represented *inter alia* by *Frankfurter Allgemeine Zeitung*. In early July 1991, however, a major change occurred as recognition of Croatia and Slovenia became part of official German foreign policy, the argument being that a disintegrating state could not be held together from abroad. In order to preserve Western European consensus, an EPC meeting was organized in The Hague on 5 July. At the meeting Germany found herself completely isolated, *Allein gegen Alle*.

During autumn 1991, the recognition issue caused several controversies. It became increasingly difficult to preserve Western European consensus, which was only saved by a gradual change in the French position (Stark, 1992). Recognition was discussed as a general issue and a commission set up to formulate general principles concerning democracy and minority rights, but as it turned out, the Community practice did not follow the principles. The Badintér Commission concluded that Croatia did not qualify, but it was recognized anyway. Macedonia qualified but was not and has not yet been recognized. The Community response to the independence of Macedonia has been severely hampered by Greece, which has effectively blocked any progress. The core of the problem seems to centre around the viability of the Greek government, which has determined the response of the Community (Pettifer, 1992). The tragedy following the recognition of Bosnia-Hercegovina in April 1992 may also have contributed to the reluc-tant, yet embarrassing paralysis of the Community. It has been argued that the recognition of Croatia and Slovenia came too late to influence develop-ments. Early recognition without effective guarantees to the newly recog-nized states would not have changed the situation, however (Glenny, 1992). The third alternative, no recognition, would presumably also have led to war. Yet the dilemma of Bosnia-Herzegovina would have been less acute. In general, however, the influence of recognition has been vastly overem-phasized. The policy was, rather, one example in a longer chain of symbolic political-diplomatic moves.

Slovenia was only briefly involved in the Yugoslav War. Therefore EC relations with Slovenia have been gradually developed since Slovenia's recognition in January 1992. An EC delegation was established in Ljubljana later in 1992 and a trade and cooperation agreement is now being negoti-ated. For Slovenia, however, the long-term goal is membership of the Community. For the medium term Slovenia is striving for an association agreement, arguing that Slovenia is a European country having other European states as the most important partners (Svetlicic and Bucar, 1992).

Assessment of Community response

The response of the Community can be characterized both as highly successful and as an outright failure. The failure is clear, even when meas-ured by the standards of stated objectives. It has proved impossible to de-escalate the conflict and to preserve the unity of the Yugoslav state. Even the recognition of Croatia and Bosnia-Hercegovina can be regarded as failures, as neither Croatia nor Bosnia-Hercegovina has been able to survive within their former borders. In short, the Community has been able to influence developments in Yugoslavia only to a limited degree, and Western European disagreements are among the most important causes for the lack of leadership. It is tempting to recall the British historian Medlicott's caustic comment on the Concert of Europe and translate it into experiences with the common European foreign policy. In his opinion 'there was a Concert of Europe when the action of the great powers was concerted, and when it was not, there was not' (Clark, 1989: 129). Today we may conclude that, 'There is a European foreign policy when the action of the West European great powers is concerted, and when it is not, there is not'. In fact, this is how the Community was viewed in the beginning of the 1980s: 'What we do have in Europe is a concert of states, whose basis is an area of perceived common interests among the major powers, and which is reinforced by wider processes of consultation involving the smaller powers and international organizations' (Bull, 1982: 163). This approach reappears in modern American studies of multilateralism where it is termed 'minilateralism' (Kahler, 1992). Diversity of positions within the Community, however, is not the only reason for failure. It is possible to identify at least three factors at the Community level as well.

First, the Troika system displayed most of its inherent weaknesses. None of the three Troika members (Luxembourg, the Netherlands and Portugal) in the decisive second half of 1991 had Eastern Europe or the Balkans among the key areas of concern in their national foreign policy. With Britain in the Troika, it consisted of the coalition of Community members which had during the last decade consciously and consistently impeded the development of a common European policy towards the East.

Second, in autumn 1991, the Dutch Presidency was also responsible for the Maastricht process. With Foreign Minister Hans van den Broek more often in Yugoslavia than in The Hague and Brussels, clear signs of over-extension became visible. This was also indicated by the disastrous response to the Dutch draft on European Union in September 1991. It is also noteworthy that the bigger Community members had difficulty in accepting the rules of the EC Presidency institution. The unspoken argument was that great powers have bigger responsibility and bigger competence in the handling of intricate and difficult conflicts such as that in Yugoslavia.

Third, EC crisis management is a contradiction in terms. International crisis management is normally associated with centralized decision making, something which is clearly lacking in the Community polity. Except for the small EPC secretariat, a European polity in the area of foreign and security policy hardly exists. To sum up, the Community has only to a limited degree been able to conduct the type of coercive diplomacy that might have de-escalated the conflict in its early phases (George, 1991; Gow, 1992, Gow and Smith, 1992). The Maastricht Treaty will not change this situation, as the statements concerning security policy, with a few exceptions, constitute only changes of nuance from the provisions found in the Single European

Act of 1986. In fact, the intergovernmental conference on Political Union was a continuous exercise in watering down proposals concerning foreign and security policy (Ungerer, 1991; Noël, 1992: 14–20). Disregarding the new principles concerning majority voting, adopted at the Lisbon Summit (*Agence Europe*, 1 July 1992) in June 1992, major change was postponed until 1996. Furthermore, the practice and codification of a common European security policy have rarely developed at the same speed.

A common foreign and security policy in post-Cold War Europe will have to be qualitatively different from the type developed through the 1980s. The common perception that the Community response has been a failure needs to be tempered by some other considerations, however. First, even if the Brioni Agreement of July 1991, according to which the Yugoslav Army withdrew from Slovenia, is of minor importance in a broader perspective, it saved Slovenia from a full involvement in the Yugoslav War. More important though, is the Community's rather successful use of coercive diplomacy which was used several times from the beginning of the conflict and with positive results (Gow, 1992: 198–202). The puzzling question is what factors kept the Community from further use of coercive diplomacy?

Finally, the West Europeans have been wise enough to prevent a situation of competition among individual West European states over whether to support the various Yugoslav entities (Guéhenno, 1992). This makes the Yugoslav war different from the Spanish Civil War of the 1930s. It was significant that one of the first decisions to be taken concerned an embargo on arms supplies to Yugoslavia. This prevented controversies among the Community member states over which Yugoslav republics to support with arms, as none of the West European states could supply their favourite with arms without harming the established norm. Furthermore, the conflict was not allowed to spill over into the Maastricht process, or on to the German–French relationship. In the view of some observers, the main reason for France moving closer to the German position on recognition was simply to save the Maastricht Treaty and the bilateral relationship with Germany (Stark, 1992). From the perspective of narrow self-interest, the Community response might be deemed successful. This internal function of the Community had a price though, and some observers have been quick to emphasize that it has been 'more important for the Community to achieve consensus than to design a third party policy helpful for the peoples in Yugoslavia in their predicament' (Galtung, 1992: 29).

The question of military intervention

The institutional distinction between the EC and the WEU has become increasingly irrelevant since 1989. In the practice of Western European foreign policy, the distinction exists to a lesser extent than ever before. Hence, political and defence responses were developed in parallel during the Gulf War. Furthermore, the WEU relief action for the Kurds in Iraq in the spring of 1991 was requested by the EC, thereby anticipating the careful wording of the Maastricht Treaty. The same procedure was followed in September 1991, when the Dutch EC Presidency asked the German WEU Presidency to develop plans for an eventual military action in Yugoslavia. Yet any action by the WEU, whether peace-keeping or peace-creating, would have the European great powers as main contributors. The military inaction is often explained by pointing out factors in Yugoslavia (topography, etc.). Yet the present great power configuration in Europe is among the most important factors.

From the very outset of the conflict, Germany held that some sort of action by the WEU should be considered. Yet according to the prevailing interpretation the German Constitution does not allow German forces to participate in such actions. Even had such legal obstacles not existed, the long shadows of history precluded the deployment of German forces in Bosnia-Hercegovina or Croatia. The German Minister of Foreign Affairs, Klaus Kinkel, has stated this very clearly. The German policy is often interpreted as an example of new assertiveness in foreign policy (Salmon, 1992). The German recognition policy is, however, better characterized as an *Ersatzhandlung*, a policy designed to show the public that something is being done, although the 'something' is assumed to have little effect (Wagner, 1992: 37–8; Newhouse, 1992: 63–6). Even the deployment of the German destroyers *Bayern* and later *Hamburg* in the Adriatic Sea for monitoring missions caused major domestic debates. In this perspective, the *lack* of German great power behaviour can provide part of the explanation for West European military inaction.

Great Britain has consistently worked against military intervention. The British argument is that assessments show that 40,000 soldiers or more will be needed for an appropriate military force. Furthermore, experience with civil war in Northern Ireland has also caused some reluctance. Outside Great Britain, it is rarely realized how extensive and costly is the British military engagement in Northern Ireland. The lack of American leadership during the first two years of the Yugoslav conflict may also help to explain the British position. This runs counter to expectations (or hopes) in some neo-realist studies of the new Europe (Mearsheimer, 1990). Finally, any action by the WEU in Yugoslavia would have had effects on European security architecture and the Maastricht process, and effects certainly contrary to British priorities. According to one analysis (Guicherd, 1991), the fierce political competition between Great Britain and France concerning the European security architecture has been focused on, among other things, the question of European defence, so far with conclusions largely in favour of the British position.

With respect to France, it may be helpful to look back at the French response to the short civil war in Romania in December 1989. During this crisis, France was among the few to raise the relevant question: whether the Romanian conflict marked the end of the revolutions in Eastern Europe or the beginning of general instability in post-Yalta Eastern Europe. France was also among the few EC members to suggest some sort of military intervention from abroad. The French response to the conflict in Yugoslavia has been quite similar, and France has been pushing for a full-scale peace-keeping force. If French intervention in numerous African states is taken into consideration it is clear that France shares the British experience of civil war. Yet in the case of the former Yugoslavia France's position is different from that of the UK. The French response, however, has oscillated between a purely military policy and a more humanitarian-oriented policy, including versions in between. In September 1992, France argued for military escorts for humanitarian convoys. Considerations concerning potential changes in the position of the United States as well as domestic public opinion and forthcoming elections help to explain the oscillation (Deubner, 1991; Moïsi in *International Herald Tribune*, 18 January 1993). From an instrumental point of view, a WEU force in Yugoslavia would effect developments towards a closer relationship between the Community and the WEU, precisely the outcome France preferred in the Maastricht negotiations.

To sum up, the present configuration of European great powers seems to exclude joint military action. A joint European defence policy simply dissolves in a structural stalemate somewhere in the triangle between Bonn, Paris, and London.

The broader Balkans policy of the Community

The threatening spread of the war in former Yugoslavia has prompted the Community to change its policy towards other states in the Balkans. The prospect of Europe Agreements with Romania and Bulgaria is usually considered the most important of the long-term institutional links. In September 1991, the Council asked the Commission to open exploratory talks with Bulgaria, noting that similar talks with Romania 'could begin once the current political situation returned to normal' (CPR 8400/91). In December the Council concluded that conditions were 'normalized', and exploratory talks began (CPR 10323/91). Yet directives for further negotiations were still being discussed in April 1992. Finally, the actual negotiations started in May, when the Commission opened negotiations with Bulgaria and Romania (CPR 6326/92). In October, the importance of bringing these negotiations to a rapid conclusion was confirmed (CPR 8858/92). The Europe Agreement establishing an association between the Community and Romania was signed on 1 February 1993, while the Agreement with Bulgaria was initialled in December 1992 and signed later in 1993.

Of equal importance is the fact that the Europe Agreement negotiations were supplemented by several short-term measures in order to support the economic reform programmes and to ensure continuation of transition. In October 1991, the Textile Agreements were amended, allowing a minor enlargement for 1991 (2 per cent for Romania and 8 per cent for Bulgaria). Parallel negotiations on quantitative restrictions concerning coal and steel products did not prove the contradictory policy of the Community. The restrictions, rather, reflected the problems in the European steel industry. In July 1991 the Community approved medium-term financial assistance (up to Ecu 375 million) to support Romania's balance of payments. The adoption of these measures, however, caused problems, as support from other members of G24 was not as forthcoming. In November the Community noted:

> that contribution of other G24 members did not equal that of the Community. Consequently, in view of the conditions it had set itself as regards burden sharing, the Community would be unable, unless these conditions were relaxed, to grant these two countries (Bulgaria and Romania) the aid which it had promised, at the very time when they needed substantial financial help to back up the necessary reforms of their economic system (CPR 9131/91).

In December 1991, the Community concluded that exceptional assistance from the Community and other G24 members was crucial for the support of the implementation of reform programmes in both Romania and Bulgaria. Consequently, the Council agreed to depart from the rule of equal sharing between the Community and the other G24 members of the contributions to the balance of payments support for Romania and Bulgaria for 1991 (CPR 9551/91). The Community would try later to ensure an equal share of the financial contributions. The need for foreign assistance becomes clear when Romanian production and trade figures are examined. Production is down 30 per cent from 1989 and Romania–East trade is now only some 5–10 per cent of total trade, compared to half before 1989 (*International Herald Tribune*, 11 September 1992).

In September 1992, additional medium-term financial assistance was granted to Bulgaria, provided specified problems were solved (CPR 8854/92). The Council subsequently adopted further medium-term financial assistance for Bulgaria (maximum Ecu 110 million) in order to support the Bulgarian balance of payments. Both the Europe Agreements and short-term measures have been adopted despite the slow reform process. The third Romanian government after Ceausescu, for example, announced a 'social market economy', i.e. a gradual approach taking into account social costs (*Financial Times*, 12 December 1992). In contrast, the reform process in Bulgaria has been much quicker, making the Europe Agreement less surprising. It thus seems that the EC's once rigid emphasis on political and economic reforms has been consciously downgraded, and being replaced as first priority by stability.

The elections in Albania in March 1991 implied a change of political leadership and made possible a new Community approach towards Albania. In autumn 1991, the Community and Albania established economic and diplomatic relations, thereby completing the network of Community relations within the former Eastern Europe. The change in the political system occurred at the same time as a general collapse of Albanian society and economy (Bibiraj, 1991; Zanga, 1992). Within some six months more than 50,000 refugees had landed in Italy, only to be sent back. The Community then engaged in several emergency actions in Albania. Throughout autumn 1991, the food situation remained critical, and supplies of agricultural products were provided at a value of Ecu 35 million. The Community also proposed to extend the PHARE Programme to include

Albania. In December 1991, some quantitative restrictions were eliminated, and in February 1992 the GSP was accorded to Albania. In May an aid programme of maximum Ecu 20 million covering industrial imports to Albania was implemented. In June, a second emergency food-aid measure was decided. In July, Albania revealed the existence of a deficit of US$ 165 million covering the subsequent year and requested international assistance. The EC response was favourable, although the Community preferred a solution within the framework of G24. The EC pointed out that during the past twelve months some Ecu 200 million had already been extended to Albania by the Community. The readiness to continue with other donors, however, was confirmed 'in support of the democratically elected Government's efforts to maintain stability' (CPR 7676/92). In other words, it was recognized that something ought to be done, but the Community was looking for partners. Subsequently, the Community decided in September 1992 to provide financial assistance (Ecu 70 million) to Albania 'in order to help support the balance of payments and strengthen reserves'. In general, Community relations with Albania are placed on the same footing as relations with the Baltic states, and so far relations have been improved with the same speed and scope.

Table 5.2 Institutional links between the EC and the Balkan States

1970	Trade Agreement between the EC and Yugoslavia
1980	Trade Agreement between the EC and Romania
	Trade and Cooperation Agreement between the EC and Yugoslavia
1990	Meeting of EC-Romanian Commission (March)
	Trade and Cooperation Agreement between the EC and Bulgaria (May)
	Trade and Cooperation Agreement between the EC and Romania
	1st meeting of Joint EC–Bulgarian Commission (November)
1991	1st Meeting in Joint EC–Romanian Commission (May)
1992	EC recognition of Slovenia and Croatia (January)
	EC recognition of Bosnia-Hercegovina (April)
	Trade and Cooperation Agreement between the EC and Albania (May)
	EC Commission Delegations established in Albania, Croatia and Slovenia (September)
1993	Europe Agreement between the EC and Romania (February)
	Europe Agreement between the EC and Bulgaria (1993)

Sources: Various issues of *Bulletin of the European Communities*, *Agence Europe*, and *General Report on the Activities of the European Communities*

In the long-term perspective, the trade and cooperation agreement is more important. The Commission was authorized in September 1991 to open negotiations, and a trade and cooperation agreement was signed on 11 May 1992. The agreement included a joint declaration on political dialogue, one of whose aims was to provide mutual information on foreign policy (CPR 6166/92). The dialogue, intended to be institutionalized at ministerial, senior official, and parliamentary levels, is modelled on the dialogue with the Baltic states. The war in former Yugoslavia has severely effected Albanian foreign relations. The large Albanian population in Kosovo has been increasingly suppressed by Serbian authorities during most of the past decade. Furthermore, problems with minorities in the Vorio Epirus region complicate Albanian relations with Greece (Pettifer, 1992: 195).

To sum up, EC priorities in the Balkans have gradually changed since the outbreak of the Yugoslav War. One observer is content to note that:

> thanks to action by the Twelve, Europe managed to contain the crisis within the territory of former Yugoslavia. It is because the European Community offered former Yugoslavia's neighbouring countries prospects of security, economic recovery and, eventually, in the more or less long term, integration that they managed to remain above purely national interests, sometimes quite legitimate, which would at any other time have involved them in armed confrontation (WEU Doc. 1342: 3).

Even if this gives the Community too much credit, the point should not be ignored that the broader Community policy has worked quite well.

EC policy regarding the Soviet Union and the successor states of the Soviet Union

In the Community Eastern policy, the Soviet Union and later Russia have been singled out as being somehow different, requiring some sort of special relationship. This is repeatedly emphasized in policy statements and also in various studies. Four factors may explain this special relationship.

Historically, Russia (and later the Soviet Union) constituted the Eastern pole of the multipolar European security order. To continental European powers such as Germany and France, relations with Russia (and the Soviet Union) were of crucial importance to the European balance of power. Yet when the independent European security dynamics were 'overlayed' by the superpowers, 'Europe' was, over a period of four decades, practically re-duced to an object in world politics (Buzan *et al.*, 1990). Developments in Europe were never completely determined by the superpowers, but even when pooled in a Community, the European influence on world politics remained very limited. Compared to the Soviet Union, the Community was a minor political entity. Yet the economic side of world politics tells a rather different story, as the Community constituted a powerful entity in trade negotiations, as a donor of aid, and in economic performance in general.

The third explanation for the special relationship between the EC and Russia lies with the gradual change from 'object' to 'subject' in European and global politics. This was, and is, by no means a painless transformation. A thorough redefinition of Western European foreign policy, as well as of the intricate balance between national and multilateral European foreign policy, is essential. The collapse of the Soviet Union has so far mainly implied a dramatic increase in the national foreign policy of *Handlungsspielraum*; in other words it has not brought about a significant change in multilateral European foreign policy. The three West European great powers are all in a phase requiring changes in their former foreign policy priorities. Clear answers should not be expected in the near future (Vernet, 1992; Heinrich, 1991). If this interpretation of foreign policy at the national level is correct, one cannot expect a clear, consistent multilateral foreign policy. Finally, the sheer size of Russia makes it an uncomfortable economic and political entity in Community external relations. Russian membership of the Community is deemed impossible, although some sort of association will be a necessary component of any new and stable European order.

The coup in Moscow in August 1991 demonstrated the fragility of the political regime in the Soviet Union. In fact, it was the beginning of the end of the Soviet state. Guidelines on how to assist the Soviet Union became the object of internal debate in the Community during the autumn of 1991. This debate involved issues of both medium-term assistance and requests from the Soviet Union for food aid. In this connection close coordination and burden-sharing with the other Western countries has often been emphasized by the Community. Pleas for a concerted approach in the G7 were frequently expressed, for example in October when the Community suggested a 'balanced breakdown of the costs', that is, one-third to be borne by the Community, the United States and Japan, respectively.

In December an EPC Declaration on the Ukraine was issued, which commented on the independence referendum. Hence, 'the EC and its member states call upon the Ukraine to pursue with the Union and the other republics an open and constructive dialogue intended to ensure that all the Soviet Union's existing international obligations and commitments are carried out' (CPR 9558/91). Later another EPC Declaration was adopted concerning guidelines on recognition of new states in Eastern Europe and the former Soviet Union (CPR 10324/91). This was an ambitious attempt to create a Community position on recognition of all the new East European states. Compared with Yugoslavia, the guidelines concerning the successor states to the Soviet Union proved to be more successful.

Community relations with CIS members were still marked by the superpower status of the Soviet Union and even though the total amount of European assistance exceeded American aid, initiatives tended to remain American. Thus the initiative to organize a multilateral conference on assistance to the former Soviet Union accelerated considerations in the Community, as the Community wanted to participate on the basis of a joint position (CPR 4022/92). Procedures enabling those states to become party to the Bretton Woods institutions were considered and the EC decided to support membership of the IMF for both the CIS and the Baltic states (CPR 4392/92; 4502/92).

At the subsequent Lisbon Conference on assistance to the CIS, problems associated with risks of nuclear technology proliferation were dealt with by establishing an International Science and Technology Centre in Moscow (CPR 6326/92). The conferences in Washington and Lisbon failed, however, to produce the comprehensive strategy needed by the fragile political and economic situation.

Trade relations with CIS republics were discussed in September 1992 and the Commission was later authorized to open negotiations with a view to the conclusion of partnership and cooperation agreements with the independent states of the former Soviet Union.

Within the worldwide network of Community external relations this continues to be a policy of strategic importance. Yet the Community has not developed a consistent long-term policy. Instead a gradual approach has been developed, so far with aid as the most important component. This is understandable as the dynamics of change in the area makes policy making extremely difficult.

The Community and the Baltic States

The independence of the Baltic states relieved the Community from a dilemma between supporting their independence and supporting the reform process in the Soviet Union. The decision to hold referenda in February 1991 was welcomed in an EPC Declaration (CPR 4476/91). The Community underlined the significance of the referenda and the 'legitimate aspirations' of the Baltics were reaffirmed. Furthermore, the Community urged 'an early opening of a serious and constructive dialogue between the central government of the Soviet Union and the elected Baltic authorities' (CPR 4862/91).

Table 5.3 Institutional links between the EC and the Soviet Union, CIS members and the Baltic States

1988	Joint EC–CMEA Declaration
1989	Trade and Cooperation Agreement between the EC and the Soviet Union (December)
1990	EC Commission Delegation established in Moscow
	1st meeting of Joint EC–Soviet Commission (May)
1992	EC recognition of Baltic States (Latvia, Estonia, Lithuania)
	EC recognition of former Soviet Republics in CIS
	Trade and Cooperation Agreements between the EC and the Baltic states, Latvia, Estonia, Lithuania (May)
	EC Commission Delegations established in the Ukraine, Kazakhstan and Georgia (September)
1993	Trade and Cooperation Agreements between the EC and CIS members

Sources: Various issues of *Bulletin of the European Communities, Agence Europe*, and *General Report on the Activities of the European Communities*

After the Baltic states had regained independence in August 1991 relations developed along rather traditional lines. A joint meeting of the EC and the Baltic states' foreign ministers was organized in September 1991 'to mark the restoration of sovereignty and independence of the Baltic states'. The meeting was regarded as a 'seal of the establishment of diplomatic relations with them' (CPR 7456/91) and the prospect was emphasized of benefits from G24 and PHARE programmes as well as Trade and Co-operation agreements. Exploratory talks concerning Trade and Cooperation Agreements commenced in September and it was also decided to grant GSP (CPR 8400/91). In November 1991 the Council authorized the Commission to negotiate Trade and Cooperation Agreements with the Baltic states and put forward the directives (CPR 8943/91). After about six months the Trade and Cooperation Agreements between the Community and the Baltic states were signed in May 1992 (CPR 6326/92).

Meanwhile the Council adopted regulations on emergency food aid (Ecu 45 million), eliminated quantitative restrictions, and suspended non-specific restrictions (CPR 10324/91). Short-term assistance continued throughout 1992. Thus, in September 1992 the Council gave 'favourable consideration to investigate loans (Ecu 220 million) in order to help support the balance of payments' (CPR 8854/92).

Balance of payments problems are well known throughout Eastern Europe, and the Community methods of dealing with the problems tend to be quite similar from one country to another. In general, Community relations with the Baltic states have been put on an equal footing with those of Albania.

The dilemma of Community eastern policy

Half a decade after the new Eastern policy of the Community was initiated it is still marked by ambiguous objectives. A certain gap between rhetoric and reality fuels the growing disillusionment in Eastern Europe and influences political discourse in Western Europe. Furthermore, in Community affairs the intricate balance between national and Community foreign policy remains profoundly problematic. Useful time was bought by the decision at Maastricht to postpone the matter till 1996. *Vis-à-vis* the urgent problems in post-Yalta Europe, the practice of Western European foreign policy might prove once again to advance quicker than the codification of a common foreign policy in various treaties. Yet external challenges have often been double-edged and disunity is as likely as unity. In the case of Yugoslavia the Community has, despite its intentions, been on the side-line of events. In spite of the strategic importance of relations with the former Soviet Union, perplexity and an *ad hoc* approach to strategy prevail over consistent comprehensive policy making. Whether the failures will be transformed into important lessons or will breed further perplexity remains to be seen.

The difficult choices inherent in the dilemma of trade vs. aid remain an important dimension in Community Eastern policy. A less protectionist Community policy would signal a genuine interest in the development of these countries (Weidenfeld and Huterer, 1992: 326–8; Vogel, 1992). Plans for an Eastern Payments Union, drawing on experiences with the European Payments Union established after the Second World War, have been outlined as a means to stimulate trade within Eastern Europe. Readiness to depart from former priorities was aired in a Commission report to the Edinburgh Summit in December 1992 and backed by some member countries. Yet it is quite predictable that those Community members who are most exposed to competition from Eastern Europe will resist such changes.

In general, the approaches chosen to support the transition in Eastern Europe have been heavily marked by the dominant mode of economic thinking in the international institutions. Experiences with the European Recovery Program after the Second World War, the Organization for European Economic Cooperation (OEEC), or the reconstruction of the Federal Republic of Germany are not considered relevant for the current transition in Eastern Europe. Proposals for the establishment of a pan-European reconstruction organization exist only on the margins of the debate (Weidenfeld and Huterer, 1992). As a consequence, current EC policy seems to have created a new European semi-periphery and a new type of dependency.

With the 1989 revolutions in Eastern Europe, the Yalta Order collapsed. It was the end of divided Europe and the end of divided Germany. For the Western European states the adaptation to this post-Yalta European order has proved to be very difficult, and the Maastricht process was just one among several answers. It also takes time to adjust to the fact that the superpowers have a less prominent presence in Europe than previously – and certainly, one less than the other. However, the break-away of the Baltic states seemed for a while to indicate that the post-Yalta order would be identical with the pre-Yalta order. Yet it would be misleading to conclude that we have returned to the European states system created at Versailles in 1919.

The break-up of Yugoslavia and Czechoslovakia makes it impossible to confine the changes in Europe to the terms of the Versailles system, and the collapse of the Soviet Union makes it less obvious to try. After all, the Versailles system was to a high degree a Western European response to the simultaneous collapse of the Habsburg Empire and the rise of communist Russia. France and Great Britain were among the creators of the Versailles system.[5] If it was difficult to adjust to the realities of the post-Yalta order, it is even more difficult to accept developments pointing beyond the Versailles system. Worries about the European balance of power remain among the primary concerns and the foreign policies of Community members remain, inconsistencies notwithstanding, an important element of Western European foreign policy making.

Notes

1. The PHARE programme is the European Community's part of the entire G24 programme on assistance to Eastern Europe.

2. *Towards a Closer Association with the Countries of Central and Eastern Europe*, Report by the Commission to the European Council, Edinburgh, 11–12 December 1992.

3. Several chronologies of events exist. Presumably the best is to be found in Appendix 1, WEU Document 1294, 1991; and in WEU Document 1337. Supplementary Draft Recommendation, pp. 22–43, December 1992.

4. The convening of the conference was confirmed at an extraordinary European Council meeting on August 27, 1991 (WEU Document 1294: 367). Problems arose, however, because the Netherlands and Great Britain 'wanted it delayed' whereas

France, Germany and Italy preferred to 'proceed as soon as possible' (Salmon, 1992: 250).

5. The Versailles system comprises the peace treaties of St. Germain-en-Laye (1919); Neuilly (1919); Trianon (1920); and Lausanne (1923).

References

Balasz, P. (1989) 'The Single European Market 1992: Changes and Tasks for Hungary', *Trends in World Economy*, no. 62, Budapest: Hungarian Scientific Council for World Economy.

Bibiraj, E. (1991) 'Albania at the Crossroad', *Problems of Communism*, XL (5): 1–16.

Bull, H. (1982) 'Civilian Power Europe: A Contradiction in Terms?', *Journal of Common Market Studies*, vol. 21, pp. 149–64.

Buzan, B., Kelstrup, M., Lemaitre, P., Tromer, E. and Wæver, O. (1990) *The European Security Order Recast. Scenarios for the Post-Cold War Era*, London: Pinter.

Carrington, L. (1992) 'After the Death of Communism', *Studia Diplomatica*, vol. 43, pp. 3–10.

Clark, I. (1989) *The Hierarchy of States. Reform and Resistance in the International Order*, Cambridge: Cambridge University Press.

Deubner, C. (1991) 'Herausforderungen an der Ost- und Südflanke Europas', *Dokumente*, vol. 47, pp. 386–9.

Galtung, J. (1992) 'Reflections on Peace Prospects for Yugoslavia', in Kuzmanic and Truger (eds), *War in Yugoslavia*, Ljubljana, pp. 19–34.

George, A. (1991) *Forceful Persuasion. Coercive Diplomacy as an Alternative to War*, Washington: Institute of Peace Press.

Glenny, M. (1992) *The Fall of Yugoslavia. The Third Balkan War*, London: Penguin.

Gow, J. (1991) 'Deconstructing Yugoslavia', *Survival*, vol. 33, pp. 291–311.

Gow, J. (1992) 'The Use of Coercion in the Yugoslav Crisis', *The World Today*, vol. 48, pp. 198–202.

Gow, J. and Smith, J.D.D. (1992) *Peace-making, Peace-keeping: European Security and the Yugoslav War*, London: Brassey's

Guéhenno, J-M. (1992) 'Sicherheit und Verteidigung in Europa', *Dokumente*, 48 (2), pp. 121–7.

Guicherd, C. (1991) *A European Defence Identity: Challenge and Opportunity for NATO*, CRS report for Congress, Washington: Congressional Research Service.

Heinrich, A. (1991) 'Neue Deutsche Aussenpolitik. Selbstversuche zwischen Zagreb und Brüssel', *Blätter für deutsche und internationale Politik*, pp. 1446–58.

Jørgensen, K.E. (1991) *Vesteuropas Østpolitik. En analyse af vesteuropæisk multilateral østpolitik i 1980erne*, Aarhus: Institut for Statskundskab.

Jørgensen, K.E. (1992) 'The End of Anti-politics in Central Europe', in Paul G. Lewis, *Democracy and Civil Society in Eastern Europe*, London: Macmillan, pp. 31–60.

Kahler, M. (1992) 'Multilateralism with Small and Large Numbers', *International Organization*, vol. 46, pp. 681–708.

Kuschel, H.-D. (1992) 'Die EG-Abkommen mit Polen, Ungarn und der CSFR', *Wirtschaftdienst*, vol. 72, pp. 93–100.

Laux, J.K. (1991) *Reform, Reintegration and Regional Security: the Role of Western Assistance in Overcoming Insecurity in Central and Eastern Europe*, Ottawa: Canadian Institute for International Peace and Security.

Lippert, B. (1991) 'EC–CMEA Relations: Normalisation and Beyond', in Geoffrey Edwards and Elfriede Regelsberger (eds), *Europe's Global Links*, London: Pinter, pp. 119–40.

Mearshimer, J.J. (1990) 'Back to the Future. Instability in Europe after the Cold War', *International Security*, vol. 15, no. 1, pp. 5–56.

Mertes, M. and N. Prill (1992) 'Europäische Strukturen: Ein Plädoyer für institutionelle Ökonomie', *Europa-Archiv*, pp. 143–52.

Newhouse, J. (1992) 'The Diplomatic Round (Yugoslavia)', *The New Yorker*, 24 August, pp. 60–71.

Noël, E. (1992) 'Reflections on the Maastricht Treaty', *Government and Opposition*, vol. 27, no. 2, pp. 148–57.

Pettifer, J. (1992) 'Greece: into the Balkan crisis', *The World Today*, vol. 48, pp. 194–5.

Pinder, J. (1991) *The European Community and Eastern Europe*, London: Pinter.

Rummel, R. (1982) *Zusammengesetzte Aussenpolitik. Westeuropa als Internationaler Akteur*, München: Engel Verlag.

Salmon, T. (1992) 'Testing Times for European Political Cooperation: the Gulf and Yugoslavia, 1990–1992', *International Affairs*, vol. 68, pp. 233–53.

Stark, H. (1992) 'Dissonances franco-allemandes sur fond de la guerre serbo-croate', *Politique Etrangère*, vol. 57, pp. 339–48.

Svetlicic, M. and M. Bucar (1992) 'The Strategy of International Economic Cooperation of Slovenia', *Development and International Cooperation*, vol. VIII, pp. 57–73.

Ungerer, W. (1991) 'European Perspectives and Central Europe', *Studia Diplomatica*, vol. XLIV, pp. 41–51.

Vento, S. (1992) 'The Disintegration of Yugoslavia', *Relazioni Internazionali*, vol. 56, pp. 30–38.

Vernet, D. (1992) 'The Dilemma of French Foreign Policy', *International Affairs*, vol. 68, pp. 655–64.

Vogel, H. (1992) 'Integration und Disintegration: Das europäische Dilemma', *Europa-Archiv*, pp. 433–8.

Wagner, W. (1992) 'Acht Lehren aus dem Fall Jugoslawien', *Europa-Archiv*, pp. 31–41.

Weidenfeld, W. and M. Huterer (1992) 'Der Westen und Stabilisierung der demokratien in Osteuropa', *Europa-Archiv*, pp. 325–34.

Zanga, L. (1992) 'Albania: Between Democracy and Chaos', *Radio Free Europe/Radio Liberty Research Report*, vol. 1, no. 1, pp. 74–7.

Other sources

CPR. Council Press Releases, Brussels: The Council Press and Information Office.

EPC. European Political Cooperation Documentation Bulletin, Florence and Luxembourg.

General Report on the Activities of the European Communities, Luxembourg: Commission of the European Communities.

WEU Doc. *Assembly of Western European Union Proceedings*, Paris: Western European Union.

6

The post-Soviet Newly Independent States and The European Community: Prospects for Trade, Investment and Aid

OLE NØRGAARD

The simultaneous disintegration of the Soviet Empire and integration of the European Community (EC) was no coincidence. It was the result of a general change in the basic conditions for both internal and external policies at the end of the twentieth century. Yet the changes had quite opposite impacts on the two societal systems, which had until then existed on the two sides of a divided Europe. Externally, the basic conditions were changed by their increasing interdependence in almost every sphere of the economy, communications and the environment. Internally, the conditions changed because of the demands which a changed society made on the political, administrative and economic elites. In Western Europe, this metamorphosis of the external and internal environment created internal political turbulence in a number of countries. It also created a renewed drive towards Western European integration (Schmitter, 1969). In Central and Eastern Europe and in the Soviet Union, the same factors, i.e. interdependence and a changed society, produced the final collapse of the political and administrative systems and the disintegration of the Soviet economic and political empire.

Within this context, this chapter will examine the policy options which the changed conditions have created for the EC and for the newly independent states (NIS) of the former Soviet Union. The first section attempts to identify the legacies which the previous pattern of relations has left for present-day policy makers. The second section focuses on the visions, goals and policies of the EC concerning the former Soviet states, while the third section concentrates on the Russian perspectives on Europe which have evolved following the disappearance of the Soviet Union. The fourth section examines the prospects for the development of the post-Soviet states and the implications for EC policies. Finally, the last section discusses the key policy options facing the European Community.

The traditional pattern of EC–USSR relations

For almost thirty years, the EC and the Soviet Union (as the major actor in the Soviet and East European trade organization, the Council for Mutual Economic Assistance or CMEA) had almost no formal contact with each other. The bipolar international system, in conjunction with economic structures, ideology and domestic political interests, led to frozen positions that resulted in what has been called 'the dialogue of the deaf' (Lippert, 1990: 124).

The dialogue of the deaf

The global bipolar system, based on military deterrence, limited the capacities of a 'civilian power' such as the EC to act independently. The success of the EC countries in shaping the content of 'Basket Three' (The Human Dimension) of the Helsinki Final Act of 1975 was mostly of a conjunctural nature, in which the military detente of that period left a somewhat wider margin for civilian powers like the EC to exert influence. The outbreak of the 'second cold war' in the late 1970s caused a decline in the external influence of the EC generally, and its ability to influence Eastern Europe and the Soviet Union in particular. The mutual isolation of the EC and the USSR was furthermore bolstered by their insignificant economic relations, which provided little incentive for altering the trade regime. Parallel with the economic and political constraints, relations were furthermore impeded by Soviet ideology and policies. At that time, the foreign policy ideology of the Soviet Union still focused on the USA as the major global capitalist and imperialist power (Adomeit, 1988). Within this vision, Europe in general and the EC in particular had neither institutional autonomy nor political influence. Europe and European institutions were perceived as being agents of American global power with at best an indirect influence on relations between the superpowers.

This focus on the US produced considerable Soviet hostility towards the idea of European integration. Soviet resentment was further nourished by an implicit fear of an emerging European power bloc, which the old Soviet generation feared would be controlled by a militarized Germany. Up through the 1960s the official attitude remained sceptical, and up to the early 1980s the Soviet Union's perceptions of the EC remained unchanged. In Soviet writings, the EC was described as a tool used by the capitalists of Europe to suppress the workers. Furthermore, Soviet researchers claimed that the EC was disintegrating and becoming a 'less politically coherent and more loose grouping than in the 1960s and even the 1980s' (Shiskov, 1982: 18). Official documents neglected the EC up to the adoption of the Single European Act in 1985, and the general change in foreign policy perceptions during the perestroika period. Within the EC, positions also remained locked. A recognition of the CMEA would be an implicit recognition of the division of Europe and was met by strong resistance, especially from Germany.

Positions remained frozen until 1984 when the CMEA, in the context of political changes in the Soviet Union and mounting Soviet economic problems, issued a communiqué expressing the wish for new negotiations. In June 1988 the negotiations led to mutual recognition between the EC and the CMEA. This recognition signified for the first time a common approach by the EC, by the CMEA, and by the Soviet Union.

Hence, a combination of global power policies, Soviet ideology and domestic political structures, in conjunction with a lack of concrete economic incentives, lay behind the paralysed positions which persisted until the mid-1980s. It was the precarious, inconsistent change in the same factors which led to the first formal agreement between the EC and the CMEA in 1989.

The first Agreement

The signing of the Agreement on Trade, Commercial and Economic cooperation between the EC and the Soviet Union was the culmination of a process which had begun with the joint declaration between the EC and CMEA in June 1988, and had continued with bilateral agreements between the EC and the individual Central and Eastern European countries. In early November 1988, the first preparatory meeting between delegations from Moscow and the Commission took place in Brussels, resulting in a decision to start negotiations on an agreement on economic and political cooperation (*Agence Europe*, 29 October 1988). In the spring of 1989 there occurred a number of contacts between the European Parliament and the Soviet authorities, and in July 1989 the first formal negotiations opened in Moscow. The very first meeting showed a basic understanding about the outline of the agreement, although Soviet ambitions, especially regarding liberalization of trade and the scope of cooperation, were noticeably higher than those of the EC. Without major problems, the agreement was signed to take effect on 1 April 1990.

The Agreement was a typical first generation agreement, similar to the ones signed by the individual Eastern European countries. It established a most favoured nation for certain types of trade between the two sides, provided for the elimination of some quantitative restrictions on Soviet exports to the EC and formulated a price clause designed to take effect in the case of Soviet dumping on the EC market. Furthermore, the agreement institutionalized cooperation in the domains of customs control, patent legislation and nuclear safety. From a Soviet perspective, the major limitations of the agreement were the quantitative restrictions which remained in sensitive product areas such as textiles, coal and steel, and the slow speed of the abolishment of quantitative restrictions.

However, the Soviet side was eager to expand this first agreement further. The ideas developed in Moscow during the first six months of 1991 showed an interest in strengthening political cooperation, taking into account the increasing independence of the Soviet republics. For that purpose, the Ministry of Foreign Affairs and the Ministry of Foreign Economic Relations prepared a draft agreement on 'Partnership and Cooperation with the EC' during the Summer of 1991.[1] It had been decided at government level to present this proposal to the EC, but the attempted coup in August prevented any further action. However, the draft proposal, although never published, was a clear indication of the high ambitions of Soviet–EC cooperation which were circulating in political quarters in Moscow at that time. The objectives persist under today's new conditions, where a number of major provisions from the would-be agreement of 1991 are replicated in the draft agreement presently being negotiated.

Cooperation and aid

The signing of the 'Agreement on Trade and Commercial and Economic Cooperation' between the EC and the Soviet Union proceeded simultaneously with the deepening economic crisis in the Soviet Union, the collapse of the CMEA, and the increased drift towards independence on the part of the Union republics. All three developments were to have a decisive impact on Soviet–EC relations.

The first important effect was the growing relative importance of economic relations with the EC, reflecting the general decline in foreign trade, the reunification of Germany and the steep decline in trade with the former CMEA partners. A second effect of the USSR's economic crisis was EC economic assistance to the Soviet Union. The issue was first brought up on a formal level at the European Council meeting in Dublin in June 1990 (*Agence Europe*, 27 June 1990). Germany and France argued for immediate aid of $15 billion, but were opposed by British Prime Minister Margaret Thatcher, who wanted assistance to be linked to the progress of domestic reforms. Up to the Council meeting in December 1990, two groups gradually crystallized. Germany, France and Italy generally supported rapid and general economic assistance and saw the assistance as important to the success of reforms in the Soviet Union. Great Britain, Denmark and Holland were more reluctant and wanted the reforms to be in place before any substantive aid was given (*Frankfurter Allgemeine Zeitung*, 5 December 1990; *Le Monde*, 6 December 1990).

The decision taken at the European Council meeting on 14 December 1990 in Rome, which marked the launching of the EC's economic assistance to the Soviet Union, was a compromise between these two groups inside the Community. The aid programme, which Germany had criticized before the meeting as being much too modest, was to be linked to concrete projects, and the implementation of the programme was to be monitored closely by the Commission (*Frankfurter Allgemeine Zeitung*, 11 December; *Le Monde*, 12 December 1990). The purpose of the programme was 'to assist economic reform and recovery ... in the Soviet Union ... aimed at bringing about [the necessary conditions for] the transition to a market economy (*Official Journal of the European Community*, no. L 201/2, July 24, 1991).

Due to several political and technical problems, it was only in mid-June that the first shipment of food aid arrived in the Soviet Union, where it was distributed by private relief organizations (*Agence Europe*, 17 June 1991). At the same time, it was decided that the programme concerning technical assistance should support five types of activities: (1) training of public and private managers, (2) development of the financial sector, (3) the energy sector, (4) transportation and (5) distribution of food (*Agence Europe*, 21 June 1991). However, unlike its role in Central and Eastern Europe, the EC did not seek to become the major aid donor to the Soviet Union. The Commission was not prepared to take responsibility for the coordination of aid. The question about the coordination of aid to the former Soviet states was finally settled at the Tokyo Conference on Aid to the Former Soviet Republics in October 1992. It was decided that future coordination would lie within advisory groups (one for each republic) under the responsibility of the World Bank. Russia, however, would not accept the World Bank as coordinator because of its specialization in Third World countries, the Bank being perceived as unsuitable for dealing with these problems in Russia. Instead, an *ad hoc* group was to be set up, the secretariat of which would be provided by Russia (*Agence Europe*, 6 November 1992). It should, however, be observed that the proportion of aid donated by the EC was significantly less than the aid donated and coordinated by the individual member states, with Germany playing the most important role.

EC policies towards the newly independent states (NIS)

The Soviet Union finally collapsed with the signing of the Minsk Agreement on 5 December 1991, the decision of the Alma Ata meeting on 21 December and the resulting decision of the remaining Soviet republics to form the Commonwealth of Independent States (CIS) (the three Baltic republics having been recognized as independent five months earlier). The EC was now faced with three problems: (1) the problem of formal recognition and the conditions under which this should take place, (2) the problem of future relations with the individual republics; and (3) how to organize aid and assistance under the new (and still unsettled) structures.

The question of formal recognition was first approached on 16 December, 1991 in the statement by the Council of Ministers containing 'Guidelines on the Recognition of New States in Eastern Europe and in the Soviet Union' (*Agence Europe*, 18 December). The conditions, which in practical terms followed the statement by President Bush in his Paris speech on 16 December (Saeter, 1992: 22), demanded that the republics observe human rights and the treaties and agreements concluded by the Soviet Union. These conditions were followed on 23 December by a statement containing *de facto* recognition of Russia, as the Community pledged to 'continue the dealings with Russia' taking into account the modification of her constitutional status' (*Agence Europe*, 23–24 December 1991). The EC was also prepared to recognize the remaining republics constituting the Commonwealth as soon as assurance was received that the republics were prepared to follow the commitments included in the 'Guidelines'. These commitments followed in early January. Only Georgia, where civil war prevented effective government, had to wait until late May for EC recognition.

Simultaneously with the question of recognition, the EC institutions were deliberating the basis of future relations with the emerging states within the NIS. As early as mid-January 1991 at the Washington Conference on aid to the Soviet Union, Frans Andriessen, the Commissioner responsible for external relations, repeated what was to become a major issue in EC relations to the Commonwealth: the need to maintain the highest possible level of cooperation between the states within the Commonwealth (*Agence Europe*, 24 January 1991). At the same time, direct membership of the EC by the former Soviet states was ruled out by the EC at an early stage. The vision of such membership had been aired by Russian Foreign Minister Kozyrev in mid-March, when he stated that Russia wanted to become a member of the EC 'one day' (*Agence Europe*, 11 March 1991).

However, speaking at a meeting of the EC Foreign Ministers on 10 January, Andriessen excluded the possibility of NIS membership of the EC – or even an agreement between the post-Soviet states and the EC, similar to the association agreements established with the Central European Countries. This policy was further underscored by Chancellor Kohl at a meeting in Bonn on 3 February when he outlined the core of a future *Ostpolitik* (Parks, 1992). Kohl stated that the former members of the Soviet Union should not be allowed to join the EC. He said that the eastward expansion of the EC should stop with the accession of Poland, Hungary and Czechoslovakia. Instead, he urged the NIS to adhere to their own zone and develop a second economic group which could act as a 'bridge from Europe to Asia'. This policy was finally formulated in the decision of the meeting of the Council in early April, which confirmed

> the will to contribute to the political, economic and social stability of the republics, and to encourage by all means at the Community's disposal democratic reform, the introduction of a market economy and regional cooperation among the different republics (*Agence Europe*, 3 April 1992).

The problem with Russia's relation to the European community was, as observed by Saeter (1992: 12), to find a model which ties Russia to European integration, while taking into account the great power status of the country. It is not realistic to expect Russia to be restrained by structures on whose design it has no influence. The exclusion of Russia from the European process, however, would have obvious negative consequences for the other ex-Soviet republics, and their chances to obtain some kind of link to the European integration process.

The solution to this dilemma has been the gradual development of a concept for a future agreement, a concept characterized by the Commission and the Council as 'going beyond first generation trade agreements and establishing political dialogue' (*Agence Europe*, 13 January 1992), and by one former Russian Deputy Prime Minister as 'another type of cooperation ... according to our third model (the two other being, on the one hand trade and cooperation agreements, and the other, European association agreements' (*Agence Europe*, 9 May 1992). Finally, in early June, basic principles of the agreements were discussed when Delors visited Moscow. During his talks with President Yeltsin, it was agreed that the future agreement should provide for 'regular political consultation, economic cooperation and cultural understanding' (*Agence Europe*, 1/2 June 1992). In July the Commission characterized the coming agreements as 'partnerships and cooperation agreements that would be somewhere between simple cooperation agreements and association agreements. This would include in depth political dialogue and economic, financial, etc. cooperation' (*Agence Europe*, 16 July 1992).

On the basis of these principles, the Commission was authorized, in the beginning of October, to start negotiations aimed at partnerships and cooperation agreements with the ex-Soviet states (*Agence Europe*, 7 October 1992). The agreement was first to be negotiated with Russia, the Ukraine, Belarus, Tajikistan and Kyrgyzstan. The first round of negotiations took place in Brussels on 26 November. It was agreed to base the negotiations on common values such as 'respect of the CSCE commitments, the rule of law, respect of human rights, free and democratic elections'. During the first negotiations, it became clear that the agreement with Russia should give rise to close economic and trade cooperation, but that it would not have a preferential nature and not lead to a free trade area (*Agence Europe*, 6857, 28 November 1992). Negotiations with republics selected for the first round were further postponed as it became increasingly clear that they lacked the elementary technical expertise needed to conduct the negotiations.

A final problem was how to handle economic and financial relations with the ex-Soviet republics and especially the aid programme which had been designed for a unified Soviet system. Regarding the latter, the EC's 1992 budget included three types of assistance to the Soviet Union: funds for humanitarian aid, for technical assistance and loans for purchase of food. The first two types of assistance could without difficulty be divided between the individual republics on the basis of size. The medium-term loan guarantee of 1.250 million Ecu, granted by the EC in December 1991, caused difficulties, however.[2] Because the loan was provided on a commercial basis, by a consortium of European banks, backed up by a guarantee from the EC, the EC set three conditions for the republics who wanted to benefit from the loan: (1) recognition of joint liability of the debts for the former USSR; (2) ensuring payments of interests; (3) agreeing to waive the clause of sovereignty (*Agence Europe*, 14 March). Whereas most states had accepted these conditions by mid-March, Russia rejected the waiving of the sovereignty clause. It was only after the intervention by the European Parliament (in July) that the problem was solved, with a compromise which respected Russia's reluctance to commit its foreign possessions as security for the loan (*Agence Europe*, 21 October 1992; *Izvestija*, 16 September 1992).

The technical assistance programme TACIS (Technical Assistance to the Commonwealth of Independent States) differed in some important respects from the Indicative Programme, which it had replaced in 1992 (European Commission, 1992). Firstly, although TACIS reiterates the ambition to develop 'effectively-functioning market economies based on private ownership and initiatives' (ibid., 1992: p. 3) it also emphasizes 'a speedy integration into the world economy as well as the development of a civil society'. This slight modification of priorities is reflected in the focal sectors which were now identified as: human resources; food production and distribution; networks: energy, transport, telecommunications; enterprise support services and nuclear safety.

The Russian vision of the new European architecture

When the Soviet Union disappeared in December 1991, the foreign policy legacy left to the new republics varied between the individual republics in at least two respects. First of all, Russia monopolized almost all foreign policy and foreign economic expertise located in the huge former union institutes in Moscow and Siberia. Second, the new states found themselves in different international environments, dependent on their geographical location and cultural affiliations. From a European perspective, however, it is Russia which is of primary interest. In Russia the debate over foreign policy has a more solid conceptual base than in other republics, as the ancestral divide between Westerners (*zapadniki*) and Easterners (*slavophiles*) is replicated under new historical circumstances. As during the perestroika period, it is this domestic context which will ultimately determine the foreign policy of Russia. And it is the foreign policy of Russia which will ultimately define the foreign policy options of those post-Soviet states which are economically and politically oriented towards Europe.

The new foreign policy perspectives

The foreign policy philosophy of post-communist Russia has been characterized by Checkel as 'new political thinking plus' (Checkel, 1992: 18). The foreign policy of the Yeltsin administration, epitomized by Foreign Minister Kozyrev, continues the changes begun in the Gorbachev period: the supremacy of common human values over international class struggle, the broader understanding of national security, and – in the regional context – the vision of a 'common European house', which also includes the post-Soviet republics. However, where Gorbachev worked for accommodation with the West, the ambition of the Yeltsin government is complete integration into the Western world and into Western political and economical institutions. Yeltsin does not fear the intrusion of Western capital, but sarcastically invites the West to economically 'conquer' his land: 'Please conquer our land, we cordially invite you to do so' (Timmerman, 1991: 571). He strives for the integration of his country into all the primary institutions of the Western world.

This quest for integration into the West has been challenged from various quarters (Crow, 1992a): by 'Eurasians', who favour a specific geopolitical role for Russia as a bridge between Europe and Asia, by those who seek increased stress on relations with Third World countries (Goncharov, 1992), and by neo-conservatives, who in general oppose increased contacts with the West. This conservative group accepts the present need for financial and technical assistance, but perceives the relations as a conjunctural phenomenon which Russia can exploit (Sirotkin, 1992). For the time being, however, the 'new political thinking plus' continues to comprise the conceptual basis of post-Soviet Russian foreign policy, despite numerous speculations about opposition forces located particularly among conservatives in the Congress of Peoples' Deputies.

Furthermore, the ongoing debate is also a replication of the old debate about Europe or the US as the major focus of Russian foreign policy. This debate is far from settled. On the one hand, we find a tendency to see Europe as the sole and natural partner for the new Russia. 'Russia is at last rejoining Europe, from which it has long been separated, but to which it has always belonged', as it was recently stated by President Yeltsin.[3] A similar belief is prevailing among the majority of the Russian intelligentsia. On the other hand, an independent group of experts recently presented a somewhat dissenting view. They claimed that it is in the interests of Russia to maintain the USA as a partner, and to use this partnership as a leverage for Russian influence in Europe.[4] And further:

> The long term interest rests with the largest possible approachment to the EC, in the ultimate integration in the European economic and political space, the core of which will be the EC. This does not, however, imply full convergence between the interests of the Community and Russia. Russia is interested in keeping its freedom of manoeuvre in the multidimensionality (*mnogopoljusnost*) of European policy, in the limitation of the military functions of the EC. From here follows the long-term interest in the continuation of NATO and development of partnership with that organization ('Strategija dlja Rossii. Nekotorye tezisy dlja doklada soveta po vneshnej i oboronnoj politike', *Nezavisimaja Gazeta*, 18 August 1992).

It is within this evolving global perspective that we should understand the attitudes and values of post-socialist Russia towards the EC.

Although the Yeltsin government's present domestic economic strategy lacks a well-defined social base, its European orientation seems to be built on more solid support. Among the social and political groups which support, and benefit from, the Europe-oriented Yeltsin government we find parts of the intelligentsia, the evolving business community and financial circles (often inseparable from the intelligentsia), and parts of the working class (especially the highly skilled sections and those organized in independent unions and strike committees). In addition to these groups support also comes from those large segments of the younger generation which are oriented towards Western culture and civilization in general (Timmermann, 1991: 72).

For the time being, it therefore seems reasonable to conclude that the long-term westward orientation of Russian foreign policy is firmly grounded in domestic structures and ideology. It is this base within a structurally transformed society, embedded in the framework of a changing global system, which makes the present opening to the West quite different from previous openings attempted by Russian/Soviet leaders.

The attitudes and policies towards the EC seem overshadowed by a firm belief that the EC's economic and political integration will progress at an accelerated pace and that the Community will become a new economic superpower.[5] Although it is often considered that at the present stage bilateral agreements with Western European countries are as important as agreements with the EC, it is expected that as European integration proceeds, the Community will take on the responsibility for an increasing number of policy areas. The present difficulties are characterized as transient problems, which will give way to the inevitable integration fostered by the technological and economic development. Hence, visions of the future EC heralded by many Russian specialists often seem more optimistic than do those of many West Europeans.

Departing from this understanding of the future development of the EC, two fundamental interests lie at the basis of Russian European policies: to avoid isolation from this European process and to avoid becoming a Third World[6] supplier of energy and raw materials to the new Europe.[6] The response to both these concerns is to obtain the highest possible participation in the European integration process in a way that promotes Russia's industrial development and entrance to the new markets.

Russia's ambition as articulated by these new policy makers is to develop economic and political cooperation so that there will be established a free trade area or a European Economic Space which includes Russia. It is a matter for particular concern that Russia's future relations to the EC be as favourable as the conditions obtained by Hungary, Poland and Czechoslovakia in their Europe Agreements from 1991. In this context, Russian specialists repeatedly stress the importance of institutionalizing the political dialogue which has evolved since the signing of the 1990 agreement. The fear of ending up as a Third World periphery on the orbit of Europe is especially noticeable in the Russian debate over the European Energy Charter. The Russian position here is that the charter, which is currently being negotiated, should be seen as a first step on the road to Russia's integration into the Western economic system. Hence, the charter should not only provide for Western investment opportunities in the Russian energy sector, but should also include provisions which can alleviate the development of the Russian industrial sector and improve its access to the European market.

This attitude of 'trade instead of aid' also lies at the basis of discussions of the EC aid programme. Although the programme has been evaluated generally in positive terms, it has been observed that the present quantitative restrictions on exports to Western Europe are only partly compensated for by the aid and credits granted by the EC. Russian experts have observed that the major part of aid consists of commercial credits rendered under normal market terms (Shochkin, 1992).

Future relations between the EC and the NIS

Both in the former Soviet states and in Western Europe there have been – and remain – great expectations as to the mutual benefits to be derived from increased trade and economic cooperation. However, the prospects of economic cooperation with the EC vary widely between the individual republics. They vary according to their foreign trade potentials seen in relation to the West European markets and, hence, their prospects. They also vary in relation to their prospects for a successful transition to a market economy, with consequences for Western European private investment.

The NIS as future economic partners for the EC

When the Soviet structures collapsed in the spring of 1992, they accelerated the economic disintegration which began in the last years of the perestroika period. And the dissolution of the centralized system of economic planning and management and the ensuing collapse of inter-republican trade reinforced the economic consequences of the breakdown of the CMEA.

Hence, to a still increasing degree, prospects for economic cooperation with the former Soviet republics depend on their individual economic potentials. These potentials can be described from two perspectives: (1) internal resources and (2) foreign trade capabilities.

Table 6.1 summarizes some macro-indicators of the relative economic strength of the individual ex-Soviet republics.

Table 6.1 Economic potential of the former Soviet Union. Breakdown by republics and regional groupings (1990, per cent)

	Russia	Ukraine Belarus Moldova	Kazakhstan Uzbekistan Tajikistan Turkmenistan Kyrgyzstan	Azerbaijan Georgia Armenia	Lithuania Latvia Estonia
Territory	76.2	5.3	16.9	0.8	0.8
Population	51.3	23.1	17.3	5.5	2.7
National income	61.3	21.7	9.6	3.8	3.2
Industrial production	66.4	20.9	6.5	3.7	2.7
Agricultural production	46.2	30.6	14.9	3.8	4.5
Import	67.5	18.8	6.5	3.8	3.4
Export	69.7	20.0	6.4	2.0	2.2

Source: Goskomstat SSSR. Narodnoe khozjastvo SSSR v 1990 g. Moskva. Finansy i statstica. 1991. (From Boris Pichugin, *Economic Space of the Former USSR and Prospects for Market Reforms*, unpublished manuscript, 1992).

The table demonstrates the dominant position of Russia, occupying 76.2 per cent of the territory of the previous Soviet Union, inhabited by 51.3 per cent of its population, producing a disproportionate share of the national income and industrial products, and responsible for an equally disproportionate share of foreign trade. Only in agricultural products is Russia a net importer. This reflects an inter-republican trade pattern whereby Russia has supplied the other republics with energy and raw materials and has in turn received agricultural products and some manufactured consumer goods.

This inter-republican division of labour has important consequences when we examine the foreign trade potentials of the individual republics. The first, and hardly surprising, conclusion is the privileged position of

Russia. In 1991 Russia was the only NIS with a foreign trade surplus. This surplus, originating from the export of energy and raw materials, was large enough to offset the deficit incurred by the other ten smaller NIS (not including the Baltic republics) ('The Emerging Picture of Foreign Economic Relations of NIS Member Republics', *PlanEcon Report*, 13 March 1992: 11). This picture is probably too generous to Russia, however, because it re-exported natural resources and some manufactures from other republics, a re-export activity that will probably cease under the new conditions. This might be one reason why Russia faced a trade deficit of $2.2 billion in the first nine months of 1992, attributed to a fall in exports by 35 per cent and in imports by 17 per cent compared to 1991 (*Izvestija*, 26 November 1991).

Despite recent declines, however, inter-republican trade still plays a more important role for the economies of the NIS states than does foreign trade. In 1990, inter-republican trade exceeded Soviet exports to the outside world more than twice. Inter-republican exchanges in 1990 produced more than 20 per cent of the USSR's national product (Pichugin, 1992). Hence, to assess the future economic prospects of the NIS, and the macroeconomic conditions under which structural forms can be expected to unfold, one also has to take account of inter-republican economic links under the new economic conditions. An attempt to estimate the foreign economic position of the republics has been undertaken in Figure 6.1, which uses world market prices to rank the per capita foreign trade balance (the import/export ratio) of the NIS in order to indicate the strength of the NIS in the new economic environment.

On the export side, 'the republics with the highest per capita export in 1989 – Belarus, Latvia, Estonia and Lithuania – have in common the fact that the bulk of their exports consists of machinery, equipment and non-food consumer goods. They are likely to lose their lead once more realistic, internationally based, relative prices prevail in the region's trade.'[7] On the import side, this finding implicates comparatively poor short-term export prospects for Estonia, Lithuania, Latvia and Belarus, meaning very sharp contractions in per capita imports in 1992 (*PlanEcon Report*, 13 March 1992: 29). In summary, the per capita trade balance provides a clue as to the future strength of the post-Soviet republics in the new economic environment. As concluded by PlanEcon: 'Those endowed with natural resources – Russia, Azerbaijan (oil), Turkmenistan (gas) – are likely to suffer less during the painful period of economic transition' (*PlanEcon Report*, 13 March 1992: 30). This pattern has implications for the future economic relations between the EC and the individual NIS states. The short- and medium-term prospects for trade between the NIS and the West largely follow the pattern outlined in Figure 6.1. In the best position to develop future trade are those republics endowed with natural resources: oil, gas, minerals, etc. In this category are Russia, Azerbaijan and Turkmenistan. In a middle position are Kazakhstan (unexplored reserves of oil) and Uzbekistan (gold deposits). With these countries the EC might develop medium-term mutually advantageous economic relations, e.g. within the framework of a European Energy Charter.

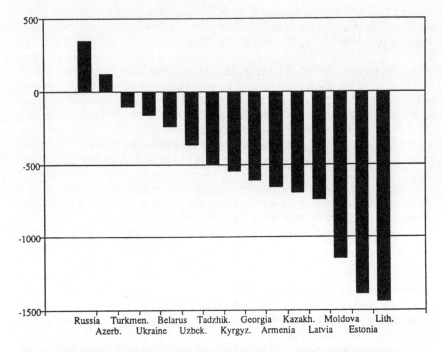

Figure 6.1 Ranking of former Soviet republics by per capita trade balance (including inter-republican trade) at world market prices in dollar terms in 1989
Source: *PlanEcon Report*, number 9–10, 13 March 1992, p. 26.

The remaining republics find themselves in a precarious foreign trade position. Moldova and the Ukraine, with their large food production sector, will have great difficulties in obtaining access to Western markets which are booming with cheap food. The Ukraine, whose food produce alone could put Western European agriculture in severe crisis should trade barriers fall, is likely to be kept out of the West European markets as long as possible. For other states, whose products consist of machinery and equipment (e.g. Belarus), metal products (Georgia, Tajikistan), chemicals (Kyrgyzstan) and textiles (Tajikistan, Uzbekistan), hard times lie ahead. Either their products will be uncompetitive on the Western markets (machinery, equipment), or they will face import restrictions (metal products, food, textiles). Hence, if the trade regime is not liberalized for these states, aid will be more important than trade for the short- and medium-term. The Baltic states are in a similar difficult position, producing all the 'wrong' products. Their position, seen from a foreign trade perspective, may be somewhat brighter, however, due to the special treatment by the EC (inclusion in the PHARE programme) and their privileged position *vis-à-vis* the Nordic countries.

Transition to a market economy in the former Soviet states

The prospect for cooperation between the EC and the NIS is only partly dependent on their economic potentials. Of equal importance, particularly in the long term, are their prospects for internal economic reforms. First, it is EC policy that economic aid and political cooperation is conditional on the development of market economies and pluralist democracies. Second, experience from Eastern Europe shows that a decentralized market economy is an imperative for any significant development of trade with the West, and for attracting Western investment in these countries. In the present context, the question of economic reforms in the NIS can be approached on two levels: the level of macro-conditions and the level of politics. There exists an obvious linkage between the macro- and micro-level in that republics with weak economic structures tend to produce conservative economic policies as a defensive political reaction to the social costs of economic transition.

On the macro level, three factors seem of relevance for the prospects of economic reforms in the NIS.[8]

1. The general level of development as measured by normal indicators of social and economic modernization. The higher this development, the higher the probability of a successful transition to market economy.
2. The degree of austerity to be expected during the transition period. The depth of this 'valley of tears' will have an effect on the timing and scope of the political backlash, which seems inevitable in all cases (Przeworski, 1991: 136–87).
3. Nationality or regional conflicts can paralyse the economic transition. The more heterogeneous the population, the higher the costs of transition, because high compensations have to be provided to achieve a broad support for reform. If heterogeneity is connected to nationality, it will cause severe political tensions, which might hinder the transition.

On the political level, it has been shown that the success of an economic reform programme is associated with what can be termed 'borrower ownership', i.e. the extent to which adjustment programmes are based on solid domestic political support ('Borrower "Ownership" of Adjustment Programmes and the Political Economy of Reform', *IBRD*, 1992, mimeo). As summarized by Portes (1992: 17), ownership is defined by the focus of the initiative for the programme, the degree of policy makers' intellectual conviction behind it, the public expression of political support by the leadership, and their efforts to build a broad consensus behind the policies.

If we tentatively apply these somewhat conflicting criteria to the NIS, the prospects for adoption and implementation of market economic reforms seem bleak.[9] Russia, so far the most advanced on the road to economic transition, scores fairly high on the first of the two ownership criteria. However, the Russian political elite is openly divided over the design and speed of the reforms. And the reformers have completely neglected the need to build public understanding and support behind the reforms.

In the Baltic states, the privileged treatment by Western governments (gaining inclusion into the PHARE programme) is a major catalyst behind the reforms. The nationality question in Estonia and Latvia, however, is a severe obstacle to reforms, as the inequalities produced by the reforms tend to follow national lines and thus intensify national tension.

In the Ukraine, the reforms have already been restrained, although the surprising initiatives of the new Prime Minister Kuchima might indicate reversal of its economic policy. In Belarus and Moldova, reforms have hardly left the ground. In the Caucasus the implementation of reforms has so far been impeded by fighting and national tensions. In some of the Central Asian republics, the generally low level of development has fostered a gradual and slow approach to economic transition, although impressive reform plans designed after Asian models have been launched by capable political leaders, especially in Kazakhstan.

If we combine these observations with the foreign trade potentials of the individual NIS, the prospects for short- and medium-term Western economic cooperation with the NIS can be summarized as in Table 6.2.

Table 6.2 Prospects for economic cooperation between the EC and the NIS

Prospects for economic reforms	Foreign economic potentials		
	High	Medium	Low
High			
Medium	Russia Azerbaijan Kazakhstan	Ukraine Uzbekistan Kyrgyzstan Belarus	Estonia Latvia Lithuania Moldova
Low	Turkmenistan	Georgia	Tajikistan Armenia

This is not the place for a detailed discussion of the precise position of each republic, which is provisional in any case. Nevertheless, the two dimensions included in the table have implications for the economic relations of the NIS *vis-à-vis* the West. In the short-term perspective, mutually advantageous economic relations can only be expected with those NIS having high (or medium) foreign trade potentials and high (or medium) prospects for economic transition. Especially for those NIS which score medium in the 'reform' category, foreign trade can reduce the social costs of transition and thus enhance the chances for the economic transition. Hence, it is important in future policies to distinguish between the individual NIS. Such distinctions have been neglected, for example by the Center for European Policy Studies, which in a recent paper concludes that 'for Central Europe trade is more important than aid whereas for the successor states of the Soviet Union aid is, in the short run, more important than trade'.[10] Those NIS having good (medium) prospects for economic reforms, but with low foreign trade potentials, are probable economic partners in the long- (or medium-) term perspective. However, they require massive economic support during the economic restructuring in order to alleviate the social costs and to create the infrastructure of a market economy.

Finally, the republics which score low on both foreign trade and reform dimensions should be seen as developing countries, with only limited possibilities for balanced trade relations with the capitalist West in the foreseeable future. One exception may be the republics endowed with rich natural resources, such as Turkmenistan. Exploiting these resources may allow them to engage in trade and achieve economic development without radical reforms. The price, however, might be a permanent position as a Third World supplier of raw materials.

Conclusion

Recent data for Russia[11] and other NIS indicate an accelerated decline in the output of most export commodities, industrial production and food-stuffs. Add to this general decline the ongoing disintegration of CIS structures, which have been outside the scope of this chapter,[12] and it takes little imagination to foresee a number of worst-case scenarios which might threaten the reforms and political stability in Russia and other NIS, in Central and Eastern Europe, ultimately constituting a threat to the stability of Western Europe. From this perspective, an effective response of the West in general and Western Europe in particular becomes ever more urgent.

As a premise for the discussion about EC policies towards the former Soviet republics, it should be recognized that neither the EC nor any other Western institution or country possesses the means to alter the general trend of developments. The sheer size of the former Soviet Union, of the economy, and the complexity of the conflicts all make it unlikely that Western policy can have anything but marginal impact. The economic disintegration of the former Soviet Union – for purely economic reasons – will probably continue whatever the West thinks or does as individual republics evolve their various reform models.

At the same time, however, it should be recognized that the stakes for Western Europe are enormous. The spectre of mass migration from the NIS frequently haunts West European mass media. Political instability in the NIS might easily spread into Central and East European countries, with severe repercussions for Western Europe (Layard et al., 1992). On the positive side, the former Soviet Union offers enormous possibilities for Western Europe. As has become clear in the discussion about the European Energy Charter, the huge natural resources in some republics (particularly Russia) are of obvious interest for Western Europe. For the long term, if the reforms succeed, the vast markets of the NIS would provide new opportunities for Western Europe. The problem is the transition period.

In this process, the EC could play an important role. Western Europe, as described in a previous section, is now the major economic partner of

Russia and other European republics in trade, investment and aid. The EC is furthermore perceived as a socio-economic model, which is closer to the visions of most NIS than are other capitalist models in Asia or North America. In the internal struggles among the NIS, the EC has become a geo-political pole of attraction, although the EC will obviously be competing with other regional structures when the former Soviet states, for economic or political reasons, seek relations with neighbouring regions and regional organizations.

Taken together, these roles leave the EC with a certain leverage *vis-à-vis* most NIS, which it could use to escape these worst-case scenarios. Through its political rather than its economic resources, the EC could prevent inter-republican conflicts from turning violent, through economic cooperation it could help solve bottlenecks in the food distribution system and continue with the technical assistance already undertaken in the TACIS programme. It could help develop new economic links among the NIS, although it is an illusion to believe that the 'political and fiscal levels' of the EC can alter the general evolution of inter-NIS structures. Furthermore, it would probably be counterproductive if 'aid and political cooperation [was] made conditional on "reasonable" behaviour in terms of interrepublican trade relations' (Centre for European Policy Studies, *The EC and Central and Eastern Europe*, 27 March 1992: 21).

For the time being, the ultimate record, membership of the EC, does not seem within the reach of most NIS, although one should 'never say never' as the head of the EC's Mission in Moscow, Michael Emerson, answered when asked about the possibility of Russia joining the European Community (*Nezavisimaja Gazeta*, 18 November 1992). However, other arrangements could be found which tie the NIS still closer to Europe. Economically, the upcoming Partnership and Cooperation Agreement should contain provisions no worse than those found in the Europe Agreements with Hungary, Poland and Czechoslovakia. Otherwise there exists a real danger that a new barrier will appear further to the East concurrently with the liberalization of trade with Eastern Europe. Such a barrier could provoke negative political reactions in the NIS, and especially in Russia. Although the opposition from vested interests in Western Europe to market access by the NIS can be expected to increase proportionally with the economic potentials of each NIS (Frey, 1984), a process of increased access should be initiated.[13] A recent example of the EC's trade policy was the recently announced anti-dumping duties on imports from Czechoslovakia. In that country the duties caused irritation and distress. But the reform process at least in the Czech Republic is so solidly anchored in the internal and international system that it cannot be contested. In the case of the newly independent states, and especially in Russia where the reform process is much more precarious, a continuation of such rigorous protectionism could constitute the wave that tips the reform boat.

Politically, the cooperation councils which are envisaged in the new agreement presently being negotiated should be made multilateral to include all the NIS. Such an arrangement would provide the EC with a major instrument whereby it could mediate conflicts among the NIS. Concerning aid programmes, political conditionality should be continued, although developments should be perceived in a long-term perspective, leaving room for the fluctuations which must inevitably occur in the difficult transition from one-party state to pluralist democracy. Correspondingly, ordinary economic conditionality should acknowledge the immense differences which exist between the individual NIS and, hence, their abilities to comply with stringent adjustment programmes.

Finally, one could rethink the balance between the various categories of aid programmes, each reflecting different conceptions as to what constitutes the major obstacles to marketization and democratisation. Fortunately, no one today believes in the orthodox developmental model where enormous financial resources were transferred to a country without incurring any systemic change; a model which in the 1970s led to the ruin of Poland. There now exists a broad consensus, also reflected in the EC's aid programmes, that the problems are based on institutional failure and on cultural legacies, rather than on lack of economic resources.

Hence, the question is to find a balance between programmes which aim at institutional change and programmes which are more directly focused on changing values and attitudes. In this respect, a case can be made that there exists a difference between the strategy to be pursued in Eastern and Central Europe and in the former Soviet states.

To a much larger extent than Central and Eastern Europe, the former Soviet states were kept isolated from Western influence. And the rapid industrialization in many parts of the Soviet Union produced a civil society even less developed than those of Eastern Europe. Today the eagerness of educated strata in the post-Soviet states to obtain access to the previously forbidden world is correspondingly larger. In the sphere of research, education and culture, such a partnership could be realized with relatively limited investments. The concrete benefit of exchange programmes, research cooperation and tourism might be intangible. Yet they would serve to communicate the perspective of partnership to broader layers of citizens in a situation where further economic hardships will be inevitable for large portions of the population.

This is not to argue against large-scale economic assistance, which is another matter with implications not only for the EC. Rather it is an argument in favour of a more balanced perspective which should recognize the role of cultural factors in both facilitating and inhibiting socio-economic transformation. Coordinated educational programmes, research cooperation, and exchanges between institutions and organizations should all nourish the gradual rapprochement of the post-Soviet societies (as well as polities) to Western Europe. In the case of the NIS, many of which have for centuries been balanced between East and West, such programmes could have an even greater political significance than in Central and Eastern Europe, which are already politically and culturally more solidly anchored in the Western hemisphere. In the NIS, such EC assistance programmes are the obvious way to maintain the support of those social strata which provide the political support for the present pro-European orientation.

Notes

1. Interviews with former officials of these two ministries.

2. The loan was distributed (million Ecu) as follows: Russia: 499; the Ukraine: unknown; Uzbekistan: 129; Belarus: 103; Georgia: 70; Azerbajdzjan: 68; Kazakhstan: 55; Turkmenistan: 45; Armenia: 38.

3. From President Yeltsin's speech at a press conference after the Munich G7 summit on 8 July 1992. Quoted in Frazer, 1992: 1.

4. Suzanne Crow described this policy paper as a fundamental conservative break with the foreign policy ideology of the Yeltsin administration. I do not share this view. See Crow, 1992b.

5. This section is based mainly on interviews with experts and politicians in Moscow conducted in late November 1992.

6. This issue was extensively discussed in *MEMO*, 7, 1992, 'Obrecheny li my stat' tret'im mirom', pp. 86–106.

7. This conclusion is quoted from the *PlanEcon Report*, 13 March 1992: 28.

8. I have taken these factors from the experiences in Eastern Europe as summarized in Nørgaard, 1992.

9. The following observations are based on *PlanEcon Reports*, vol. VIII, nos. 9 and 10, March 13 1992, and vol. VIII, nos. 11–13, March 27 1992; *IMF Economic Review* (the individual NIS), Washington D.C., 1992; *Report on the USSR and Eastern Europe*, various issues; BBC: *Summary of World Broadcasts*; *Izvestija* (various issues); *Nezavisimaja Gazeta* (various issues), *Litteraturnaja Gazeta* (various issues).

10. 'The EC and Central and Eastern Europe. Issues for Discussion', paper, 27 March 1992.

11. Data for Russia were published in 'Vazhnejshie pokazateli, kharakterizujushchie social'noekonomicheskoe polozhenie Rossii', *Izvestija*, 26 November 1992.

12. For discussion of the future of CIS structures, see for example Sheeny, 1993; Shishkov, 1992: 78–86; Borko, 1992.

13. See also, *Towards a Closer Association with Countries of Central and Eastern Europe*, Report by the Commission to the European Council, 11–12 December 1992.

References

Adomeit, Hannes (1988) 'Gorbatschows Westpolitik', *Osteuropa*, 6, pp. 421–34.

Borko, J. (1992) 'Bporu li sodruzhestvu uroki soobshchestva', *Svabodnaja Mysl*, 12.

'Borrower "Ownership" of Adjustment Programmes and the Political Economy of Reform', IBRD, 1992, mimeo.

Checkel, Jeff (1992) 'Russian Foreign Policy: Back to the Future', *Report on the USSR*, vol. 1, no. 41, 16 October, p. 18.

Crow, Suzanne (1992a) 'Competing Blueprints for Russian Foreign Policy', *Report on the USSR*, vol. 1, no. 50, 18 December.

Crow, Suzanne (1992b) 'Russia Debates Its National Interests', *Report on the USSR*, vol. 1, no. 28, 10 July, pp. 43–6.

The European Commission (1992) 'Partnership with the Commonwealth of Independent States and Georgia: TACIS – Technical Assistance and Cooperation Agreements': Brussels, 18 November.

Frazer, Perdita (1992) *The Post-Soviet States and the European Community*, London: Royal Institute of International Affairs.

Frey, Bruno S. (1984) *International Political Economics*, New York: Basil Blackwell.

Goncharov, S.N. (1992) 'Osobye Interesy Rossii', *Izvestija*, 2 February.

Layard, Richard, Oliver Blanchard, Rudiger Doonbush and Jane Krugman (1992) *East–West Migrations: The Alternatives*, Cambridge, Ma.: MIT Press.

Lippert, Barbara (1990) 'EC–CMEA Relations: Normalisation and Beyond', in Geoffrey Edwards and Elfriede Regelsberger, *Europe's Global Links: The European Community and Inter-Regional Cooperation*, London: Pinter, pp. 119–40.

Moresco, March (1992) 'The European Community, Eastern Europe and the USSR', in John Redmold (ed.), *The External Relations of the European Community*, New York: St. Martin's Press.

Nørgaard, Ole (1992) *Comparing Economic Reforms in the Baltic States*, Aarhus: Institute of Political Science.

Parks, Christoffer (1992) 'Kohl Urges Bar on Ex-Soviet States from EC Membership', *Financial Times*, 4 February.

Pichugin, Boris (1992) *Economic Space of the Former USSR and Prospects for Market Reforms*, Unpublished manuscript, Institute of Europe, Russian Academy of Sciences.

Portes, Richard (1992) 'The European Community's Response to Eastern Europe', *The Economic Consequences of the East*, IBRD.

Przezworski, Adam (1991) *Democracy and the Market. Political and Economic Reforms in Eastern Europe and Latin America*, Cambridge: Cambridge University Press.

Sæter, Martin (1992) 'Oppløsningen av Sovjetunionen og alleuropæiske integrationsperspektiver', *Internasjonal politikk*, 50, pp. 11–23.

Sheeny, Ann (1993) 'The CIS: A Shaky Edifice', *Report on the USSR*, vol. 2, no. 1, pp. 37–40.

Shiskov, Juri (1982) 'EEC: The Crisis Continues', *International Affairs*, 3, pp. 13–21.

Shishkov, Ju. (1992) 'Budushchee SNG', *Narodnyj Deputat*, 10, pp. 19–26.

Schmitter, Philippe C. (1969) 'Three Neo-Functional Hypotheses about International Integration', *International Organization*, vol. 23, no. 2, pp. 161–6.

Shochkin, Vladimir (1992) 'Ravnopravnaja torgovlja s Evropoj vygodnee chem nyneshnaja pomoshch ES', *Izvestija*, 16 September.

Sirotkin, Vladlen (1992) 'Evropa bez granic', *Izvestija*, 15 February.

'Strategija dlja Rossii. Nekotorye tezisy dlja doklada soveta po vneshnej i oboronnoj politike', *Nezavisimaja Gazeta*, 18 August 1992.

Centre for European Policy Studies, *The EC and Central and Eastern Europe*, 27 March 1992: 21.

'The Emerging Picture of Foreign Economic Relations of NIS Member Republics', *PlanEcon Report*, 13 March 1992: 11.

Timmerman, Heinz (1991) 'Russland und Europa', *Osteuropa*, p. 571.

7

The EC Policy of the Visegrad Countries

METTE SKAK

Introduction

The revolutionary changes throughout Eastern Europe are also foreign policy changes. The former Council of Mutual Economic Assistance (CMEA) countries have acted swiftly in reformulating their policy towards the European Community (EC) from merely seeking trade into pursuing EC membership and full market access. Relations with Eastern Europe have thus become an element in the enlargement problem of the Community (Skak, 1991; Pinder, 1991; Pedersen, 1992).

This chapter seeks to explore the new EC policy of East Central Europe. The object of analysis is Hungary, Poland, and Czechoslovakia (including the independent Czech Republic and Slovakia). As the front-runners among the post-Communist countries in the pursuit of EC association and membership these countries, known as the Visegrad countries, enjoy the EC's special attention. However, little is known about the particular background of their EC policy. In an attempt to fill this gap, the differing features in domestic situations and approaches to the EC will be exposed as well as the approach to reintegration, which they more or less have in common.

A few words on the Visegrad cooperation among the formerly three, now four states seem warranted. The institutionalization of cooperation took place on 15 February 1991 in the Hungarian town of Visegrad north of Budapest, the site of a similar gathering in 1335. The aim of the summit was to work towards the simultaneous return to Europe (The Visegrad Declaration, 1991). Visegrad cooperation thus became a tool in the participants' EC policy and has served to strengthen policy coordination. During the Prague summit in May 1992 the three countries agreed to jointly submit their applications for EC membership with a view to initiate entry negotiations in 1996 (*Reuters*, 6 May 1992). On 21 December 1992, they signed a free trade agreement (ibid., 21 December 1992). However, the Visegrad countries continue to struggle with the economic and social consequences of the transition towards the market economy and feel rebuffed by the insufficient market openings in the Europe agreements of association with the Community. To make matters worse, the division of the Czech and Slovak federation threatens to breed new instabilities of significance for the entire region and to aggravate economic disparities.

Analysing the change in the EC policy
of the former communist states

It is beyond the limits of this chapter to examine the complex phenomenon of change throughout the communist world. Suffice it to say that analysts focus their explanation on developmental dynamics in general or political entrepreneurship at the elite level (Pye, 1990; Hough, 1989/90). The idea is to examine the situation following the establishment of post-communist regimes, and more specifically the formulation of an EC policy of gaining membership.

The explanatory framework borrows from the French historian Jean-Baptiste Duroselle. He distinguishes between a causal setting, the *système de causalité*, i.e. the structural factors outside the control of the decision maker, and *the système de finalité*, representing the intentional setting, i.e. the aims, strategies and perceptions of the decision makers themselves (1964: 296). Factors from both explanatory settings will always operate, but the fact that they intermingle does not rule out the need to weigh their relative significance. What is important, then, is to allow for causation at both levels.

It may be fruitful to hypothesize in advance concerning which specific factors could serve to explain the reformulation of Eastern European EC policies. Within the *système de causalité*, one could cite general factors like interdependence or the anarchic nature of the international system. Arguably, the end of bipolarity heightens the importance of the regional context, and here the relevant factors are the integrative dynamics of the EC, the unification of Germany and the collapse of the CMEA and the Soviet Union. Relevant *système de finalité* factors are the ideologies of Europeanization and reintegration of the new post-communist elites and other foreign policy perceptions (Skak, 1991: 4–26). Europeanization refers to the goal of returning to Europe, to participate in West European cultural, political and economic exchange, and to emancipate society from the communist past. Reintegration can be seen as the organizational dimension of Europeanization. Reintegration here entails the pursuit of membership in key Western organizations of economic, political and military cooperation: the EC, NATO, the WEU, the Council of Europe, OECD, etc.

The following analysis will seek to explain the shift by Hungary, Poland and Czechoslovakia to an explicit policy focused on obtaining EC membership by distinguishing dimensions of *causalité* and *finalité*. Thereafter, the strategies and developments within the respective EC policies will be described. Finally, the normative theory of reintegration inherent in the thinking of the political elites of the Visegrad countries will be discussed. Since there are better materials available for analysing Hungary's EC policy than for the other Visegrad countries, there will be a bias in the data towards Hungary. The Hungarian case will also be used as a general introduction to EC policy deliberations in the Visegrad countries.

The EC policy of post-communist Hungary

Hungarians resent the 'most similar systems' approach of the Community in its policy towards the Visegrad countries. In the Hungarian view, Hungary is the only East European country which has followed a consistent, long-term policy of EC rapprochement. Hence, Hungary is seen as having a competitive edge in adaptation to EC standards, as well as in the field of reform. The policy of the government of Joszef Antall has thus been to make Hungary the first post-communist country to gain full EC membership.

EC policy determinants in the realm of système de causalité

Since 1989, Hungary's foreign policy situation has improved considerably. Hungary sought contacts with the EC as early as the 1960s and also attempted in vain to gain a first generation agreement like Romania's. But it is only now, following the CMEA–EC basic agreement of 1988 and Gorbachev's subsequent abandonment of the Brezhnev doctrine, that Hungary is free to pursue its interests in relation to the West. In the words of Csaba Csáki, 'our relationship to the European integration can no longer be restricted merely to the adaptation of the outsider' (1990: 80).

Despite the fact that the emancipation of Hungary's neighbours from Soviet tutelage places Hungary in an anarchic and far from mature security environment, Hungarian analysts cite *interdependence* rather than anarchy as the compelling condition of international relations. The more balanced Western networks of interdependence, notably the EC, have come to be synonymous with welfare in the Hungarian perception (Palankai, 1991: 73). In the analysis of the World Bank economist Alfred Tovias, the specific impact of interdependence in Hungary's relationship with the EC is related to the following four developments (1991: 292ff.):

1. the entry of Spain and Portugal into the EC;
2. the incorporation of the GDR into the EC via German unification;
3. the completion of the EC's Internal Market;
4. the revision of trade schemes with EFTA, other CMEA countries, etc.

Hungarian economists maintain that the EC's trade concessions to third partners such as the new EC members Portugal, Spain and the ex-GDR erode the value of the trade access gained by Hungary as a result of the first EC–Hungarian agreement of September 1988. This, combined with general trade diversion effects of the Internal Market, works to the detriment of Hungary (ibid., p. 301). Hungary faces tougher competition and greater difficulties in penetrating the EC market. As anticipated by Tovias, Hungary's association with the Community does little to eliminate this problem as the association treaty is most restrictive in areas where Hungary has its competitive advantages, above all in agriculture.

This conspicuous shortcoming in the association treaty has not limited the attraction of the EC. Hungarian economists see EC membership as the ultimate solution to Hungary's problems in the field of agricultural exports, as it would open the Common Agricultural Policy (CAP) for Hungary. For the time being, however, 'Hungary and other East European countries have no alternative than to sign the association agreements that promise concessions on market access' (Kiss, 1992: 9). Kiss further fears that the Hungarian agricultural sector will be adversely affected by the gradual opening of the Hungarian market. This may be an exaggeration, but clearly the problems surrounding Hungarian exports to the EC market constitute important *système de causalité* factors, the CAP being a 'neuralgic point' (Csáki, 1990: 87). Hungary's competitiveness stems from high-quality arable land/high crop yields, low labour costs and relatively modern farming methods. By 1990, the EC's share of Hungarian agricultural exports was 34.7 per cent, having climbed up from a share of 23.1 per cent in 1983 (Kiss, 1992, Table 3). Conversely, the importance of the CMEA including the Soviet market has fallen, from a share of 58.3 per cent of Hungarian agricultural exports in 1983 to 43.1 per cent in 1990.

Despite the decreasing role of former CMEA countries as partners for Hungary, these figures document the decisive role of trade with CMEA and, hence, the significance of the loss of the Soviet market as another factor in Hungary's reorientation towards the EC market. The drop in Soviet imports, notably agricultural goods, by 80 per cent in 1991 was a serious blow to Hungarian producers (Dabrowski, 1991: 31–2). On the other hand, this factor should not be exaggerated. Laszlo Csaba insists that there was no real loss in the economic sense. Citing the utterly abnormal character of CMEA cooperation from the point of view of economic integration, Csaba sees the development in Hungarian trade around 1990 almost as a recovery. On the collapse of CMEA trade he comments:

> Anecdotal evidence of individual dealers suffering market losses, or individual employees losing their jobs, deserve sympathy but will hardly invalidate the overall macroeconomic conclusion (1992: 45–6).

Hungary's trade reorientation took place before the collapse of the CMEA and of the Soviet Union in 1991. The EC surpassed the CMEA as trade partner for Hungary in 1990. In other words Hungary took the initiative in bringing about reintegration in the world economy before being pushed into this restructuring. Important additional factors in the Hungarian push for trade with the EC are the decline in the purchasing power of the Hungarian domestic market as well as the 500 million dollars lost due to the Gulf War (Kiss, 1992: 8–9; Palankai, 1991: 4).

German unification has affected Hungary. The political significance of this event is highlighted in the following statement by Gaspar Tamas Miklos from the Alliance of Free Democrats:

> The formerly unimaginable German unification is emerging, and the existence of a powerful Germany may have a decisive influence in the region. Our new government has to take an entirely different foreign policy for balancing that. We must not commit ourselves in one direction again, and we have to build close relations with France, Britain, and the United States, because an independent Hungary can only exist in this way. (*Arena*, February 24, 1990; here quoted from Palankai, 1991: 76–7)

Yet the German factor belongs just as much to the *système de finalité*, the context of motives behind Hungary's EC policy. Besides, Hungarians do not nourish the same apprehension towards Germany as do Czechs or Poles.

EC policy determinants in the realm of système de finalité

One conclusion to be drawn from this is that the signing of the association agreement cannot be explained by Hungarian economic interests alone, as economists fear the economic impact upon Hungary. The explanation must also be sought at the political and institutional levels. Regarding these aspects, the political scientist Attila Ágh presents a normative of theory of reintegration which builds upon the logic of *Einbindung,* familiar from deliberations concerning how to handle the challenge from German unification:

> The point is that it is above all out of political necessity that we need the EC association ... The political future of the country is still open and a positive political coercion is ... necessary for us ... Europe is ... a protection against proponents of parochialism, who are not weak, but gaining strength day by day ... Evidently, the democratic transition can only be finished and political and economic consolidation take place inside the EC. (*Népszabadság,* 15 February 1992).

It is the post-communist political forces which are seen here as targets for a binding web of international cooperation. There is a further dimension of learning to this: 'The closer we get to the European process of integration, the better we get to know the specific provisions and tasks ahead for joining the EC and the better we will understand how difficult it is [to join the EC]' (ibid.). Likewise, foreign ministry officials dwell on the broader impact of Hungary's gradual incorporation into the European Political Cooperation: 'Effective cooperation will promote better mutual understanding and increasing convergence of positions on international issues as well as on matters likely to have substantial effects on one or the other party' (Mohi, 1992: 13).

The decisive argument for signing the association treaty is the conviction that this is the road to full EC membership, the *real finalité* in Hungarian EC policy. The formulation of this goal represents the foreign policy innovation of the post-communist government of Antall. As explained by Hungarian Foreign Minister Geza Jeszensky, it forms part of a general strategy of reintegration:

> Full membership in institutions that provide political, economic and military security – organizations like the Council of Europe, the European Community and NATO – is essential for consolidating Central and Eastern Europe (*International Herald Tribune,* 22 October 1992).

The leitmotif of returning to Europe is an emotional, but no less operational factor in Hungary's EC policy. Emphasis on the European identity is a typical feature of the Visegrad region. The isolation from Europe in the post-war years was widely perceived as one of the most painful effects of sovietization. In 1928, Western Europe accounted for 70.5 per cent of Hungary's exports, the three most important partners being Austria, Germany and Czechoslovakia (*Danish Economy,* 1992: 116). Accordingly, the return to Europe is viewed as a *return to normality.* But Hungarians are increasingly realizing the hard economic and political realities, the gap between their level of development and the *acquis communautaire*. Politicians still believe that adaptation will be easier inside the EC than from the outside and so, the determination to join the EC remains the same (*Frankfurter Allgemeine Zeitung*, 23 October 1992).

As already shown, it is the prospect of interdependence relationships with the Western world and the promise of the Internal Market for Hungarian exports which constitute economic sources of attraction for Hungary. Another important economic motive concerns the need to attract foreign investment, a motive highlighted by Tibor Palankai in connection with the association treaty (1991: 16). At present, the countries undergoing the difficult transition from communism are in a Catch-22 situation: 'Foreign capital is distrustful towards us, and refers to the lack of stability. But the creation of stability is impossible without the help of this capital' (*Népszabadság*, 24 February 1990). One way to break this chicken-and-egg situation would be to endow the post-communist countries and their prospective foreign investors with institutional guarantees that these economies are going to be parts of the Community Market. For this reason, the political elites of the Visegrad countries insist on making the perspective of EC membership explicit, and they demand a timetable.

Hungary's EC policy: strategies, tactics and developments

The examination of the *système de finalité* behind Hungary's EC policy has demonstrated fairly articulate thinking about reintegration and Europeanization. Although other Visegrad countries are catching up, Hungary has pursued the most offensive EC policy, attempting to set an early date for entry as a full EC member. Antall originally proposed 1 January 1992 as entry date, the operational target being 1995 or later as revealed by one of his advisors (*DPA*, 18 December 1990; *Népszabadság*, 27 November 1990). At an early point in the negotiations on the association treaty, Hungary demanded a clear commitment to future Hungarian EC membership in the treaty's preamble, but the outcome was a rather vague statement (*MTI/E*, 10 April 1991). However, prior to the European Council in Edinburgh, the EC Commission issued a paper addressing the demands of Hungary and its Visegrad neighbours, which was noted with satisfaction by *Népszabadság* (9 December 1992; see *Towards a Closer Association* 1992). Later, following the summit's failure to squarely adopt these principles, *Népszabadság* responded with a bitter editorial which argued that Hungary still remains in a peripheral position (ibid., 15 December 1992).

As mentioned earlier, Hungarians have tried to argue their case on the basis of their actual eligibility as EC member, pointing to the country's pioneering reforms. However, Hungarians also point out that when the EC decided to admit membership of Spain, Portugal and Greece, economic considerations were not decisive; the main concern was bolstering their democratization (cf. Hedri, 1990). This argument of the Mediterranean precedent is also used in Poland and Czechoslovakia.

At one point, Hungary announced that it would submit its application for EC membership in the spring of 1992 in order to enter in 1996 together with Sweden and Austria (*TT*, January 29, 1992). However, no application was submitted, perhaps in a display of loyalty towards the decision of the Visegrad countries to apply jointly, and as a sign of greater realism. Another plausible factor is the cool German reaction to the Hungarian style, as witnessed by Hans-Dietrich Genscher's failure to offer Hungary 'unlimited support' in its pursuit of EC membership at a German–Hungarian meeting in 1991 (*Frankfurter Allgemeine Zeitung*, 5 June 1991). Notwithstanding fears of Germany, Hungary and its Visegrad partners attach great importance to their bilateral relationship with Germany as a Europeanization and reintegration partnership (Skak, 1992). Furthermore, Hungary wants to turn the Hungarian–Austrian relationship into an integration partnership on the basis of a pact on cooperation in integration management in order to profit from Austria's experiences in the EC membership negotiations ahead: 'We do not want economic aid, but technical assistance in preparing the integration ... What is particularly important is that Austria has begun the process of legal adaptation' (*Népszabadság*, 12 June 1992).

As a result of the perceived shortcomings in the association treaty, Hungary and its Visegrad neighbours are seeking supplementary export outlets and free trade agreements, of which the treaties with EFTA are the most important. However, neither Hungary nor other Visegrad countries appear to take the so-called EFTA option (seeking membership of EFTA in order to adapt slowly but systematically to future EC membership) seriously in their EC policy. This was reiterated by the Geneva-based economist Richard Baldwin, who points to the dismal performance of the Visegrad economies (*Financial Times*, 9 November 1992).

Hungary's attitude towards Visegrad cooperation and other concepts of regional cooperation such as the Carpathian Basin and the Central European Initiative (formerly Hexagonale) is evidently ambivalent. On the one hand, Hungary looks upon these regional schemes as a complementary EC policy, a contributing integration and as 'vital elements of the overall European integration' (Jeszensky, 1991). On the other hand, the fear exists that too much regional integration may work against Hungary's aim of joining the EC. This sceptical view is shared by the Czech prime minister Vaclav Klaus, who calls Visegrad cooperation 'an artificial process created by the West' (*RFE/RL News Briefs*, 11–15 January 1993: 12).

The crisis surrounding the Maastricht Treaty and the soul-searching mood inside the EC has had its echo in Hungary. The feeling has surfaced that there might be a problem of alienation and erosion of national identity in relationships of integration. One author urges Hungary to seek closer relations with other European small states such as Sweden, Portugal, Greece and Holland, reasoning that 'these countries will have exactly the same problems as us in relation to the mechanisms of integration' (*Népszabadság*, 6 June 1992). Perhaps this marks a change in Hungary's attitude towards a 'Nordic' preference for regional cooperation as closer to the citizen, less bureaucratic, etc. in contrast to top-level EC cooperation. However, the official Foreign Ministry declaration on the French ratification of the Maastricht Treaty in the September referendum saw the outcome as definitely 'helpful' for Hungary (*The Independent*, 22 September 1992).

The association treaty was ratified by the Hungarian parliament with only two votes against and no abstentions. The Minister of International Economic Relations, Béla Kádár, motivated the proposal by stating:

Thanks to the EC, the principle of levelling has been applied, which gives us various reliefs so that in a few years of time the last barriers to free trade will be removed ... The present transitory period gives the Hungarian economy the opportunity to live up to the challenges from the European economies. (*Népszabadság*, 17 November 1992).

In other words, there were, after all, important concessions. Hungary would have been worse off without the association treaty, but public attitudes on the EC as reflected in the media are still impatient, and the state of the economy is not normalized despite increasing exports to the EC.

The EC policy of post-communist Poland

With almost forty million people, the Polish economy makes it the biggest of the cases examined here. The division of Czechoslovakia will only add to Poland's regional weight, but the Polish economy is notoriously crisis-ridden. Poland's partners, including the EC, remain somewhat sceptical towards partnership with Poland. Despite this, Poland is vigorously pursuing the goal of EC, NATO and WEU membership. What is more, the increase in Polish industrial production in 1992 was widely interpreted as the first real sign of economic recovery throughout the post-communist world (*Financial Times*, 14 October 1992).

EC policy determinants in the realm of *système de causalité*

On the surface, there are many similarities between Hungary and Poland in the way both were caught by the logic of interdependence in a reversal of previous unilateral dependence on the Soviet Union. Yet the dimension of crisis makes the Polish case special. Poland's post-war economic and political history can be viewed as one of continued crisis with 1956, 1970, 1976, 1980, 1981 and 1989 as the high points. In other words, the Polish problems can be traced back to the Stalinist era, but it seems that it was the credit-financed imports of technology and consumer goods of the 1970s under the Gierek regime that were responsible for dragging the country down. From then on, Polish debts soared: from $1.1 billion in 1970 to $11.3 billion in 1976, $24 billion in 1981 and $48.5 billion by 1991 (Höhmann, 1985). While technology imports helped to bolster growth during the 1970s, it came to a standstill around 1980.

The real *annus horribilis* was 1990, the year of a record drop in industrial production of minus 24.2 per cent compared to 1989 (*Danish Economy*, 1992: 96).

Not that 1991 was much better. Polish authorities link two-thirds of the drop in production to the collapse of the Soviet market. Russian 'tourists' profiting from zloty convertibility drained Polish currency reserves of some $80 million each month (Dabrowski, 1991). Factors like these were a most powerful catalyst for the Polish switch to an EC-oriented foreign policy as a matter of necessity.

EC policy determinants in the realm of système de finalité

This does not mean that Poland's turn towards the EC was involuntary, however. Poles have felt the separation from Western Europe just as painfully as have the Hungarians. Poland was very frustrated about not being accepted as a member of the Council of Europe, after Hungary and subsequently Czechoslovakia were accepted as members. In the field of joint ventures there was an attempt to open the economy while the Communist Party was still in power.

A decisive catalyst for Poland's EC orientation was the unification of Germany, because of the traditional Polish perception of being placed in a geopolitical squeeze between the Soviet giant and a potential German giant. Yet, while independent Polish economists are very frank about the motive of *Einbindung* of Germany behind Poland's support for EC cooperation and integration, Polish top politicians carefully observe diplomatic etiquette. After all, Germany accounts for 80 per cent of Poland's foreign debt (partially written off in 1991). Before his visit to Germany in 1991, the then Prime Minister Jan Krzysztof Bielecki emphasized Germany's role as partner for Poland in its push for EC membership, declaring that 'our path to Europe lies in Germany' (*Reuters*, 6 March 1991). Likewise, Polish Foreign Minister Krzysztof Skubiszewski chose not to mention Germany directly when exposing the security motives determining Poland's new policy of joining European integration (Skubiszewski, 1991).

The twin motives of *Einbindung* and balance also found in Hungary are accompanied by similar reasoning concerning the 'Einbindung' of domestic extremist and ultra-nationalist forces into networks of international cooperation (Lamentowicz, 1992: 25). The Polish Minister for European Integration, former Prime Minister Bielecki, deserves to be quoted for his formulation of the nexus between EC membership commitment and foreign investment: 'The signal has to be made explicit *vis-à-vis* foreign investors that the EC really wants to include Poland. It is not a question of entry now or tomorrow. It may take up to 10 years, which may be the best for us' (*Weekendavisen*, 27 November–3 December 1992).

Poland's EC policy: strategies, tactics and developments

The Polish style in communicating its EC policy has at times been dramatic, as when Lech Walesa spoke of the Iron Curtain being replaced by a 'Silver Curtain' dividing a rich West from a poor East (*Guardian*, April 4 1991). Walesa complained about the lack of reciprocity in trade relations, reminding his audience that Polish shops were full of Western goods, while no Polish goods were available in Brussels. Despite discouraging signals from the EC, Poland put the year 2000 as deadline for its EC entry (*Guardian*, 8 March 1991). Subsequently, there were threats of suspending the talks on the association treaty if the EC Commission did not make concessions on agricultural goods. The current Polish Prime Minister Hanna Suchocka has warned Brussels against a wait-and-see attitude (*Agence Europe*, 10 October 1992).

Most remarkable for Poland is the nationalist-inspired opposition to the conclusion of the association treaty. It manifested itself in the spring of 1992, when Minister of Agriculture Gabriel Janowski from the Peasant Alliance demanded a renegotiation of the treaty, as he feared hefty competition from EC producers on the Polish home market (*Information*, 2–3 May 1992). He was joined by other parties, and only the Democratic Union, headed by former premier Mazowiecki, and Bielecki's Liberal Democratic Congress were unreserved in their endorsement of the treaty. The Polish parliament ratified the treaty on 4 July, with 238 votes for, 78 against, and 20 abstentions (ibid., 21 September 1992). Among the sceptics was Vice Premier Henryk Goryszewski, who cast his vote in favour of the treaty, albeit 'with a heavy heart'. Goryszewski's critical views are now directed against the Maastricht Treaty:

> The small peoples of Europe who are going to be the first to lose their national identity will never permit this ... Poland will never become part of Maastricht-Europe ... the Europe of the Twelve will ultimately be a Europe of the German nation (*Frankfurter Allgemeine Zeitung*, 3 September 1992).

This attitude could be indicative of a change in popular attitudes towards the EC in the post-communist world, when the effects of integration with the EC begin to intermingle with the domestic economic travails in a complex transition with no end in sight. The influential *Zycie Warszawy* wrote in connection with the French Maastricht referendum that 'the French dilemma shows Poles are not less "pro-European" than West European people, whereas Bielecki pointed to the dangers in a reawakening of nationalism' (*The Independent*, 22 September 1992).

The EC policy of post-communist Czechoslovakia

For many years, Czechoslovakia was an entirely anonymous country in international affairs. This changed dramatically as a consequence of the Velvet Revolution, when a foreign policy along the lines of reintegration was launched. What makes Czechoslovakia unique is the regional division of its EC policy into two separate halves. With the division of the country into two sovereign states, it has become irrelevant to speak of Czechoslovakia's EC policy. It is, therefore, necessary to address the EC policy of the two new states. Czechoslovakia's vision was to copy the example of Spain, and it is likely that the Czech Republic will succeed in this. The back side of the medal is the almost inevitable accentuation of economic disparities, and hence political tension between the two independent republics because of Slovakia's lower level of development.

EC policy determinants in the realm of système de causalité

In contrast to Poland, Czechoslovakia was not catapulted into a foreign economic policy oriented towards the EC because of an acute domestic economic crisis. The level of Czechoslovakia's debt was insignificant ($8.1 billion by 1990) and the population enjoyed stable living standards with stable supplies of goods. However, the country depended on CMEA trade, which meant that Czechoslovakia was ill prepared for the situation following its collapse. At one time, the then Minister of Finance Vaclav Klaus compared the situation to that facing South Korea and Taiwan if the US market closed overnight (*Financial Times*, 2 April 1991).

Three-quarters of the initial drop in the industrial production in 1991 (minus 21 per cent) was attributed to the collapse of the CMEA (Dabrowski, 1991: 33). German unification forced Czechoslovakia to give up a total of 500 mill. transferable roubles owed by the GDR and there was competition from ex-GDR firms. The Slovak economy was hit particularly hard by the contraction of arms sales, of which Czechoslovakia was the world's leader when measured on per capita basis. Energy supplies dropped drastically. Czechoslovakia found itself in a vacuum and had to turn to the EC in order to revive production. However, the swiftness of Czechoslovakia's foreign economic reorientation suggests that dissident and semi-dissident economists like Vaclav Klaus were well aware of the dynamics of EC integration as both a challenge and an opportunity for Czechoslovakia.

EC policy determinants in the realm of système de finalité

A typical description of Czechoslovakia's new orientation towards the EC is found in a brochure issued by the Prague Institute of International Relations:

> It is only the single market of the EC that can constitute a natural economic centre of the market economies arising ... Voices of Western experts can be heard very often bidding us not to prematurely liquidate the CMEA structure ... We are of the opinion that these suggestions proceed from misunderstanding: our mutual cooperation should first of all consist in a cooperated dismantling of the CMEA structures ... the multilateral cooperation among the East European ... countries has its justification only as related to the adaptation to the conditions prevailing in the European Communities (Stepanovsky, 1990: 6–8).

In addition to viewing EC membership and market access as goals in themselves, Czechs in particular stress the motive of *Einbindung:*

> The process of European integration should not stop at the reunification of Germany; it should go on. Only then will Europe be a safe place for Germany. Only then will Germany be a safe place for Europe. (Havel, 1990).

As for economic motives, it is tempting to postulate a hidden agenda in Czechoslovak Foreign Minister Jiri Dienstbier's concept of triangular trade, i.e. deliveries of machinery, food and consumer goods from the Visegrad countries to the Soviet Union sponsored by the West (1990). It looked like a concept for the resumption of CMEA trade based on export credits provided in practice by the EC. To the dismay of the Visegrad countries, however, the concept has come to play the role as *substitute* for EC market concessions, without providing for genuine breakthroughs in exports to countries like Russia.

Czechoslovakia's EC policy 1989–92: strategies, tactics and developments

Post-communist Czechoslovakia's foreign policy was characterized by a development from idealism to realism which had the effect of making the country's EC policy more offensive. During the Paris CSCE summit in November 1990, President Vaclav Havel challenged the alleged contradiction between 'integration in depth' and 'integration in breadth' (*Agence Europe*, 21 November 1990). At a news conference at the European Parliament, Havel outlined his vision for Czechoslovakia's relationship with the EC:

> We could even become full members earlier. It may be that we could become something in between an associate and full member. Political integration might proceed faster than economic links, depending on what happens to the Community's progress on economic and monetary union (*Reuters*, 20 March 1991).

Foreign Minister Dienstbier was quoted as saying that Czechoslovakia preferred the EC to a Central European free trade zone. While acknowledging the advantages associated with Czechoslovak–Polish–Hungarian cooperation, he stressed the need for concentrating on preparing the country for EC membership (*Report on Eastern Europe*, April 19 1991: 26).

Negotiations on association were less tough than in the case of Hungary and Poland, but it is Czechoslovakia that suffers from the safeguard clause on steel exports, which led to an anti-dumping customs of 30.4 per cent on seamless tubes beginning by 15 November 1992. The Czechoslovak foreign trade company for steel exports subsequently protested against the measures (*CTK-Business News*, 19 November 1992). Slovak Premier Vladimir Meciar claimed that Slovakia's losses from the export restrictions surpassed the figure for economic assistance given to Slovakia (ibid., 26 November 1992). Worse still is the prospect that Slovakia and the Czech Republic will be forced to accept even tougher safeguard measures in this field when they are to negotiate their own new association treaties as separate states. This is suggested by the Commission's enforcement of stronger steel safeguards regarding Bulgaria and Romania than was the case with the Visegrad countries.

The final stage in the Czech and Slovak Federal Republics' EC policy was devoted to upholding the trade provisions of the interim treaty of association, until separate arrangements for the independent Czech and Slovak republics are ready.

The EC policy of the Czech Republic: the basic approach

The initial Czech attitude towards Slovakia's self-assertion, which included pretensions of separate EC membership, was irritation and fear that it might delay the association of the Czechoslovak Federal Republic (*Report on*

Eastern Europe, 8 November 1991: 37). However, soon the attitude became one of letting go of the Slovaks in anticipation that the independent Czech Republic might fare better alone. The Czech perception gained support in an economic analysis of the Visegrad candidates for EC membership published by the London Centre for Economic Policy Research, an analysis which drew the attention of Czech media (*CTK-Business News*, 8 October 1992). According to Vaclav Klaus, the Czech Republic could join the EC already within five years (*CTK*, 6 November 1992). Klaus has pointed out that the foreign trade ratio is comparable to the EC ratios and claims that tax and wage policies will soon be at the Community level. The Czechs seem intent on cultivating their relationship with the EC and also have more expertise than the Slovaks.

The division of Czechoslovakia nourishes Czech apprehensions *vis-à-vis* Germany, but Vaclav Klaus is aware of the possibilities inherent in the Europeanization partnership with Germany inherited from the now defunct Federal Republic. According to the *Financial Times*, considerations about Germany inspire him to show restraint in public utterances of his critical views in relation to the Maastricht Treaty (7 October 1992). Otherwise, it is precisely this controversial profile which deserves attention. In contrast to his Visegrad counterparts, Klaus was reserved in his comments on the French referendum, pointing out that the close French vote could force the Treaty's drafters to return to the drawing board. Attempts to form a single currency had no chance to succeed in the near future because the economic situation of the different countries varied so much (*The Independent*, 22 September 1992). Prior to the French referendum, the Czech daily *Mlada Fronta Dnes* carried an interview with Klaus, who stated that:

> Maastricht, which was an artificial and, in my opinion, unnecessary attempt to accelerate West European integration, is causing many problems such as the Danish rejection ... the Czech government has resolved to refrain from intervention and there is no need to reinstate it through the EC. (*CTK-Business News*, 8 September 1992)

Likewise, Czechoslovak foreign policy advisor Martin Danes observes a critical attitude towards 'the excessive powers of Brussels bureaucrats' (*Le Monde*, 13 October 1992). Czech political scientists interpret this as a shift towards a 'British' approach to EC cooperation in the Czech government, an approach focused on the EC as a market. The sceptical attitude towards the political visions may originate in Czech disillusionment over French President Mitterrand's project of a European confederation raised at the Prague summit of 'les Assises' in June 1991. Nevertheless, it also falls into the pattern of Czech monetarism and Thatcherism personified by Vaclav Klaus. Danes formulates Czech public opinion as follows: 'Maastricht is far away. Vukovar is right here' (*Le Monde*, ibid.).

The EC policy of the Slovak republic: the basic approach

Full separation from the Czech Republic was not what the Slovak nationalists wanted, but Slovak demands for autonomy within the federation made it difficult to construct a viable entity. The differences in approach to reform were too big to make any sense of a 'confederation' as proposed by Slovakia. The Czechs cite Slovak Prime Minister Vladimir Meciar's goal of making Slovakia an independent subject of international law as justification for why the federation was doomed. The Slovak position is difficult to understand. One underlying factor is that the political leader implementing independence (Meciar) is not the same person who appears to have masterminded Slovakia's policy of independence, namely former Prime Minister Jan Carnogursky. Carnogursky's independence policy focused on the EC relationship as an instrument for gaining autonomy and independence and less on the direct relationship with Prague. This is in contrast to Meciar, who made himself more vulnerable to a Czech secession from Slovakia.

As early as 1990, before taking office as Prime Minister, Carnogursky expressed his ambition for a separate Slovak membership of the EC (*Reuters*, 4 June 1990). A year later, he spoke of acquiring independence by the year 2000 as a result of Czechoslovakia's EC membership. Carnogursky warned that if the EC favoured a unitary Czechoslovakia, Slovakia would force the issue by seceding (*Report on Eastern Europe*, 2 August 1991: 47). He wanted to use separate Slovak (and Czech) access to the EC as a means to subsequently dissolve the Czechoslovak federation 'according to the Maastricht principle of subsidiarity' as his political colleagues say (personal communication). Carnogursky himself says that it is the cool attitude of the EC towards Slovakia's desire for separate EC membership that fuels Slovak aspirations towards independence . This coolness on the part of the EC

> illustrates that the EC does not understand our problems, the EC does not have a coherent Central European policy. The EC is really Western Europe and has shown itself unable to overcome the East–West divide. The EC must realize the national issue (personal interview, October 1992).

In Carnogursky's view (as well as in Meciar's) Slovakia has an 'Eastern option': 'Slovakia prefers a linkage to the West but if the West – that is, the EC – takes a negative attitude, Slovakia will be able to go to the East and then the West loses an important buffer' (personal interview). Carnogursky uses the imposition of the special anti-dumping customs on steel to argue for the competitiveness of Slovakia's industries. He and Meciar are emphatic about the strategic significance of Slovakia and its attraction for foreign investors (*CTK-Business News*, 26 November 1992). Carnogursky explains Slovak nationalism as the same feeling of vulnerability concerning national identity which also inspires West Europeans. Taking notice of these new attitudes, Slovaks also want to secure themselves inside the EC (personal interview, October 1992).

Given the fact that Slovakia now has to negotiate its own relationship with the EC, views like Carnogursky's – however far-fetched and delusory they may seem – will become more influential in shaping policy. However, the harsh realities of independence are making themselves felt; Meciar cited 1993 unemployment rates of 18 per cent (*CTK-Business News*, 26 November 1992).

The implicit theory of reintegration of the Visegrad elites
and its policy implications

The revolutionary change in the EC policy of the Visegrad countries towards an aggressive pursuit of membership is not just a question of regime change. Key causes are the collapse of trade with the Soviet Union, the EC market as an export option and the attraction of Community integration or domestic crisis (in Poland). *Système de finalité* factors are equally significant. It is at this level that the motives and arguments behind the policy of turning towards the EC are formulated for the decision makers themselves, which then serves to consolidate reorientation. A general feature in Visegrad EC policy is the nationalistic determination, which parallels the quest of the East Asian Newly Industrializing Countries. This serves to put the challenge into perspective. The Visegrad countries' quest for EC membership and market access is a similar dual quest for the reassertion of national pride and the achievement of international reintegration.

There are differences across countries in the relative weight of the two types of decision frameworks. In so far as Hungary continues a long-term policy of opening its economy, the main explanation for Hungary's turn to the Community lies at the level of *système de finalité*. *Système de causalité* factors have worked almost as intervening variables, reinforcing the determination; e.g. the negative effects of the CAP upon Hungarian exports. A more outspoken case of determination from the *système de finalité* is Slovakia's pursuit of independent EC membership.

Whereas Hungary tried at an early stage to take the initiative in a policy of reintegration and ultimately succeeded, Czechoslovakia was pushed into it. However, the Czechs rapidly formulated an offensive EC policy. Czech policy today is characterized by a Thatcherist or functionalist approach to integration which is critical of the political union of the Maastricht Treaty. Indeed, the turmoil surrounding Maastricht has mobilized undercurrents of second thoughts and critical reflection in the Visegrad countries. This is especially true in Poland, where the perception of shortcomings in the association treaty mix with nationalistic anti-German perceptions and fear of an EC 'superstate'. Still, the dominant theme in today's EC policy in Poland and elsewhere is to push for specified and uniform membership provisions while upholding the criticism of the market access contained in the association or Europe agreements. In other words, the quest for reintegration on EC terms remains the leitmotif. Figure 7.1 summarizes the main points in the approach to reintegration inherent in the deliberations presented earlier. The figure shows the relationships perceived as necessary and sufficient for reintegration. Western thinking on the reintegration of the post-communist world is preoccupied with the changes within the post-communist world itself, politically and economically as well as institutionally. The dimension of change is also accepted by the post-communist elites as a necessary precondition for bringing about reintegration. This is the insight which came to dominate even the ruling Hungarian Socialist Workers' Party as a cognitive catalyst for the Hungarian transition from authoritarianism to democracy. The focal point is that domestic change is not a sufficient precondition for returning the post-communist world to the prevailing European order. The criticism raised by the Visegrad elites in their approach to the EC and other West European fora is that the issue of access has to be addressed far more systematically in the West's response to the changes in the former Communist world.

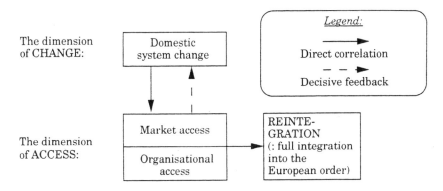

Figure 7.1 Reintegration – elite perceptions in the post-communist world

We are thus confronted with a challenge that touches the entire complex of theories of democratization and consolidation in the post-communist world. It presents itself as a necessary corrective to this field of social science. Is it fair to accuse studies of transition from communism of having ignored the dimension of access, the international dimension of system change? Yes, it is. At any rate, this dimension seems to be taken for granted as it is left out, for instance in Adam Przeworski's otherwise convincing exposition of the political economy of democratization (1991). The exception that proves the rule is Jack Snyder's contribution concerning how to avert anarchy and praetorianism in the post-communist world, which contains a vision of a Western policy aimed at economic assistance and reintegration (1991). Otherwise, it is mainly economists – including officials in the EC Commission! – who are genuinely aware of this dimension: 'The most lasting form of aid that the West could give Central-East Europe is to facilitate its reintegration into the world economy by means of improved access to Western markets' (Senior Nello, 1991: 183).

The crux of the matter is liberalization of international economic relations as a concomitant to liberalization of the domestic economies. The argument of the post-communist elites concerning organizational access, i.e. close cooperation and eventual membership of the EC, OECD, NATO, the Council of Europe, etc., is a variation of this theme of liberalization of international relations. Yet it has a further dimension of *Einbindung* to it; *Einbindung* of local extremist or praetorian forces.

Is market access so important? Has this question not been blown out of proportion by the post-communist elites in their understandable zeal to demonstrate that they differ in outlook from their communist predecessors?

Such psychological mechanisms cannot be disregarded, but this does not mean that there is no substance to their case.

In reality there are three basic arguments concerning the necessity of access to trade. First, there is the loss of export outlets and hence incomes from the collapse of the CMEA as a compelling factor for orientation towards the Western markets.

Second, there is the trade or export-boosting effect of the domestic system change. It is often forgotten that the economic model of the centrally planned economies was one of extreme import substitution or trade minimalization (Holzman, 1974). This means that the shift towards a 'normal', more export-oriented model would itself entail a net upsurge in trade. This is the reality created by the system change in the East, to which the international system must face up and to which it must adapt.

The third is a political argument, which concerns the role of the middle class. Theories of democratization generally acknowledge that the middle class holds the key to the consolidation of democracy. This stratum has a self interest in the workings of liberal society – mobility and competition, the observation of law and order, respect for private property, etc. (Herz, 1982: 286). The lack of a middle class in the post-communist world is the central concern of David Ost (1991; cf. Schöpflin, 1991: 249). Relying on Red Barons (i.e. former communist managers acting as real private managers for their firms) can only be a temporary solution to the problem of a lack of a middle class because of the uncertainties surrounding their 'democratic instinct'. What is needed is to create a middle class whose prosperity originates from new production and new forms of property associated with the new society being created, a self-made middle class with vested interests in the system change and democracy.

However, the emerging middle classes cannot rely on domestic customers because of their weak purchasing power; a problem that will increase because of the inevitable lay-offs and growing unemployment in the post-communist world. For this reason export earnings become the primary economic lever for this new social stratum. Moreover, export earnings constitute a crucial lever for the entire system change as they breed incomes which may be subject to taxation, a precondition for an effective social security system.

All this combines to make the question of market access as important as that of organizational access. These twin dimensions of access have to be addressed more systematically in Western policy in order to manage the challenge from anti-reform forces, nationalism and revisionism in post-communist foreign policy (Skak, 1992). The eruption of armed conflict in Yugoslavia and elsewhere in the post-communist world demonstrates the urgency of this task. As for the vital Western stake in responding in a way that really contributes to reintegration, it is worth quoting Francois Heisbourg, former director of the International Institute of Strategic Studies:

> If reform fails because of a lack of financial support, or through a lack of openness to Central European exports to Western Europe, or because of excessive reticence toward membership in the EC system, then we will all pay in security terms. (*International Herald Tribune*, 30 May 1991).

Hence, markets and institutions are the crucial weapons in Western *security* policy towards the post-communist world. This places the EC in the role as executor of security policy. What is needed more specifically is to look into the possibilities of additional market openings beyond the limits and provisions settled in the Europe agreements of association. The questions of the timetable, the beginning of entry talks and the specification of entry criteria must also be addressed. As can be seen from the Commission's report *Towards a Closer Association with the Countries of Central and Eastern Europe*, the Achilles heel is not the Commission, but the individual EC members. They are subject to general recession, to pressure from powerful lobbies, etc. These are very real challenges for all EC countries.

Given the obvious difficulty in achieving a real breakthrough in market access in the sensitive areas of agriculture, steel, and textiles, the task is also one of channelling PHARE funds more effectively into helping post-communist countries to diversify their production profile *away* from these areas. In other words, it is necessary to help them speed up the process of creating a more complex East–West division of labour, which might also be instrumental in creating a more viable East–East division of labour. This could prove the key to consolidate, for instance, Visegrad cooperation.

References

Csaba, Laszlo (1992) 'How to Survive Reorientation and Liberalization: The Example of Hungary', in John Flemming and J.M.C. Rollo (eds), *Trade, Payments and Adjustments in Central and Eastern Europe*, London: RIIA/The European Bank for Reconstruction and Development, pp. 45–56.

Csáki, Csaba (1990) 'Hungaran Agriculture and the European Integration', *AULA. Society and Economy*, vol. 12, pp. 80–94.

Dabrowski, Patrice (1991) 'East European Trade (part I): The Loss of the Soviet Market', *Report on Eastern Europe*, vol. 2, no. 40, 4 October, pp. 28–37.

Danish Economy (1992) 'Copenhagen: Det økonomiske Råd/ Formandskabet', May.

Dienstbier, Jiri (1990) 'Die Aussenpolitik der Tschechoslowakei in einer neuen Zeit. Vorschläge zur wirtschaftlichen Gesundung Osteuropas', *Europa Archiv*, no. 13-14, 25 July, pp. 397–407.

Duroselle, Jean Baptiste (1964) 'La nature des conflits internationaux', *Revue Française de Science Politique*, no. 2, pp. 295–308.

Havel, Vaclav (1990) 'The Chance that Will not Return', *U.S. News & World Report*, February 26 (reprinted by the Prague Institute of International Relations in the brochure *Europe: Czechoslovak View*).

Hedri, Gabriella Izik (1990) 'Economic Cooperation and Reform in Europe', *Bulletin of Peace Proposals*, vol. 21, pp. 183–93.

Herz, John (1982) *From Dictatorship to Democracy. Coping with the Legacies of Authoritarianism*, Westport, Connecticut: Greenwood Press.

Höhmann, Hans-Hermann (1985) 'East European Economies 1981-84. Growth, Reform and Foreign Trade Problems', *Berichte des Bundesinstitut für ostwissenschaftliche und internationale Studien*, no. 5.

Holzman, Franklyn (1974) *Foreign Trade under Central Planning*, Cambridge Massachusetts: Harvard University Press.

Hough, Jerry (1989/90) 'Gorbachev's Politics', *Foreign Affairs*, vol. 68, pp. 26–41.

Jeszensky, Geza (1991) 'Security in the New Central Europe' (excerpts from an address at the Johns Hopkins University, Bologna Center on 17 May, in *Hungary:*

Democracy Reborn, Budapest: Ministry of Foreign Affairs, pp. 51–9.

Kiss, Judit (1992) 'Joining the EC - Agricultural Implications for Hungary', Budapest: Institute for World Economics, *Working Paper*, no. 6, April 1992.

Lamentowicz, Wojtek (1992) *Political Instability in East-Central Europe: Domestic Threats to European Security and Integration*, Paper for the Inaugural Pan-European Conference on International Studies, Heidelberg, 16–20 September.

Mohi, Csaba (1992) 'Rules for Political Cooperation of the Association Agreement between the Community and Hungary', in *European Conference on Similarities and Differences in the Adaptation of the Countries of Central Europe to the European Community, Budapest November 28–30*, Budapest: Euration, pp. 12–15.

Obrman, Jan (1990) 'Putting the Country back on the Map', *Report on Eastern Europe*, vol. 2, no. 51, 28 December, pp. 10-14.

Ost, David (1991) *The Generation of Interests in Post-communist East Europe: Solidarity, the Incipient Bourgeoisie, and the Crisis of Liberal Democracy in Poland*, Paper prepared for the 15th IPSA World Congress, Buenos Aires, 21–5 July.

Palankai, Tibor (1991) *The European Community and Central European Integration: the Hungarian Case*, Institute for East–West Security Studies, Occasional Paper Series no. 21, Boulder, Co.: Westview Press.

Pedersen, Thomas (1992) *Integration and Enlargement. Challenges to the EC in the 1990s*, Paper presented to the Inaugural Pan-European Conference in International Studies, Heidelberg, 16–20 September.

Pinder, John (1991) *Towards a Wide and Federal Community: A Secure Symbiosis of East and West in Europe*, Paper for the 15th IPSA world congress, Buenos Aires, 21–5 July.

Przeworski, Adam (1991) *Democracy and the Market. Political and Economic Reforms in Eastern Europe and Latin America*, Cambridge: Cambridge University Press.

Pye, Lucian W. (1990) 'Political Science and the Crisis of Authoritarianism', *American Political Science Review*, vol. 84, March, pp. 3–19.

Schöpflin, George (1991) 'Post-Communism: Constructing New Democracies in Central Europe', *International Affairs*, vol. 67, April, pp. 235–50.

Senior Nello, Susan (1991) *The New Europe. Changing Economic Relations between East and West*, Harvester Wheatsheaf, Hemel Hempstead.

Skak, Mette (1991) *East Europe, the Soviet Union and Europeanization: A Challenge for the European Community*, Paper for the 1991 Annual APSA meeting, Washington D.C. 29 August–1 September.

Skak, Mette (1992) 'Post-Communist Foreign Policies. Initial Observations', *Cooperation and Conflict*, vol. 27, pp. 277–300.

Skubiszewski, Krzysztof (1991) 'Problems of Foreign Policy at the Threshold of 1991', Speech delivered in the Sejm of the Republic of Poland on 14 February. (mimeo.)

Snyder, Jack (1991) 'Averting Anarchy in the New Europe', updated version in Sean M. Lynn-Jones (ed.), *The Cold War and After. Prospects for Peace*, Cambridge, Mass.: MIT Press, pp. 104–40.

Stepanovsky, Jiri (1990) *Czecho-Slovak Foreign Policy*, Prague: Institute of International Relations (Brochure).

Towards a Closer Association with the Countries of Central and Eastern Europe (1992) Report by the Commission to the European Council, Edinburgh, 11–12 December 1992 (Communication from Vice-President Andriessen to the Commission in Agreement with the President).

Tovias, Alfred (1991) 'EC–Eastern Europe: A Case Study of Hungary', *Journal of Common Market Studies*, vol. 29, pp. 291–315.

The Visegrad Declaration (1991), 'Declaration of the Cooperation of the Republic of Hungary, the Czech and Slovak Federal Republic and the Republic of Poland on the Road to European Integration'.

PART THREE

The EC and the Developing Countries: Still Partners?

JØRGEN DIGE PEDERSEN

Introduction

Relations between the European Community and developing countries constitute one example of asymmetrical interdependence among groups of nations. Whatever impact recent developments in Europe may have, it is not likely to alter the lack of symmetry in relations between the EC and the developing world. What may change, and I contend *will* change, is the precise nature of interdependence. This chapter is devoted to an attempt to sketch the contours of these changes as they can be gauged from identifying important trends in the evolution of past relations and to make a projection based on policy changes within the EC and on reactions from developing countries. The changes will be further illustrated by brief studies of the relations between the EC and two of the major non-associated developing countries, India and Brazil.

The structure and evolution of the EC's relations with developing countries

The most conspicuous fact about EC relations with developing countries is its complex and many-faceted nature. First, it is important to distinguish between those relations managed bilaterally by the member states and those managed by EC institutions. We are concerned here only with the latter. Second, the system of interrelations managed by the EC is itself highly complex. The EC is in charge of external trade policy, and the management of trade with developing countries is of obvious importance for overall relations. Actual trade, however, is also influenced by measures taken by member states and by other policies of the Community, notably the Common Agricultural Policy (CAP). Third, elements of trade policy have been integrated with the policy on development cooperation with some developing countries. Finally, relations with developing countries, in particular aid relations, are administered and financed through different sets of agencies within the Community. This complex network of relations between the Community and developing countries has been termed a 'Pyramid of Privilege' (Mishalani *et al.*, 1981) indicating the differential nature of relations with various countries of the Third World.

The 'Pyramid' was constructed in the mid-1970s as a consequence of the first enlargement of the Community. At the apex of the pyramid lay some of the poorer African, Caribbean and Pacific countries from the British Commonwealth together with African countries previously associated through the Yaoundé agreements. The Lomé I convention, concluded in 1975, provided these countries – the ACP group – with a privileged position in terms of preferential access for their exports, stabilization measures for their earnings from the export of primary products (STABEX), and access to financial resources from the Community, mostly in the form of grants. The next layer of the pyramid included countries in the Mediterranean area, whose association provided them with less preferences than ACP countries. At the base of the pyramid came the remaining developing countries, mostly in Asia and Latin America, who did not possess special privileges in their relations with the Community except through the benefits which they could derive from the 1971 Generalized System of Preferences (GSP) in trade in manufactures, from the limited aid resources introduced into the Community budget in 1976, and from a number of special trade agreements concerning specific products (Cosgrove-Twitchett, 1976).

The arrangement with the ACP countries under Lomé I and subsequent agreements have stood apart for several reasons: its separate financing (mainly) through the European Development Fund instead of the Community budget; its ethos of being an agreement between independent sovereign partners rather than a clear-cut donor-recipient relationship; and its administration by a separate directorate, the DG VIII, under the charge of a single commissioner. In contrast, relations with non-associated developing Asian and Latin American (ALA) countries have in recent years been administered by the Directorate for External Relations, DG I, headed by another commissioner; cooperation activities have been financed through the annual budget; and relations have been organized around individual, bilateral agreements with distinct donor-recipient attributes (Commission, 1991).

Since its establishment, in the mid/late 1970s, the system of cooperation with developing countries, though still intact in its formal structure, has gradually changed in several respects. One obvious change has been the expansion of the system's coverage in terms of countries included and the expansion in terms of the amounts provided as foreign aid. The fourty-six countries included in Lomé I have now become sixty-nine in Lomé IV. In addition there are the Mediterranean countries, and the number of ALA countries included in EC programmes has increased from around ten to more than forty. In all, well over a hundred developing countries have today established links with the EC. This expansion has gone a long way in changing the EC–developing countries relationship from a regional arrangement into a truly global programme.

The means to sustain these relations have also increased, although hardly in similar proportions. Annual net flows of official development assistance were stagnant for long periods, and rose significantly only during a brief period in the late 1970s and more consistently since 1985. From around 5 per cent of total OECD (DAC) development assistance in the mid-1970s, EC aid has increased its share to 7.7 per cent by 1991.[1]

The globalization of EC development cooperation programmes has gradually changed the geographical focus of policy towards developing countries.
The establishment of links with more countries, many of which contain EC
offices (delegations), has meant increased attention being given to these
countries to the relative detriment of ACP countries. In terms of aid
resources, however, the shift has been much less marked, as can be seen
from Figure 8.1.

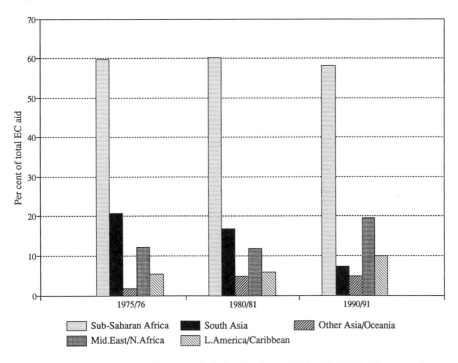

Figure 8.1 Geographical distribution of EC aid, 1975–90
Source: OECD, *Development Cooperation*, Paris, various years

While the African share of total disbursed aid from the EC has only
marginally declined, South Asian countries have lost out to Latin American
and Mediterranean countries. The increase in the share of Latin American
countries reflects to some extent explicit changes in EC aid priorities, in
particular following Spain and Portugal's entry into the Community in
1986.[2]
A third change in the policy towards developing countries can be described as a selective transfer of principles from the Lomé conventions to
cooperation with non-Lomé countries, or as gradual harmonization of the
cooperation policy. The integration of trade and investment issues with aid
policy that has constituted one of the salutary features of the Lomé arrangements has been partly incorporated into the new agreements with other

countries through the inclusion of new forms of economic cooperation (trade promotion, trade and investment information, promotion of techno-logical collaboration, and aid programmes). The aid–trade coupling has considerably expanded the scope of the original non-preferential trade agreements. Some of the poorer ALA countries have in addition benefitted since 1984 from a STABEX-like system of compensation for losses in export earnings. In 1988 the EC established a modest-scale investment promotion programme, the EC International Investment Partner Programme (IIP) (EC, 1988). The European Investment Bank has also been authorized to extend loans on a modest scale to ALA countries (*Agence Europe*, 11–12 May 1992).

Some of the administrative features of the Lomé cooperation programmes have also been imitated. Five-year programmes similar to the indicative programmes under the Lomé arrangements have recently been suggested, and a five-year financial package for the whole ALA programme covering the 1991–95 period has been prepared (OECD, 1991).

What has *not* been imitated in the cooperation with ALA countries is the principle of equality between cooperating partners and the separate set of institutions expressing this principle that has made the Lomé convention a unique form of international agreement (Cosgrove and Laurent, 1992). There is also reason to doubt whether the principle will survive the expira-tion of the present Lomé IV.[3]

Finally, the cooperation policy has gradually changed its official aims and the means to achieve these ends. Broadly speaking, the rhetoric has changed in accordance with dominant trends in the international debate on devel-opment issues, and EC aid programmes have increasingly included various policy conditionalities. The rhetoric of the development cooperation policy that lay in the design of Lomé I and in the first set of policy guidelines for the enlarged Community has clearly changed.[4] Missing is the emphasis on the equality of partners and the achievement of economic self-reliance. The notion that 'the solution is not for donors to impose stricter conditionality on aid' (Memorandum, 1982) has certainly disappeared. Indications of this changing climate in development cooperation could be found in the Lomé III convention, signed in late 1984, which included references to human rights issues and instituted a policy dialogue on sectoral development and import policy. Lomé IV (1989) strengthened these elements with the intro-duction of strong references to democracy and human rights and a facility to support structural adjustment programmes. Combined with a stronger emphasis on private sector development, efforts to promote and protect foreign investments, plus the inclusion of a range of new issues such as environment and population, Lomé IV represents an important stage in the redefinition of development cooperation policy. A Council Resolution of 28 November 1991 on 'Human Rights, Development and Democracy' made respect for human rights and democracy in all recipient countries both an objective and a condition for cooperation policy (*Bulletin of the European Communities*, 11/1991). Human rights provisions have since been a stand-ard part of all new cooperation agreements, including the new guidelines for cooperation with ALA countries.

A recent policy document on development cooperation (Commission, 1992) confirms the policy changes. It emphasizes that development aid can be utilized as leverage for economic and political reforms; it de-emphasizes economic interdependence and stresses interdependence in areas like environment, drug trafficking, population and AIDS; and it recognizes development cooperation as constituting only one part of the external policy, the aim of which is to defend the Community's interests and project its global presence.

Table 8.1 EC trade with developing countries, 1973, 1980, 1990 (1989)

	Africa	Latin America	Middle East	Asia	All developing countries*
1. EC share of region's export (%)					
1973	54.2	22.8	39.5	16.9	31.2
1980	42.8	18.8	32.3	15.1	27.1
1990	58.9	22.4	24.5	16.2	23.1
2. EC share of region's import (%)					
1973	47.3	21.6	36.9	14.4	26.0
1980	51.1	15.8	36.3	12.2	25.1
1990	50.3	17.2	40.3	14.1	23.4
3. Region's share of EC export (%)					
1973	9.6	6.8	5.6	5.0	27.4
1980	14.0	6.5	11.4	6.0	38.0
1990	7.2	4.3	7.6	9.8	31.0
4. Region's share of EC import (non-oil) (%)					
1973	7.3	8.3	1.3	7.0	24.4
1980	5.8	7.0	1.4	9.6	24.1
1989	3.7	6.2	1.8	13.9	27.1

* Including Oceania. For a small share of trade destination can not be determined.
Source: UNCTAD, *Handbook of International Trade and Development Statistics*, various issues. (Own calculations)
Note: Intra-EC trade is excluded. China is not included in Asia.

Apart from the various cooperation agreements, the Commission executes its role as manager of the Community's trade with developing countries primarily through the administration of the common external trade policy. The 1971 GSP system and agreements under the Multifibre Arrangement (MFA) have been the most important instruments for influencing imports from developing countries, keeping in mind the significant, if unmeasurable, impact of the CAP on trade in agricultural products. Use of anti-dumping measures and other discretionary instruments at the disposal of the Commission have also been important in regulating imports.

The general principle in the operation of the GSP and other trade instruments seems to have been to erect barriers against exporters who threaten weaker European industries, like textiles, footwear, electronic consumer goods, chemicals and steel. Unfortunately, these branches are generally those in which developing countries embarking on industrialization are most likely to concentrate their efforts. As a consequence, most barriers to imports have focused on developing countries exporting manufactures.

The resulting commercial relations between the EC and developing countries have experienced both stability and change.[5] The EC trade with different regions of the Third World has generally been quite balanced. The share of developing countries in EC non-oil imports has been remarkably stable at around 25 per cent and, as Table 8.1 indicates, the share of the EC in imports (and to a lesser degree in exports) of major regions has been stable as well. The EC has been a dominant exporter to Africa, the Middle East and Latin America, but has been less important for Asia. It has constituted by far the largest market for exports from Africa while its share of exports from the Middle East has declined and the somewhat lower shares of Asian and Latin American exports have been stable. The overall stability, however, conceals some important structural changes in EC imports from developing countries. Non-oil imports from developing countries have changed in both commodity and regional composition. Manufactures have replaced primary products as the most important imported products and, closely related to this, the Asian countries (in particular the East Asian NICs) have come to dominate trade, while also advancing to become the most important developing country markets for EC exports.

In private capital flows, the role of the EC has fluctuated somewhat, but in general, EC countries have lost the prominent role they previously had. In many areas of the Third World, however, the EC remains the most important source of foreign capital. In aid flows, the EC plus member states have been by far the most important donors accounting for close to half of all aid from OECD countries.

The overall picture of the economic relations between developing countries and the EC, then, is clearly one of asymmetry. Developing countries may be important as suppliers of some goods or as markets for a few exports from the EC, but on the whole the EC is a vastly more important partner in trade, investments and financial flows for developing countries than vice versa. Changes in commercial relations with developing countries, however, have tended to intensify relations with countries, particularly Asian, but also Latin American, that have been less important in the cooperation policy of the Community. The gradual globalization of cooperation policies may thus be seen as an adaptation to this evolving pattern of economic relations.

1992 and Maastricht: consequences for developing countries

The launching of the Single European Market project went largely unnoticed by developing countries. It was only after the promulgation of the Single European Act in 1987 that concerns began to emerge. By comparison, there have been only a few reactions from developing countries in relation to the Maastricht Treaty. Clearly, developing countries have been most concerned about what they perceive to be of direct and immediate importance for their economic interest; i.e. the Single Market, rather than its proposed political superstructure.

Though sporadic, the reactions of developing countries to the plans for the Single Market have been basically quite similar. The South Commission noted in its report the trend towards the formation of large trading groups among developed countries and voiced a fear of an emerging 'Fortress Europe' (South Commission, 1990). Similarly, UNCTAD conducted its discussion of the likely impact of the 1992 programme under the heading 'The Drift towards Greater Protectionism' (UNCTAD, 1989). Basically, the same concerns have been voiced by individual countries and groups among developing countries.[6] Fears of a more protectionist Europe have been common, and particularly for ACP countries the potential erosion of existing trade preferences has been the dominant concern (Gakunu, 1992). For its part, the EC has since 1988 repeatedly given assurances that the Single Market would be open towards the outside world. Europe 1992 would not be a 'Fortress Europe' but a 'World Partner'.

Estimates of the likely consequences of the Single European Market for developing countries or regions thereof have generally followed the model developed by Stevens (1990). According to Stevens, the economic effects of 1992 emanate partly from market responses, partly from political responses. Trade creation may result from stronger economic growth in the EC, while diversion of trade could occur because of the emergence of more efficient production units within the EC. Trade policies, policies on aid procurements and migration policies could also change in directions either beneficial or harmful to developing countries. Estimates based on this kind of reasoning have indicated that a completion of the Single Market programme could result in net trade-creating effects for developing countries in the order of 5 per cent of current exports to the EC (Davenport and Page, 1991). Because for manufactures trade diversion would be larger than trade creation, the same study estimated that the winners among developing countries would be found among exporters of primary products, in particular exporters of oil. Detailed studies of the impact of 1992 on regional groups of developing countries do not present an encouraging picture, however. For Sub-Saharan Africa, the potential effects have been estimated to be negligible, although slightly positive (Tovias, 1990); for Caribbean countries the impact could be alarmingly negative (Stevens, 1991); for Asian developing countries a positive net impact has been suggested, in particular for the NICs (Verbiest and Tang, 1991), but other studies have underlined the fundamental uncertainty (Kreinin and Plummer, 1992) or potentially negative effects, in particular on South Korea (Han, 1992).

All these studies expect the main positive influence to come from renewed economic growth in the EC after 1992 – a growth that at the time of writing (early 1993) seems to be postponed indefinitely. A second observation, common to all studies, is that the effects of the completion of the Single European Market will only be marginally influenced by policies adopted by developing countries, but will essentially depend on policies adopted by the Community. The changes envisioned for the Community's political decision-making structures could be a crucial factor affecting policy decisions; hence the potential importance of the Maastricht Treaty.

The consequences of Maastricht for relations with developing countries, however, are hard to determine. At a formal level, development cooperation has for the first time become inscribed in the text of an EC treaty. The treaty also requires development policies to be consistent with overall foreign policy, including security policy and external economic policies. The integration of development policy into the overall foreign policy, the strengthening of which is one of the treaty's major aims, could well lead to a more 'political' use of development cooperation policies. This is in line with the observed trend towards increased use of conditionalities, and accords with previous examples of the use of cooperation policies as instruments of foreign policy, for instance, in relations with Central America. The treaty articles dealing directly with development cooperation mainly represent a codification of present practices described earlier (including the emphasis on democracy, human rights, etc.) plus the ever-present ambition for closer coordination of policies among member states, including joint actions and closer collaboration between diplomatic missions and Commission delegations abroad. The practical consequences of the treaty, however, will still depend very much on initiatives taken by the Commission and on responses to these initiatives from member states.

Some of the initiatives of the Commission and some of the recent actions of the Community in relation to developing countries, especially in the aftermath of the treaty, can offer ideas as to the direction of future policies. The Commission and the Council have recently taken new initiatives in the field of development cooperation and in the general management of external relations. First, the Commission has suggested a substantial increase in budgetary resources for external action, including resources for development cooperation, and it has proposed that funds earmarked for Lomé cooperation in the future should be integrated into the Community budget. Second, as mentioned above, new guidelines for development cooperation have been formulated and a number of new cooperation agreements have been concluded with key developing countries along the lines of the new policy. In addition, administrative rearrangements under the new Commission have brought all matters relating to development cooperation under a single commissioner, thus facilitating future integration of policies for the ACP and for ALA countries (*Financial Times*, 23 December 1992).[7] The new policy also sets some initial priorities for cooperation policies towards different regions that seem to be closely aligned with the evolution of Community interests. For Africa, the emphasis will be on economic and political reforms and it can be expected that it will primarily be African countries that will face political conditionalities. The policy towards Mediterranean countries will focus on population policies and other activities seeking to combat the threat of large-scale migration. In Latin America and Asia, efforts will be concentrated on strengthening the private sector. For Asia one of the key goals is to increase the EC's share of exports and investments (Commission, 1992). The selective application of human rights conditionality, evident from the continued cooperation with Algeria and Indonesia and the suspension of aid to some African countries (Sudan, Malawi, Togo, Zaire) already reflects the impact of economic and security policies on the conduct of development cooperation policies.

At the Council meeting in Lisbon in June 1992, development cooperation was mentioned among possible areas of joint actions under the common foreign and security policy (*Bulletin of the European Communities*, 6/ 1992). The Council meeting in November 1992 on development cooperation also asked the Commission to prepare proposals for sectoral and country-level operational coordination of development policies (*Council Press Release*, 1083/92). Development cooperation, it seems, could well be among the first foreign policy issues selected for closer coordination between member states as a consequence of the Maastricht Treaty.

For those trade policies which are so important in determining the eventual impact of the Single Market, the Community is still struggling to formulate new principles and construct new joint instruments. The outcome of the conflict over the import regime for bananas indicates a degree of willingness to safeguard traditional ACP-supplier interests (*Financial Times*, 23 December 1992), while proposals to strengthen foreign trade instruments and prolong the MFA regime and the reluctance to untie aid procurements indicate a continuation of protectionist policies (*Financial Times*, 7 October, 21 December 1992). Finally, the emphasis placed by the Community on the use of reciprocity in dealings with third countries, whether trade, investment or banking, also leaves an impression of a tough international economic negotiator willing to provide concessions only on a *quid pro quo* basis.

Recent actions and policy declarations from the Community thus add up to a clear impression that the Maastricht Treaty constitutes part of a process which *will* in fact lead to closer cooperation between member states in the conduct of policies towards developing countries, to closer integration of aid policies with economic and foreign policy issues, and, most likely, to a more aggressive and 'tough' foreign policy.

Implications for developing countries:
India and Brazil

The implications for individual developing countries of a more unified European Community with an increasingly integrated, coordinated and possibly tougher external policy can be viewed in light of the trends in EC policies outlined above. The implications, however, will also depend upon the specific situation of individual developing countries. The choice of India and Brazil as cases for closer investigation is based on an assessment of these countries' general importance, and particularly their importance within the group of developing countries not associated with the EC through preferential arrangements. Each country represents a different continent with a different international setting and a separate set of development priorities, although as we shall see they have much in common. Due to their size and stage of development, both belong to the select group of developing countries in possession of sufficient material and human resources to produce a response to external developments such as the changes in Europe. While clearly not typical developing countries in economic and political importance, India and Brazil may be viewed as spokesmen for developing countries. Hence, their experience may be taken as rough guidelines for what developing countries in general can expect from dealings with the EC.

India and the EC: change and decline?

India has in recent years faced dramatic international and domestic changes that have affected the country's economic and political prospects.[8] The end of the Cold War and the demise of a bipolar world has increased Europe's importance for India as a potential counterbalance to US dominance. The collapse of the USSR has left India in a vacuum which Russia alone is incapable of filling. Economically, the EC has also become a more important partner, although one with whom India has been running a considerable trade deficit. The deficit has contributed significantly to the accumulation of balance of payments deficits which in combination with adverse international events (Gulf crisis, collapse of the USSR) have brought India close to a debt crisis. Since 1991 the debt problems and interventions by the IMF/World Bank have forced India to embark on a major experiment in economic liberalization.

The international crisis that India is facing has been accentuated by domestic political problems which for long periods have relegated foreign policy issues to a secondary position and in some periods have virtually paralysed the government. It is in this context of fundamental crisis and uncertainty that India has to redefine her relationship with a changing Europe.

Institutional links

The institutional links between India and the EC have focused principally on economic issues, although in recent years political issues have also emerged. One can discern three broad phases in relations between India and the EC, each covering about a decade.

The start of the first phase came with the opening of an Indian Mission in Brussels in 1962 in anticipation of UK entrance into the EC. When the prospects of immediate UK membership disappeared in 1963, India's interest in maintaining close relations with Brussels diminished, and a working relationship was only established in the early 1970s, when the UK finally succeeded in joining the EC.

UK entry in 1973 marked the beginning of the next phase, which lasted until the early 1980s. A Commercial Cooperation Agreement, effective from 1974, created a Joint Commission as a forum for regular meetings on trade issues. Important multi-year trade agreements were concluded in textiles under the MFA and annual agreements under the GSP were regularly concluded for a number of products, as were separate agreements on specific Indian export items (jute, coir). This intricate system of trade agreements came to encompass a substantial portion of India's export to the Community, estimated at roughly 70 per cent by the 1980s. An early contribution to the development of India's dairy sector in 1970, as well as the arrival of emergency supplies, marked the beginning of a Community aid programme, which became institutionalized with the establishment of the general aid programme in 1976. Seen in the light of current discussions regarding conditionalities, it is ironic that the aid programme was started during the period of emergency rule, when democracy was effectively suspended and human rights violations widespread.

A third phase began with the conclusion of a comprehensive cooperation agreement in 1981. The agreement extended existing trade cooperation and broadened it to include provisions for cooperation in a wider field of economic relations, including aid programmes. The institutional links were strengthened with the 1982/83 opening of an EC Delegation in New Delhi. Economic cooperation became a major issue on the agenda of the new Joint Commission and private sector cooperation was encouraged through the creation of a Joint Business Council. A political dialogue opened in 1982, and from 1986 evolved into regular annual meetings between EC troika foreign ministers and Indian officials.

A further intensification of contacts came in 1987 with the formation of a new Working Group for Industrial Cooperation, which became the forum for renewed efforts in industrial and technological cooperation. At the same time, the EC included India in its IIP facility. By 1991, fourteen investment projects related to India had been supported by this facility. In 1992, negotiations for a new cooperation agreement were concluded (*Agence Europe*, 16 December 1992). The new agreement represents a further broadening of the scope of cooperation, including many of the Community's new concerns (human rights, intellectual property rights, emphasis on private sector) (*Commission Press Release*, 1049/92).

The main EC activity towards India has undoubtedly been the aid programme. India has traditionally been the largest single beneficiary of EC aid, but its ranking has declined in recent years. While modest compared to other donors, the volume of EC aid has been significant due to its being largely in the form of grants rather than repayable loans. The most important single aid programme – the Indian-managed 'Operation Flood' dairy development programme – has been greatly welcomed by India despite some controversy over its social impact, and is to continue through 1994. Other aid projects and programmes initially came in the form of deliveries of commodities (fertilizers) which made them commercially attractive for EC companies, but during the 1980s regular aid projects in the rural sector have become more prominent.

The overall picture of Indo-EC interaction is one of a well-institutionalized and stable relationship that must be regarded as unique in terms of EC relations with non-associated developing countries. Despite frequent minor disputes over trade issues (anti-dumping measures, etc.) institutional relations have become increasingly close. The gradual growth of the aid programme notwithstanding, the establishment of new forms of cooperation has increasingly given relations between the EC and India a stronger commercial flavour. In many respects, the EC today seems inclined to treat India more and more as a commercial competitor similar to other Asian countries, rather than as an aid-deserving poor country.

Economic ties

The evolution of institutional ties has not been fully matched by development of balanced and close economic ties. Trade between India and the EC has increased steadily during the last two decades, but the trade balance has been tilted in favour of the EC. At present, India receives more than a third of its imports from the EC while a quarter of its exports are directed towards the Community. The importance of the EC as a source of imports and a market for exports stands in stark contrast to India's negligible role in EC foreign trade. India accounts for only one per cent of total EC imports and exports. The asymmetrical nature of trade relations is also evident from the commodity pattern of trade. India's exports to the EC have increasingly been manufactured goods, but a few items have dominated heavily. Diamonds, leather goods, textiles and clothing comprise nearly two-thirds of India's export, and only in one major sector (leather goods) can India be considered a significant supplier to the EC. In contrast, India's import from the EC is composed largely of sophisticated industrial goods like machinery and other forms of capital goods. Despite this, India is still one of the EC's largest trading partners among developing countries, but the narrow trade base has given India very limited commercial bargaining power.

In the case of foreign investments, the importance of the EC for India is evident. European companies have consistently accounted for about half the collaboration agreements between Indian and foreign companies. Direct foreign investments have risen during the 1980s, and while German companies have increased their presence, British investments are still dominant. The combined share of EC companies has remained close to two-thirds of the total stock of foreign investments. One could expect that the dominance of European companies among foreign investors in India would result in increased exports to Europe. This, however, seems not to have been the case. Foreign companies have generally been unwilling to export, despite favourable export incentives provided by the Indian government.

In concessional financing, the EC and member states have rivalled the World Bank as the largest source. At present, aid from EC and member states accounts for about 40 per cent of total aid, and with respect to private bank loans and other forms of non-concessional finance, European sources have been prominent as well.

Overall, Indo-EC economic ties constitute an important and stable relationship, but one in which India has been the more eager to collaborate. However, the Europeans have dominated and have provided far fewer benefits in terms of trade creation than India has expected. The EC remains India's most important international economic partner, while India has only a modest presence in the external economic relations of the EC.

Reactions to European integration

Reactions in India to plans for the Single European Market first became noticeable some time after the Single European Act.[9] While Indian officials have been quite aware of the potential importance for India of events in Europe, public awareness and the reaction of the Indian business community has been modest. In June 1988, Indian Prime Minister, Rajiv Gandhi, during his visit to West Germany, appointed a Committee of Indian Ambassadors in Europe to study the implications of the Single European Market.[10] The report of the Committee was ready by April 1989 and when it became known in India, it prompted a keener interest in changes in Europe. The report's main conclusion was that the Single European Market offered both opportunities and challenges for India (*Ambassadors' Report*, 1989). A unified market would present new opportunities for Indian exporters, and it could enhance prospects for collaboration between EC companies and Indian firms capable of performing low-cost labour-intensive operations.

Challenges for Indian companies were found in the harmonization of standards at a high technical level and in the expected technological advances in Europe. In addition, Indian exports would be challenged by manufacturers based in poorer EC countries. The emergence of stronger European companies was another matter of concern, and in the banking sector the EC policy of reciprocity could threaten India's traditional protectionism. The Committee observed that the Indian companies' main problems were their lack of technological sophistication and their modest size. Finally, the Committee saw a need for strong, coordinated efforts by Indian authorities to support firms operating in Europe. The report concluded in an optimistic tone. The size of the domestic market would in any case make India an attractive economic partner, and this fact alone would allow India sufficient bargaining power to manage in the future.

The subsequent debate within India and in discussions between India and the EC demonstrated few changes in attitudes. While government officials have been quite confident in India's abilities to manage in the new situation, representatives of private business have been more pessimistic. Businessmen felt that the EC had been quite helpful in providing information and other services related to the creation of the Single European Market, but they also felt that the helpful attitude was not reflected in the operations of European companies. European companies were seen as being largely unwilling to associate with Indian partners, and India has expressed anxiety over future technical standards required to operate in the European market. In bilateral meetings, Indian officials have repeatedly complained about increased protectionism in the EC. The Indians, however, have also been painfully aware that India is 'a distant partner in the outermost concentric circle of the EC's external relationship' (Jain, 1989), although they have always made a point of stressing the economic complementarities and political affinities between India and the EC.[11]

Little concrete action seems to have occurred. Neither the Indian government nor Indian private companies have so far taken any decisive action to promote Indian interests in the EC, apart from the modest activities undertaken through the Joint Commission. While some Indian companies have investigated opportunities for investing in Europe, the number of successful attempts is very limited. Similarly, only a handful of Indian companies have prepared themselves by establishing quality control procedures that could facilitate their entry into the European market.

The overall impression of Indian reactions to the changing European scenario is one of a deep divide between perceptions and intentions on the one side and concrete actions on the other. One explanation for the inaction lies in India's preoccupation with domestic problems. Another seems to lie in the belief that the EC will assist India through the well-established cooperation channels should any difficulties arise. This belief has probably been nurtured by the repeated assurances from the Community. A third explanation for Indian complacency comes from the excessive reliance on the myth that 'India is too large to be ignored'.[12] While India's size will always make it an attractive market, the history of Indo-EC relations has clearly demonstrated that size is no guarantee against its becoming marginalized, both in the global economy as well as in its relationship with the EC.

India and a unified Europe

Political compulsions and important economic ties have led India to focus attention on the Single European Market. Its inaction and the globalization of EC concerns have left India in a somewhat uncomfortable position. The EC will effectively determine the distribution of costs and benefits in future Indo-EC relations. A gradual fusion of EC member states into one powerful international actor could present India with even greater problems. A coordinated effort to utilize the EC's bargaining power for furthering commercial or political interests, for example, would be hard for India to oppose. Commissioner Andriessen's recent remarks that economic liberalizations would have to 'go in both directions' and that India should adopt a 'positive attitude' towards protection of intellectual property rights are signs that the EC might be willing to use its powers to press for policy changes (*Agence Europe*, 4–5 November 1992). As most demands presented by the EC are similar to demands by the World Bank/IMF, the EC's emergence as a strong international actor will leave India with very little international room for manoeuvre, especially in the present crisis. The only actions India can take to strengthen itself in the face of a stronger European presence are those of vigorous economic regeneration or of allying itself with other Asian partners. As the prospects of either option materializing are rather dim, India's best hope for beneficial relations with the united Europe lies in changing attitudes within Europe.

Brazil and the EC: a promising partnership?

The debt crisis, the gradual liberalization of its economy and the transition to a democratic political system are dominant concerns in Brazil's domestic politics.[13] On a hemispheric level, the US 'Enterprise of the Americas Initiative', the conclusion of the NAFTA agreement and the attempt to create the *Mercosur* regional free trade zone constitute important elements. Under these circumstances links with Europe, while important, are not at the top of Brazil's foreign policy agenda. They are important because they are substantial and expanding in economic terms and because they constitute a political alternative to a dependence on the US. They are of limited interest in the sense that Brazil feels it has alternatives, both in the form of a US alliance and in the form of regional arrangements. Contrary to India's situation, Brazil's international economic and political options have not been significantly reduced in the aftermath of the Cold War. Economic problems, however, are of overwhelming importance, and it is primarily for economic reasons that Brazil is interested in developing closer ties with the EC.

Institutional links

Institutional links between Brazil and the European Community have evolved through three phases. The first link between the European Community and Brazil dates back to the 1961 agreement between Euratom and the Brazilian government, but this agreement remained an isolated case. In the early 1970s, with the establishment of the GSP and the MFA schemes, some institutional links were established. In 1974 a non-preferential trade agreement became operational, making Brazil the second Latin American country to sign an agreement with the EC. The Joint Commission created by the agreement held only three meetings during the next ten years, however, and the agreement never became operational. In the EC's aid programme from 1976, Brazil was only sporadically included, and only since 1983 have small amounts of aid been provided.

The start of the next phase was marked by a more comprehensive agreement, which took effect in 1982. The scope of the agreement, while still non-preferential in trade, was broadened considerably. Most important, industrial and technological cooperation was included. The impact of the agreement on collaboration activities was limited, however. The Mixed Commission created through the agreement held only one meeting during the first five years of its existence, and while some aid was provided, ties were generally weak. A major cooperation project involving Community institutions came through the participation, from 1982, by the European Steel and Coal Community in the Carajás Iron Ore Project. This project, like the Euratom agreement, remained a prominent, but isolated case of EC–Brazilian cooperation.

The situation changed, however, around 1986–87. The change to a civilian government in 1985 combined with the strengthening of the pro-Latin America lobby within the EC after the accession of Portugal and Spain led to renewed efforts to develop links with Latin America, including Brazil. An EC Delegation opened in Brasilia in 1986, the Mixed Commission began to meet regularly, and in late 1988 an EC–Brazilian Business Chamber was created, the aim of which was to increase private sector cooperation. Brazil also benefitted from the IIP programme and a few joint ventures are known to have been established with the help of this facility (*Agence Europe*, 17 April 1992). Through the working of the Mixed Commission and the Business Council, Brazil hoped to secure itself access to European technology via EC-funded research programmes in high-tech areas.

In recent years, especially since the G7 Houston Summit in July 1990, environmental issues have become more prominent in EC–Brazilian relations, giving Brazil some leverage in negotiations. The EC has already committed itself to helping to finance a separate fund for saving the Amazon rainforest. A third cooperation agreement was negotiated in 1992. This new agreement is far more comprehensive than the previous one, and while marked by an emphasis on respect for human rights and democracy, it clearly expresses EC interests in protection of foreign investments and intellectual property rights and Brazil's interests in industrial and technological cooperation.

Prior to the recent increase in institutional ties, the most intense contacts were those related to the supervision of trade links, and trade frictions have been frequent. The management of quotas under the GSP/MFA and anti-dumping proceedings against Brazilian exporters, particularly steel, had been the cause of many controversies. The same applies to the restrictions on imports as a result of the CAP. While the extent to which trade restrictions have damaged Brazilian exports to the EC is difficult to judge, it has been estimated that almost a quarter of total Brazilian exports to the EC can be characterized as 'managed trade'.

In sum, links between Brazil and the EC have expanded considerably in recent years, laying the foundation for more comprehensive future cooperation. To some extent this reflects the strengthening of ties between the EC and Latin America generally. From a Brazilian point of view the increasing links mean improved prospects for Brazil to realize its European option.

Economic ties

Economic links have been infinitely much stronger compared to institutional links. The trade balance has shown a comfortable surplus for Brazil since the mid-1970s, due partly to the debt-induced policy of import compression. The EC has in recent years regained its position as Brazil's largest export market, with more than 30 per cent of total exports and supplying more than 20 per cent of total imports.

The composition of trade, however, demonstrates clearly the asymmetries between the two parties. Brazil's exports consist mainly of primary products and less sophisticated industrial goods, while EC exports to Brazil are composed of advanced manufactured goods like machinery and instruments. Although Brazil accounts for less than 2 per cent of overall imports to the Community it is a significant supplier to the European markets in some agricultural goods and raw materials. Brazil counts much less as a market for European goods, however.

The EC's growing importance for Brazil is most evident in foreign investments. Since the early 1980s, accumulated investments by European companies have surpassed investments by US companies, and far exceeded Japanese investments. Like most foreign investors, European companies are concentrated in manufacturing and, although normally smaller than US companies, they play a prominent role in several important sectors. An important feature of the activities of European companies in Brazil has been their involvement in foreign trade. In 1984 Fiat was the largest single importer *and* exporter in Brazil–EC trade, and it has been estimated that EC multinationals account for more than one-third of Brazil's imports from the EC and about 18 per cent of Brazilian exports to the EC.

In relation to the debt problem, European banks have been heavily engaged in lending and presently hold a portion of the external debt comparable to that of US banks, but negotiations with the Brazilian authorities have been conducted under the hegemony of the large US banks, and the EC has played no role.

From a Brazilian perspective, the overall picture is one of important and growing ties. From the EC point of view, relations with Brazil are important enough to justify serious concern, but they are far from being of the same level of concern. In contrast to the situation in India, EC companies have contributed to the development of close trade links, but this may to some degree have increased Brazil's exposure to fluctuations in the European economy.

Reactions to European integration

The prospect of the Single European Market initially evoked widespread anxiety in Brazil. The image of 'Fortress Europe' neatly sums up the initial reactions of leading sections of the Brazilian elite. A survey conducted among Brazilian businessmen in September 1989 revealed their apprehensions, with anxiety over developments in Europe being greatest in sectors with large exports to Europe (Guimarães, 1990). Their fears have gradually subsided, however, and a more positive attitude has emerged. Both among businessmen and among diplomats one finds today a more nuanced view of risks and opportunities. Nevertheless, most Brazilians realize that an eventual positive outcome will only be achieved if Brazil adapts to whatever circumstances European developments may generate.

There were several reasons for Brazil's change in attitude: (1) the promotional work done by the EC; (2) the observed difficulties of the unification process in Europe and studies conducted on the likely impact of the Single Market on Brazil's exports; (3) the positive experience from Brazil's recently intensified dealings with the EC; and (4) the more confident position enjoyed by Brazil after the Enterprise of the Americas Initiative.

While attitudes seem to have changed during the last few years, actions taken by Brazilian authorities or Brazilian business have been sporadic, reflecting the preoccupation with domestic problems. The impulse for the creation of *Mercosur* came to some extent from the Single Market project. The *Mercosur* could then serve as a local parallel to other regional arrangements and could also increase Brazil's 'attraction power' to foreign investors. In the same manner, the new strategy of economic liberalization has been perceived as a way to make Brazilian enterprises more competitive, preparing them for the competition in the EC.

A more noticeable reaction has come from the Brazilian companies, who have invested in Europe. Brazilian investments in Europe have grown since 1987 and now exceed investments in Latin America. Most investments have been directed towards Portugal and the UK, but some companies are known to have invested in production facilities in Spain, Italy and Germany (Guimarães, 1990). Some of these projects seek to defend existing export markets, while others represent a fresh move into the EC. Automotive parts, construction, textiles, and orange juice blending are all areas where Brazilian companies have invested. In addition, Brazilian banks have also increased their activities in Europe.

While some Brazilian companies have invested in Portugal in order to obtain access to the EC, the general attitude has been that Portugal is not in a position to act as a 'back door' to Europe. Brazil clearly resents being patronized by Portugal, and Brazilian companies mostly prefer to deal directly with the larger European countries.

Generally, Brazilian reactions to developments in Europe have, after an initial period of fear, become far more pragmatic. At present Brazil is concentrating on improving ties in specific areas. Trade frictions are regarded as a normal feature of international trade, and as for the problems stemming from the CAP, a realistic view is that matters can only improve through negotiations in the Uruguay Round. Brazilians still feel a need to remind the EC of their problems. In this regard they can, and probably will, use the present concern for the environment to keep Brazil on the agenda of the EC.

Brazil and a unified Europe

The EC has definitely become more important in Brazil's external relations. Political and economic relations are being strengthened, and the EC and Brazil both display a positive interest in continuing this process. Whether the intensified institutional relations result in stronger economic ties, however, will be determined by many other factors. Most important are probably domestic developments within Brazil itself. If the government does not succeed in stabilizing the economy, and if the uncertainty about the future of the political system and of economic policy continues, it may prove difficult to improve economic relations. The EC's interest in cultivating ties with Brazil is still to a large extent shaped by the development of a policy towards Latin America in general, and Latin America has rivals in other parts of the world whose interests the EC will strive to accommodate as well. Brazil will therefore have to fight to be kept on the agenda of the EC, but recent events suggest that they may succeed in doing so.

Conclusion

Despite obvious individual particularities, relations between the EC and India and Brazil represent two different versions of past trends and two possible scenarios for developing countries' future relations with the EC. Taken together, they illustrate the trend towards globalization of the EC's policy regarding developing countries and the shifts in the content of the policy. India's relations with the EC represent a change from a relatively favoured position, based on early cultivated institutional ties dominated by donations of aid, to a more commercialized, *quid pro quo*-based relationship. Brazil's relations with the EC have moved from a distant position with weak institutional ties to a much closer relationship based on similar *quid pro quo* principles with commercial interests in the forefront. For both countries, changes in the relationship have come about through initiatives from the EC rather than through their own efforts. The prospects of a strengthened economic and political integration within the EC have probably encouraged these policy changes, and the expected integration of Member Countries' development policies will provide the EC with a greater capacity to project its policy globally.

Who will be the winners and losers among developing countries in this process? In all probability, it will be determined by the attractiveness of the country in economic and political/security terms and to a much lesser degree, by the reactions of the various countries. While government initiatives may be important, reactions from private business to the Single European Market will most likely be decisive in the long run. In this respect, Brazil seems to be slightly better prepared than India. Very few Third World business enterprises, however, could claim to be fully prepared. ACP countries, particularly in Africa, being less attractive and having lesser capacities to react, may together with South Asian countries be losing most. For developing countries as a whole, except perhaps the Mediterranean countries, much will depend on developments in Eastern Europe and the attention the EC gives to problems here. If reactions by developing countries are any indication, no one seems today to consider themselves as being on top of any EC 'Pyramid of Privilege'.[14] It may only be of little comfort, then, that events other than those in Europe, primarily the final outcome of the Uruguay Round, but also regional trade negotiations in Asia and in the Americas, may have equally important consequences for developing countries. However it chooses to enact its role as a global player, the attitude of the EC will indeed be crucial role in shaping the outcome of these processes.

Notes

1. Figures on aid and other financial flows have been collected from OECD, *Development Cooperation*, Paris, various years, and OECD, *Geographical Distribution of Financial Flows to Developing Countries*, Paris, various years.

2. Latin America's share of budgetary resources for ALA aid has gradually grown from 20 to 25 to 35 per cent (*Commission, 1991*). Allocations from other aid programmes (food aid, emergency aid) also influence the geographical distribution.

3. There have been many indications that the Community is far from satisfied with the present organization of the Lomé Convention.

4. Observers seem to agree that the NIEO debate shaped the *design* of the Lomé Convention, while the *essence* of the Convention was a continuation of colonial ties (Twichett, 1981; Ravenhill, 1985).

5. For details, see Pedersen (1991).

6. No comprehensive overview of the reactions of developing countries exists. Page (1991) and Greenaway (1992) only provide an indirect survey of the concerns of developing countries.

7. The sudden resignation of the Director-General for Development, Dieter Frisch, may indicate a downgrading of the Lomé principles. Frisch had managed the Lomé conventions for a number of years (*Agence Europe*, 8 January 1993).

8. For a detailed account of Indo-EC relations and for full references, see Pedersen (1992a). Information on Indo-EC relations was obtained through interviews with EC officials, Indian government officials and representatives of private business in India. Interviews were conducted in January 1991 (India) and in January 1992 (Brussels).

9. The Maastricht Treaty has produced virtually no Indian public reaction so far.

10. *Ambassadors' Report*, 1989, Preface.

11. N.P. Jain was then Ambassador of India to the EC.

12. See *Ambassadors' Report*, 1989, p. 20.

13. For a detailed account of EC–Brazilian relations, including full references, see Pedersen (1992b). Interviews with EC officials, Brazilian government officials and representatives of Brazilian business were conducted in Brazil (July 1991) and Brussels (January 1992).

14. The ACP group clearly feels they no longer are at the top; the ASEAN group fears 'downgrading'; India and Brazil see themselves as belonging to an outer circle, and Latin America has long felt neglected. All see the EC as more concerned with internal matters. See Redmond (1992) for ASEAN; Cosgrove and Laurent (1992) for the ACP; my own interviews cover India and Brazil/Latin America.

References

Ambassadors' Report (1989) (Report of the Ambassadors' Committee on the Single European Market 1992 and India), Bonn.

Commission (1991) *The Europe-Asia and Latin America Dialogue. Financial and Technical Cooperation 1976–1989*, Luxembourg.

Commission (1992) *Development Cooperation Policy in the Run-up to 2000*, SEC (92) 915 final.

Commission Press Releases, Brussels.

Cosgrove, Carol and Pierre-Henri Laurent (1992) 'The Unique Relationship: the European Community and the ACP', in Redmond (1992: 121–37).

Cosgrove-Twitchett, Carol (1976). 'Towards a Community Development Policy', in Twitchett (1976: 151–74).

Davenport, Michael, with Sheila Page (1991) *Europe: 1992 and the Developing World*, London: Overseas Development Institute.

EC (1988) *E.C. International Investment Partners* (brochure), Brussels: The Commission.

EC–India Perspectives in a Changing International Order (1989) (Proceedings of a CEPS–ICRIER Seminar), Brussels: Centre for European Policy Studies.

Gakunu, Peter (1992) 'The Single Market and Commercial Relations with Non-Member Countries: Views from Developing Countries with Preferential Arrangements with the EC – the ACP Countries', *Journal of Development Planning*, No. 21, pp. 163–78.

Greenaway, David (1992) 'An Overview of Concerns of Non-Member Countries about the Single European Act and Its Implementation', *Journal of Development Planning*, No. 21, pp. 91–115.

Guimarães, Eduardo Augusto (1990) *EEC 92: Reflections on Brazilian Business*, Rio de Janeiro: Fundacão Centro de Estudos do Comercio Exterior.

Jain, N.P. (1989) 'India and the European Community in a Multi-Polar World', in EC–India Perspectives in a Changing International Order, 1989, pp. 1–4.

Han, Sun-Taik (1992) *European Integration: The Impact on Asian Newly Industrialising Economies*, Paris: OECD.

Kreinin, Mordechai E. and Michael G. Plummer (1992) 'Effects of Economic Integration in Industrial Countries on ASEAN and the Asian NIEs', *World Development*, Vol. 20, No. 9, pp. 1345–66.

Memorandum (1982) 'Memorandum on the Community's Development Policy', Supplement 5/82, *Bulletin of the European Communities*, Brussels: The Commission.

Mishalani, Philip, Annette Robert, Christopher Stevens and Ann Weston (1981) 'The Pyramid of Privilege', in Christopher Stevens (ed.), *EEC and the Third World: A Survey*, London: Hodder and Stoughton, pp. 60–82.

OECD (1991) *Aid Review: The European Communities*, Paris: OECD, Development Assistance Committee (mimeo).

Page, Sheila (1991) 'Europe 1992: Views of Developing Countries', *The Economic Journal*, Vol. 101, No. 409, pp. 1553–66.

Pedersen, Jørgen Dige (1991) 'The New Europe: Boom or Bane for the Third World?', *Cooperation and Conflict*, Vol. XXVI, No. 3, pp. 145–59.

Pedersen, Jørgen Dige (1992a) *India and the EEC in a New World Order*, Paper for the 12th European Conference on Modern South Asian Studies, Berlin, September 1992.

Pedersen, Jørgen Dige (1992b) *Brazil and the EEC in a New World Order*, Paper for the Inaugural Pan-European Conference on International Relations, Heidelberg, September 1992.

Ravenhill, John (1985) *Collective Clientelism. The Lomé Conventions and North–South Relations*, New York: Columbia University Press.

Redmond, John (ed.) (1992) *The External Relations of the European Community*, London: St. Martin's Press.

Redmond, John (1992) 'The European Community and ASEAN', in: Redmond (1992: 138–60).

South Commission (1990) *The Challenge to the South*. The Report of the South Commission, Oxford: Oxford University Press.

Stevens, Christopher (1990) 'The Impact of Europe 1992 on the South', *IDS Bulletin*, Vol. 21, No 1, pp. 50–6.

Stevens, Christopher (1991) 'The Caribbean and Europe 1992: Endgame?', *Development Policy Review*, Vol. 9, No. 3, September, pp. 265–83.

Tovias, Alfred (1990) *The European Communities' Single Market. The Challenge of 1992 for Sub-Saharan Africa*, Washington: The World Bank.

Twitchett, Carol Cosgrove (1981) *A Framework for Development: The EEC and the ACP*, London: George Allen & Unwin.

Twitchett, Kenneth J. (ed.) (1976) *Europe and the World. The External Relations of the Common Market*, London: Europa Publications.

UNCTAD (1989) *Trade and Development Report*, New York.

Verbiest J.P. and Min Tang (1991). *The Completion of the Single European Community Market in 1992: A Tentative Assessment of its Impact on Asian Developing Countries*, Manila: Asian Development Bank.

From Strategic Triangle to Economic Tripolarity: Japan's Responses to European Integration

CLEMENS STUBBE ØSTERGAARD

Introduction

This chapter deals with the interplay between external, Japan-related forces and the internal integration processes of the European Community (EC). In addition, the evolving EC foreign policy network relating to Japan will be discussed.[1]

The chapter first argues that Japan-related structural change in the international system can explain not only part of the momentum of EC integration 1985–90, but also more recent aspects of integration. Secondly, it describes and discusses the EC's developing external political links with Japan, under the diffuse policy leadership of the Commission. Finally, the chapter argues that the Japanese responses to the Single Market process have – on the whole – further stimulated EC integration, thus supporting Schmitter's hypothesized externalization effect. Japanese caution has kept this effect to a minimum, but some bargains may have had to be adjusted.

The period under particular scrutiny is 1989–92, and the areas of interest are economic and political, rather than the trade frictions which originally brought the two sides together. The analysis draws on interviews conducted in Tokyo and Osaka, as well as on material in leading European and Japanese media, *Agence Europe* and government reports.

The framework is based on the assumption that integration results from elite bargains. These bargains may be a response to, or be triggered by, international structural change and the Commission's policy leadership (Sandholtz and Zysman, 1989: 95). Bargains among elites occur in response to challenges presented by international and domestic changes: when the global context changes, bargains have to be adjusted. The relevant elites for this analysis are a transnational industry coalition, a coalition of governmental elites and the Commission. There is a hierarchy of bargains: fundamental bargains (i.e. the Single European Act, the Maastricht Treaty) embodying basic objectives, and in many areas subsidiary bargains to implement them. A distinction is made between internal and external bargains, where the latter would include for instance national treatment for subsidiaries of foreign (i.e. American) firms in Europe or the auto-agreement made with Japan in 1991. At the same time external elites can benefit from the consequences of internal bargains, such as stability, growth, etc., or they may suffer due to inward-turning, protectionist attitudes. The argument is that the 1992 movement should be understood as a joint response by actors (governments and companies and EC institutions) to the shift in the relative distribution of economic power resources indicated by the USA's decline and Japan's ascent; European countries stood to lose control and influence in arenas such as technology, monetary matters and trade. To be dependent on Japan was an option quite different from that of relying on the well-known Atlantic partnership, underpinned by strategic and cultural links. The global setting can be understood in neo-realist terms, but the political processes (bargains) triggered must be analysed in other than structural terms.

International structural change related to Japan

European integration was revitalized during the 1980s in response to global developments which carried the threat of a loss of control and influence over economic power resources. Since then, Japan-related structural changes have remained an important part of the global context, leading to a need for the adjustment of elite bargains on integration. There have been other active factors: both domestic changes, such as German unification, and other international changes, such as the end of the Cold War, may be seen as having affected integration. Here we shall look mainly at two categories of structural change: 1) the distribution and character of economic power resources, and 2) the advent of a pattern of economic tripolarity.

Examining the evidence, there has been a continuation of the trends noted by Sandholtz and Zysman in areas of technology, monetary and finance matters, and trade. However, new worrying elements have been added to the overall picture presented by the international economic structure. These relate to Japan, but do not necessarily lead to a demand for further integration. Briefly, they include: the speed and costs of Research and Development (R&D) and technological development, the globalization of Japanese industry, and Japan's move to a new *stage* of industrialization. The rise of East Asia in the world economy and the leading role played in the region by Japan is also changing the global context. The return of China to two-digit GNP growth, the prospect of Taiwan joining the world's biggest trading nations, East Asia's recent average growth of 7–8 per cent GNP, and the prospect of resolving several of the Cold War-originated conflicts in the region make it obvious that the challenge, which was the catalyst for the fundamental bargain on integration, is greater than ever.

Distribution and character of economic power resources

Elements of continuity

Japan's leading positions in various key high-technology sectors have not been diminished. It has continued to advance in electronics, coming to control half the global market for chips and increasing its own competitiveness.[2] Japan has also added new areas such as biotechnology and aerospace; it is planning to put a man on the Moon in 1996 and is already able to make better fighter-planes than the US. In new materials, information technology, telecommunications, optronics and mechatronics, Japan is increasingly taking the lead (Ozawa, 1992: 269). Forefront technologies related to engineering at the atomic or molecular levels and the interplay between science and engineering in general have received much attention. Table 9.1 compares Europe and Japan in the mid-1980s.

The structure of monetary and currency relations changed still further. Japan has remained in its unique position of relative strength as the world's main source of capital and its 'lender of last resort'. Immense financial resources are under Japanese control, giving it a crucial role in macroeconomic policy coordination in the context of G5, G7, G24, annual economic summits and multilateral financial institutions. It was also the United States' financial backer for the war against Iraq. Tokyo became a leading financial centre; it even had a role propping up London's continued position as a finance centre. The world is already on a *de facto* multi-reserve currency system, including the Japanese Yen and, it is hoped, the Ecu (Kashiwagi, 1990). From 1985 to 1991, Japanese firms made overseas portfolio investments of $427 billion (Courtis, 1991: 14). Though the yen has recently become more reluctant to go overseas, it remained the only stable currency in the autumn 1992 debacle. In that year, however, the Japanese financial system was in crisis, sending shock waves around the globe. Japanese banks were trying to cope with the bad debts left over from the excesses of the late 1980s.[3] On the one hand then there has been since 1988 further evidence of Japanese superiority in the monetary and financial area, while on the other there has also been a crash in the Nikkei index, as well as large securities firms scandals, reduced lending and a reduced capacity to feed the international funds market. The EC is still unable to formulate a dynamic approach to the management of monetary problems, remaining dependent on 'the Gang of Two', Japan and the United States.

The structure of the EC's trade environment changed further over the last decade (Sinha, 1990: 229). Due mostly to increased tourism and bubble-related imports, the role of the external sector in Japan's GNP decreased from 4.85 per cent in 1985 to 1.2 per cent in 1990. With the slower growth experienced in 1991, and the huge cost-cutting investments described below, Japanese corporations again sought foreign markets, with inevitable growth in trade surpluses. However, attention is very much directed towards the high growth economies in East Asia (this trade is 25 per cent over that with the US), but also towards the expected growth potential of Europe under unification. Record trade surpluses with Europe in 1991 and 1992 were also influenced by exports of machines and components to the Japanese plants established in Europe.

Table 9.1 Japan's technology gap *vis-à-vis* Europe

	Least progressive	Less progressive	Equal	More progressive	Most progressive
Most advanced			2 technologies: optical fibres, videodiscs	2 technologies: optical elements, semiconductors	3 technologies: e.g. disaster prevention, copiers
More advanced			8 technologies: e.g. industrial robots, automatic interpreters, safety of LWRs	9 technologies: e.g. sensors, optical fibres, fuel cell power generation	4 technologies: large-scale computers, earthquake prediction, artificial heart, LSI
Equal		6 technologies: e.g. space communications, artificial satellites, seabed oil production	25 technologies: e.g. CAD/CAM, rockets, nuclear fusion, intragenic recombination, fermentation, crop breeding	9 technologies: e.g. laser printers, photo power generation, cattle breeding	3 technologies: medical R&D, housing construction, vermin prevention
Less advanced	1 technology: medical lasers	6 technologies: e.g. resource exploration, radioactive waste disposal, weather surveys	4 technologies: e.g. civil aircraft, uranium enrichment		
Least advanced	1 technology: fast breeder reactor				

Source: White Paper, Science and Technology Agency, Japan, 1985

Though the years 1985–90 saw a decrease in Japan's trade surplus with Europe, it was also the period when the extent of the crisis for Europe's automotive and electronics industries became obvious. An EC-wide agreement was reached on cars, but in the all-important electronics sector no real results were obtained. In 1991 the surplus again soared towards record heights: out of a total Japanese trade surplus of $90 billion, $29 billion was generated in Japan–EC trade (Rothacher, 1992: 1).

More recent changes

The phenomena described so far continue to underpin the bargains forming the basis for revitalized European integration. There have, however, occurred other Japan-induced changes in the character of the international economic structure.

The high-technology race has reached a stage where short product cycles, steeply falling prices and the pace set by Japan in R&D are all making it difficult for Europe and the US to keep up.[4] As new fields are entered, Japan simply outspends the competition, behaving much as President Reagan did towards the Soviet Union in the military field. Investing at double the per capita rate of the US, Japan spent more even in absolute terms. Technological development is also racing ahead of technological structural adaptation. Attempts by the Community to counter this with large-scale R&D programmes have not improved EC competitiveness with Japan, partly because the pace of market change is so fast that it leaves European firms with misallocated resources and huge losses, and partly because technology promotion schemes become bureaucratized.[5] In the crucial electronic components industry, Philips is the only European left in the global 'top ten', six of which are Japanese (*International Herald Tribune*, 13 March 1991). Large schemes like Esprit and Joint European Submicron Silicon Initiative (JESSI) were intended to develop technologies that would help Europeans compete against Japanese multinationals, but they and others became long on bureaucracy and short on engineers. It was mistakenly believed that laboratory work could substitute for efficient manufacturing and aggressive marketing. An important response by European industry may be to cooperate outside the Single Market: Volvo–Mitsubishi, Hitachi–Fiat, Suzuki–Volkswagen, Mitsubishi–Fiatavio and Nissho Iwai–Metalgesellschaft are just a few of the recent joint ventures. In the nature of such deals, not many details are known, making it difficult to evaluate their true importance. My own guess is that such international consortia will become a typical feature of the international economic system.

The second important new trend is the multinationalization of Japanese industry which is changing the global context for Europe. There are several reasons for this trend: first, the enormous R&D expenses in the present industrial stage require a presence in all major markets. Second, fear of increased protectionism and the prospective weakening of the General Agreement on Tariffs and Trade (GATT) make it desirable to become insiders in Europe and the US: regarding Europe, there also exists a desire to capitalize on growth potential in EC and Eastern Europe. Third, the

Japanese feel the need to strengthen strategic market positions now, because the Yen is likely to appreciate and competition from Europe and East Asia will sharpen. Finally, the five-year boom and financial 'bubble' provided further incentives for the recycling of current account surpluses, by making other markets seem like bargain basements (Courtis, 1991). Between 1985 and 1991, Japanese firms invested about $600 billion abroad, $427 billion in portfolio and $167 billion in direct investment. A quarter of this investment went to Europe. Thus the competitive base of Japanese industry is being globalized into a world-wide system of production. The 'Japanese challenge' is becoming less Japanese, in the words of Dunning. The trend toward globalization is far from finished. At the present low degree of multinationalisation, Japanese firms produce and sell abroad the equivalent to 5 per cent of GNP. The corresponding figure for the USA is 20 per cent, and a comparable development for Japan, say up to the German level of 15 per cent, would mean that by the end of the decade the international presence of Japan would be four to four and a half times larger than today.[6]

The third important new characteristic of the global structure is the perspective that Japan, based on its singular investment behaviour, is moving to a new stage of industrialization, shedding from the Japanese economy assembly-line-based processes which exploit economies of scale – e.g. standard autos and electronics goods – and shifting these to overseas locations, while simultaneously taking up small-lot, flexible manufacturing with 'mechatronics' to produce multi-variety, new upmarket goods for its affluent consumers. This change is possibly based on the huge capital investment undertaken by Japan during the so-called Heisei boom of 1986–1991. Investment has not just gone into capacity expansion which would create global overproduction. Thirty per cent has been spent on increased productivity, another 30 per cent on innovation, and the rest on new capacity, half of which went to establish facilities for new products and services. In other words, 80 per cent of the $3 trillion spent over the last five years was used to create an economic base for long term growth in the 1990s. Spending on rationalization and productivity raised labour productivity from index 100 in 1985 to 140 in 1991. In another instance, car manufacturers decided to aim at reducing the design cycle from four to two years in the course of the 1990s (with half the staff and at a quarter of the cost). The competitive impact is staggering. The investment going into innovation is now targeted to the domestic market and aims at giving Japan a role in the world economy similar to that of the US in the 1950s and 1960s. Japan will take on the role of new product laboratory for the world economy. Europe would be a model market for these products. The difference between investment behaviour in Japan and notably the US, but to a degree the EC, 'sets in place a dynamic that will have fundamentally important implications for international economy relations through the end of the century' (Courtis, 1991: 8). Just one consequence of the move away from mass-production to satisfy fickle consumer tastes will be that the economies of scale sought by the Single Market will decrease in importance. The long-term competitive, financial and strategic implications cannot be overestimated.

The effects on elite bargains on EC integration

We have seen a number of structural changes in the global context which are related to Japan or derive from Japanese actions: forbidding R&D costs, multinationalization of Japanese industry, Japanese investment towards a new stage of industrialization, and the ascent of East Asia. What effects do these changes have on European integration, on the need for adjustment of the bargains, and on the coalition which supports the fundamental bargains of integration? Do these developments reinforce the bargains? Do they support the implementation of subsidiary bargains and the acceptance of bargains at the mass level? What is happening to the structures of control and influence?

R&D costs may lie behind the strategic alliances now being made among EC–Japanese–US firms. It is worth noting that the sheer size achieved through the many grand scale joint ventures, mergers and share-swapping operations promoted by the Single Market process – as well as the size of the post-1992 European market – has given leverage to European firms in negotiations. Are the strategic alliance industries lost to Europe and the coalition? 'By the end of the century we won't know where Europe ends', sums up one scenario.

Multinationalization of Japanese companies: Europe will face a new wave of competitive pressures, this time within its own borders, from highly productive networks of Japanese-owned manufacturers, suppliers and service providers. There will be fresh capital in knowledge- and technology-intensive sectors. If European industry is strong enough to withstand the competition, and depending on the degree to which Japanese firms transfer innovative activities, there will occur a contribution to the restructuring and upgrading of European industry, and there could actually emerge new world-class technology centres in the region (Dunning and Gittelman, 1992: 237). An influential analyst, Terutomo Ozawa, disagrees: the Japanese are just refining their pattern of comparative advantages and keeping the interesting high-value products, in a vertical division of labour. Problems with this strategy might lead to adjustments of the external bargains with Japan, and might bring European small and medium-sized industry more clearly into the coalition. However, there also exist increased possibilities for cooperation and strategic cross-continental alliances.

Japanese domestic capital investment and the predicted resulting 'post-war US role' – at least in production – might call for closer integration, just as the original US challenge did in 1957. The handling of 'le defi americain II', in a context of no Cold War, will be a different matter. Again, however, control and influence may seem less crucial in a less militarized strategic situation. The state of the European economies and their trade balances would be an important factor in determining the outcome. In any case, it would seem important for Europe to obtain the strongest possible bargaining position through increased integration.

Emergence of a pattern of economic tripolarity

The advent of economic tripolarity is another change in the international structure, having both political and economic significance (Bergsten, 1992: 51). The combination of the continued ascent of Japan, the crumbling of the Soviet Union, the Single Market process of the EC and the persistence of the United States has changed the balance of power, and the trend towards global economic tripolarity is strengthened. The three poles also tend to be three interdependent trading groups. The question, however, is whether interdependence has increased enough for this too to be considered a structural change? The financial markets are interwoven, as are goods and services trade. Mergers, joint ventures, cooperation agreements and strategic alliances multiply.

The importance of the strategic triangle (US/USSR/China) of Cold War days, may thus be replaced by an economic tripolar world order (US/EC/Japan). This new order stresses not only interdependence, but also the relevance of 'pivot-positions', two-against-one scenarios in economic struggles, 'playing the triangle', etc.[7] There has been no lack of proposals that the US and Japan should form a G2, create a 'Pacific Century', and so on. After the end of the Cold War, however, and with the reduced importance of the American nuclear umbrella, Japan and Europe might also team up to, for instance, outflank US industry. Indeed this might be the intention behind the Mitsubishi–Daimler Benz alliance. A US–EC alliance to force Japan to 'play by the rules' is less likely, because of the high risk, because of US dependence on Japan for technology and capital and for strategic reasons. Three-player games are, unfortunately, very unstable, and the costs of failure are considerable. The certain losers, in the case where there occurred an erosion of the open world economy and the formation of blocs, would be the developing countries and the former Eastern bloc (Vernon, 1990: 67).

There are also cooperative possibilities in the triangular framework. One suggestion points out suitable areas for intensified transnational cooperation as being: 'framework conditions for the trade in technology and communications-based services, compatibility and protection of technological development and, above all, concrete economic and technological cooperation and division of labour in an effort to facilitate a balanced structural adaptation within the triangle US–Japan–Europe' (Grewlich, 1988: 230).

The triangle can function only if Europe is a roughly equal partner, economically, technologically and politically, and this naturally demands accelerating the integration process, including its foreign policy component (Pons, 1992).

Some conclusions on structural change

Can Japan-related structural change help explain not only the early momentum for renewed EC integration, but also more recent aspects of the process?

Developments in R&D may tend to weaken the importance of some of the original factors impelling the transnational industry coalition toward what became the Single Market process. The strategy for coping with the high costs of technology development could be changing to one of 'If you can't beat 'em, join 'em', i.e. the US and Japanese multinationals. This trend may also make it increasingly irrelevant for the EC to protect its market from intruders. Other factors, however, such as Japan's investment behaviour and related industrial positioning, its competitiveness and growing multinationalization and the overall importance of an East Asia dominated by Japan, should certainly reinforce the fundamental bargains on European integration. The growing recognition of tripolarity should in turn reinforce integration.

Has the transnational industry coalition maintained its aim of integrating Europe, now that economies of scale seem to be losing their importance? Is it affected by the cross-continental activities? Is it focused on other objectives? Have the Commission and the government elites been left in the lurch? These are some of the questions which might be raised at a time when the 1992 process is reaching beyond the elites to the populations of the member countries, at mass levels where it is highly questionable whether changes in the global context are fully appreciated.

The evolving EC foreign policy network relations with Japan

The image of a tripolar world has placed EC–Japan contacts on the mutual agenda. Up to now, it is the weakest link in a triangle, having the US in a pivotal position. Japan has particularly sought to counterbalance its political dependence on the US, and has wanted to see Europe as a unitary actor. For a long time Europe was reticent, but from 1991 the Commission has been making a weak attempt to take the initiative for a new external bargain with Japan. Both the EC and Japan are of course adept at rhetoric and symbolism as well as at carrying on dialogues of the deaf.

This section first describes the existing rudimentary foreign policy network with Japan, in place before 1990. It then goes on to examine Japanese initiatives for political relations, and the place of Europe in Japanese foreign policy thinking – if any. The framework for and issues of Japan–EC relations, as foreseen in the Joint Declaration of July 1991, are then discussed. The fourth section treats the Commission's report and the ensuing General Affairs Council's 'Conclusions on Future Relations' of mid-1992, which is the closest the EC has come to a Japan policy.

Pre-1990 political relations: Japanese initiatives

Long seen as a junior partner of the US, Japan only became interesting to Europe when its trade surplus burgeoned during the 1970s and it became an economic competitor. The trade relationship was politicized and came to involve the EC, which from 1970 had taken over responsibility for external trade relations of the members. The Commission's first trade policy initiative was towards Japan, and it was only when – due to safeguard clauses within Europe – the intended Japan–EC trade agreement failed to materialize in the early 1970s, that Japan gave priority to bilateral talks (Freudenstein, 1991: 11). The trade deficit remains the central aspect of the relationship. It has been attacked by the Commission with 'a substantial dose of political intervention and management of trade' (Maull, 1990: 57). The foreign policy actions involved may loosely be characterized as springing from Ginsberg's integration logic: Japan presses the EC to respond in connection with internal measures, which come to affect Japanese trade interests (1989: 185).

Besides this there have been many informal coordinating consultations in connection with the numerous economic summits, G5 and G7 meetings, work in multilateral institutions such as the IMF, GATT, the World Bank and the UN system.[8] These belong to the category of increasing 'global interdependence' used by Ginsberg to explain the growth in EC foreign policy actions (1989: 184). As US hegemony diminished, there were more opportunities for the Community and Japan to find positions of common interest in opposition to American economic and political views and actions, and an informal *ad hoc* foreign policy network grew up around these important institutions and regimes.

Formalized possibilities for foreign policy coordination or action were few. The troika foreign ministers and director-general meetings started in 1983 and petered out a few years later, only to be recommenced in 1990. They were 'nothing more than *tours d'horizon* of the political situation in the Soviet Union and the Third World' according to the Japanese, and they did lead to concrete policy coordination (Murata, 1988: 9). European Political Cooperation apparently did not pay much attention to Japan, nor were there any visits to Japan by important actors like Hans-Dietrich Genscher or Jacques Delors. Europe still did not regard Japan as a serious interlocutor in the political and security area.

During the 1980s there were a number of Japanese attempts to upgrade political relations. These included Foreign Minister Saburo Okita's improvised visit to the European Council meeting in April 1980, Prime Minister Yasuhiro Nakasone's concerted attempts at freeing Japan from the US by means of consultation with Europe on the emplacement of SS-20 missiles in the INF process (and by more state visits than any previous PM), and Noboru Takeshita's call in London 1988 for broader cooperation with Europe. Japan has been eager to see Western Europe evolve into a unitary actor, making possible a political relationship of sufficient weight to counterbalance the US. From the point of view of tripolarity, the US is in the enviable position of having strong relations with the two remaining poles – the pivotal position. The weak link between Japan and Europe weakens both, *vis-à-vis* the US.

A very clear case was made by Vice Foreign Minister Murata in 1987, when he catalogued the common Japanese–European interests towards the US, including security cooperation areas, and charted the difference in US relations with the two (1988: 60). He derived Japan's propensity for thinking trilaterally from its recognition of the revitalization of Europe and the accelerating process of integration. There were, he said, three main problems for the political relationship: Europe is not a political unit; European interest in and understanding of Japan is far inferior to that of the Americans; and the existing official consultations are inadequate in frequency and depth.

European responses and initiatives

Europe finally began to heed these calls in early 1990 when Delors lamented the 'lack of political visibility' of the relationship (visibility to whom, one might ask). By then, the Japanese Ministry of Foreign Affairs had again found its very pro-American stance,[9] and it was perhaps only the vicissitudes of the Gulf crisis, and the influence of the Europe-oriented Deputy Foreign Minister Hisashi Owada, which resulted in the preparation of an EC–Japan Joint Declaration to strengthen political dialogue. In the process, the President of the Commission visited Tokyo in June 1991 for the first time in five years, 'playing the statesman, not the car salesman' as a participant observer noted. Delors insisted on the need for substance and effectiveness of the declaration, saying it would strengthen the third side of the triangle and 'if the declaration has sufficiently dense content, the EC will not make decisions that concern Japan without consulting Japan' (Isaka, 1991). The drafting process was tough because some saw the declaration as diverting attention from the economic issues, while the Japanese felt humiliated by French attempts to impose managed trade as the price of political dialogue. This contradiction has always been a feature of the relations. The main impression, however, is that a new phase was reached, in which Ginsberg's concept of 'self-styled logic' is applicable, since the EC is finally initiating policy action based on its own internal dynamic and interest. In this case, it may have been the interest of the Commission and a number of member countries in expanding the area of foreign policy actions which allowed a response to previous Japanese overtures. In the words of the preamble, the two sides were: 'Mindful of the accelerated process whereby the EC is acquiring its own identity in the economic and monetary sphere, in foreign policy, and in the field of security'.

The Joint Declaration

The resulting declaration foresaw a battery of formal elements in the foreign policy network:

1. Existing regular consultation mechanisms, in specialized areas.
2. Annual summits between the President of the EC Council and Japan's Prime Minister (e.g. The Hague 1991 and London 1992).
3. Continuation of annual ministerial level meetings between the Commission and the Japanese government (e.g. Watanabe–Delors in January 1993, the first in three years).
4. Semi-annual consultations 'between the foreign ministers of the Community and the Commissioner responsible for external relations

(troika)' (*Japan Times*, 20 July 1991) and the Japanese foreign minister.

5. Briefing of each other's representative by the presidency on EPC (following ministerial political cooperation meetings) and by Japan on the government's foreign policy.
6. Regular review of implementation, through the above fora.

In addition to this, Jacques Delors created a special task force to find areas of cooperation,[10] Commissioners like Frans Andriessen have paid regular visits to Tokyo and, as always, members of the European Parliament meet Japanese counterparts annually. Considering the exigencies of the EPC framework, as described by Regelsberger, this is a large framework.[11] However, not much seems to be going on within it, at least not much of relevance to the issues brought up for political cooperation. With a fleeting mention of possible common diplomatic action, the general principle of the Declaration was to inform, consult, coordinate and cooperate on:

1. Strengthening the United Nations and negotiated solutions to international tensions.
2. Supporting democracy, human rights and market economy.
3. International security matters such as non-proliferation of ABC weapons, missile technology and arms transfers.
4. Strengthening the open multilateral trading system, by rejecting protectionism and recourse to unilateral measures and implementing GATT and OECD principles for trade and investment.
5. Equitable access to respective markets, removal of obstacles – structural or other -impeding the expansion of trade and investment on the basis of comparable opportunities.
6. Areas of trade, investment, industrial cooperation, advanced technology, energy, employment, social affairs and competition rules.
7. Supporting developing countries.
8. Meeting transnational challenges: environment, resources and energy conservation, terrorism, international crime and drugs.
9. Joint projects in the field of science and technology.
10. Academic, cultural and youth exchange programmes.
11. Supporting Central and East European countries.
12. Stability of the Asia–Pacific region.

From the press statement from the London Summit a year later it is obvious that the Japanese have not obtained the broad political relationship which they had sought.[12] The results of the political dialogue are totted up: joint tabling of a UN General Assembly Resolution on a register of conventional arms transfers; G24 cooperation on Central and Eastern Europe, and close collaboration towards assisting the reform efforts of CIS states; pressure exerted on North Korea to implement International Atomic Energy Agency safeguards and inspection regime; and cooperation in the Middle East peace process. Meagre results indeed, but they mirrored both the problems between the two main actors and the incompleteness and diverging interests of the coalition of government and industry elites behind this particular external bargain.

At the very moment that the declaration was made, Japan's trade surplus had again started to increase, jumping 35 per cent in May 1991 (*Asahi News Service*, 12 June 1991). It has done so ever since, leading Delors to remind Foreign Minister Watanabe in January 1993 that politics and trade cannot be separated and that the record trade surplus for 1992 would begin to create political problems.[13] The Ministry for Trade and Industry has reacted by planning regular Japan–EC trade talks, perhaps in an attempt to keep the issue separate from the political dialogue. Structural trade imbalance has once again crowded out other items on the agenda, except for a minimal programme of basic requirements for coordinating contributions to international economic and political stability – in a situation of diminished US capabilities.

Holding together the coalition in favour of expanding links with Japan is hampered by the diverse strategies of member states, which range from the confrontation favoured by France and Italy, over the cooperation and competition preferred by Germany and Holland, to the collaboration strategy of Britain and Ireland. Each of the positions has its own logic position and the consequences for integration policy differ.[14] The Commission itself has a mixed position: on the one hand, it clearly has a role as 'knight in arms' for European trade, while on the other, it clearly wants to expand the foreign policy role of the Commission. There is even a certain similarity between the Commission and Japan: both are in many ways at a similar stage of taking up their responsibilities on the world stage; both are trying to translate economic clout into international political influence, and both have an internal structure which is stretched to capacity. This helps explain Japan's seeming inability to influence coalition-building in its favour: the complexities of Brussels decision making are simply too great.

Conclusions on future relations – ignoring tripolarity

The problems of creating a political relationship seemed confirmed when the Commission published its first report since 1988 on relations with Japan.[15] Criticized by Japan, the report became the basis for the General Affairs Council's adoption of a set of 'Conclusions' on future relations with Japan.[16] The document is minimalist on political dialogue, but dwells on economic issues and in particular calls on the Japanese to rectify:

a.   the recent deterioration in EC trade position with Japan;
b.   the recent return to growth led by export rather than domestic demand;
c.   the lack of progress in opening specific sectoral markets;
d.   the slow pace of structural reforms in Japan;
e.   the growing tendency towards US–Japan bilateral arrangements which appear discriminatory.

Cooperation is mostly foreseen in the field of environment, activated by the UNCED Rio conference, and in development assistance, perhaps because the EC has agreed to increase its aid budget for Asia by 55 per cent, to $2 billion in the 1992–1995 period.[17]

The limited development of political relations with the one other state in the world, apart from the US, which is on a par with Europe is worrying. Trade friction, and the internal divisions this creates in Europe, partly explains the situation. Yet the US is able to have both tough negotiations and a strong political bond with Japan. The unclear mandate of the Commission, and the uncertain international philosophy of Japan, results in lack of a clear policy. Neither side knows how it wants to shape the bilateral relationship, and there is no cultivation of shared interests, apart from defensive and reactive *ad hoc* cooperation around differences with the US. The resulting confused agenda of economic and military issues is even less appetizing in a period of European introspection and limited EPC capacity. The end result of ignoring the tripolarity of the present international system is that both sides are left with no option but to trust in the United States.[18]

Japan's responses to revitalized European integration

Japan's responses to European integration have had both positive and negative effects on the process. The many varied responses from Japan are all based on perceptions of the Single Market process, its chances and its risks. This section analyses the views of ministries, banks, business and media, based on a series of interviews. It then goes on to chart the direct and indirect responses, or counter-strategies, of business and government. Before finally discussing possible conclusions about the stimulating effects on the 1992 process, it also briefly examines the uncertainty introduced by the economic and political situation of Japan in 1991–92.

Perceptions of the Single Market and the Economic and Monetary Union

Interviews with three ministries – Foreign Affairs, MITI, and the Ministry of Finance – found a common triangular world view. There were, not unexpectedly, different opinions, not only between the ministries, but also within the Ministry of Foreign Affairs, on how close Japan should stay to the US. Policy differences between bureaux and intra-ministerial cliques have weakened an effective foreign policy coordination. The attitude to the Single Market had changed from one of apprehension to a wide acceptance that integration would strengthen European industry, create a more dynamic economy for the Twelve, generate more competition, and make Europe more equal to the two other major economic areas in the world. Towards the EMU and Political Union officials interviewed expressed a wait-and-see attitude, as well as some surprise at the progress achieved. However, it was regarded as a natural, though ambitious, direction which would contribute to a stable world economy. The risks for Japan were small, provided openness was maintained and implemented, so that a free, multilateral, GATT-like world market would result. This was only natural in view of the globalization of manufacturing industries. Japan's strategy should be one of stressing cooperative, not conflictual elements, realizing the growing importance of the Commission and working on those problems which create an image problem for Japan: trade surplus, foreign direct investment (FDI), etc.

The Bank of Japan expected European markets to be more open, more competitive for European as well as outside companies. It would be a place for technological innovation, as well as innovation of services. The EMU seemed a stop-and-go process, but given sufficient Bundesbank initiative would be beneficial to the world economy in terms of price and currency stability. The obligation on fiscal authorities to consolidate their fiscal position was seen as a prerequisite for increasing world savings, private investment, and thus achieving higher growth rates. The problems for Japan would be that Europe might turn inwards, or that the desire for integration would affect its better judgement in world monetary affairs. The profound interdependence in business transactions would make it clear that the present EC–Japan problems are 'just a temporary mischief'. Market forces will dominate, but the risk of protectionism is not over. Deregulation, however, and not only of financial services, seems to dominate European development. Other banks realistically foresaw that when external policies clash with internal EC policies, internal policies will take priority, as had happened in the Uruguay Round and currency negotiations.[19] There could even be a period of 'double walls', one maintained by individual member states, one by the EC itself.[20] The necessary strategy was for Japanese banks to follow their corporations and go to Europe, subsidized by the Tokyo office. A single currency would be very convenient, and it was important to be cautious so as not to provoke reactions in Europe.

Interviews at two of Japan's biggest corporations, Mitsui and Matsushita, as well as at Keidanren, the Federation of Economic Organisations, revealed a desire to strengthen commercial and industrial interdependence in this weakest link of the tripolar global economy. Renewed integration, though probably caused by Japan, was understandable and has a strong future because it has a material basis. Protectionism can be avoided by caution, but the strategy is 'Get in!' and there was satisfaction that Europe's economic strength would grow. There was a hope that the free-trading Northern Europe would dominate, but Europe's need for capital and the big mergers taking place would in any case mean no closure. However, Japan had an image problem, it had to be careful not to alienate Europeans, and it lacked a central policy. The companies were looking forward to rationalizing their retail systems for Europe. They both foresaw Japanese–European commercial cooperation in South-East Asia.

The Japanese media have in the past created the impression of a peaceful, rather sleepy, far-away Europe. Coverage is still sparse, but is now very supportive of integration. The *Japan Times* thus editorialized:

> Europe has returned to the world stage with more power than at any time since 1945, and more prestige than at any time since 1914 ... All Europeans have benefited from this continent-wide renaissance, but the main beneficiary has been the European Community ... With the German superpower as anchor and the Soviet military threat receding, the EC is ceasing to be the supposed weak link in the First World entente between Japan, North America and Western Europe. (*Japan Times*, 8 January 1991)

In a long series of editorials the influential *Asahi Shimbun* has given its support to the Single Market process, the Maastricht Treaty and the EMS at every stage, pointing to the goals of growth, stability, and competitiveness, and warning of the fairly unlikely pitfalls of protectionism and regionalism.[21] Other media, like the commercially oriented *Nikkei Weekly*, are not holding back either:

> We hope the European countries will overcome their difficulties in achieving the unification presumed in the Maastricht Treaty, which is a great experiment in the history of mankind. Neither the U.S., the world's sole superpower, nor Japan, a major economic power, will be able to build a new world order alone. A European Union to be created among countries with complicated interests will be a product of European wisdom. It's also Europe's responsibility for ensuring world stability.[22]

These are only words, but they do both express and shape the perceptions of important parts of Japanese society. Let us now examine in more detail the responses resulting from these perceptions.

Reactions to the single market process

The first distinction to be made when analysing Japan's reactions to the 1992 process is that between business and government.

The major corporations are well known for their intelligence networks and their ability to adapt quickly to changing market situations. They are also good learners, and US reactions have provided ample lessons. Their responses were to move from exports to investment, to seek strategic alliances and to find ways of appeasing the Europeans. The government, on the other hand, is normally slow to develop policy and weak in its implementation (Calder, 1991: 607).

Major corporations and banks

The very first reaction of business, when the White Paper on the completion of the Internal Market was issued, was to speed up direct investment in Europe in those sectors of greatest technological and comparative advantage at the time – automotive and electronics – supplemented by investments in financial and other services.[23] With the first phase of multinationalization, this was due to happen anyway. Choices of location for new plants were made on criteria of cost, incentives offered, stability and language, the UK and the Netherlands being preferred.[24] Though businesses were forced to transplant machinery overseas to protect their existing share in export markets, they quickly turned from a defensive to an offensive strategy, trying to develop their competitive advantages in the overseas environment. In the course of this process, mergers and acquisitions were employed. In some cases – processed foods, pharmaceuticals, chemicals – this may have been done with a view to increasing competitive strength not yet acquired by the Japanese multinationals in domestic industry.

Growing European anxiety about this development led to several modifications of the overall policy. Investments were spread to more member states, including France;[25] the subsidiaries were given a little more management autonomy; R&D activities were placed in European subsidiaries; overseas design facilities meant more responsibility for product development; a few more Europeans were put in management positions; corporate philanthropy was increased towards the host country, etc. Similarly, the Japanese adapted to the EC's anti-circumvention measures on local content, country of origin, etc.[26] Direct investment has dropped since 1990, and the recent slow growth in Japan has meant that profit from FDI has been repatriated. The EC member countries have been eager to attract Japanese investment and no coordinated policy has been possible.

FDI was generally thought to have meant a reduction of Japanese exports to Europe, but several analysts find that it has meant a sharp rise in intra-industry and intra-company trade in intermediate and finished goods, particularly sophisticated components (Ozawa, 1991: 43). Whether because of this trade-expanding effect, or because of the slowdown in the Japanese economy, exports to Europe started growing and creating problems with the Commission. This was a response to slacking domestic demand rather than to integration, but part of the trade surplus results from Japan's bilateral deals with the United States which deflected its exports to Europe. It is one indication that the US remains more important to Japan and could be taken as a spur to further integration.

Strategic alliances and joint ventures were another response employed by Japanese corporations, as they cut down on FDI growth and gave priority to cooperation in international consortia. The resulting mega-cartels, like Siemens–Toshiba–IBM in chip production, are of such magnitude that they can set themselves above any competition regulation; the real effect on European integration is difficult to unravel.[27] They may, paradoxically, be simply too big to notice.

Technology transfer and technological cooperation were increasingly seen as ways to placate European demands. Even the embattled electronics industry availed itself of offers to share technologies in a controlled manner.[28] However, most of the technological cooperation was implicit in joint ventures and alliances, and not enough light has been shed on the character and conditions of this transfer in order to determine whether it is more than a smokescreen for securing continued market access.[29] MITI stresses the importance of cooperation for a stable business environment, encouraging firms to regard it as a contribution to the host society, a price to be paid to the foreign market. It creates an environment of incentives, tax benefits and administrative guidance.

Another response of industry has been to tackle the often criticized Japanese management philosophy. In early 1992 the Keidanren chairman conceded that: 'If Europe and the United States find themselves faced with a life-or-death situation, they will join together to do whatever is necessary. Japanese goods would inevitably suffer a boycott. Japan would have lost by winning too much' (Funabashi, 1992). This convinced him that the concept of symbiosis (*kyosei*) promoted by Akio Morita of Sony would be essential in the coming years for the coexistence of Japanese companies and their foreign counterparts.[30] Kyosei, according to a more extensive report released in June, is to establish a framework for fair competition by harmonizing rules and business conditions in the EC, US and Japan. While US firms could do with the long-term planning and quality control of Japan, the report accepts that its own members must change: abandoning the excessive pursuit of market shares and the opaque commercial relations with business partners, as well as reducing working hours and overtime. The changes could take a long time – the chairman of Nippon Telegraph and Telephone, Japan's largest company, estimated fifty years – but the move has important backers.

Government

On the side of government, it appeared important to counteract the feared trend towards protectionism in the Single Market, which were allayed only in late 1988. The means employed were 'packages' of market opening, macro-economic measures and deregulation, increased and vocal support to multilateral institutions and international regimes, and finally diplomatic manoeuvres.

Between 1981 and 1985 seven packages of market-opening measures made Japan the most open market as far as tariffs were concerned. The attempt of the Maekawa Report of 1986 to reduce the trade surplus lacked concrete proposals and specific goals. However, the Yen appreciation which had been agreed to earlier led to a transition from an export-led to an internal demand-led economy. In 1986 external demand made a negative contribution to growth for the first time in eight years. Measures of financial deregulation have been recognized by the EC. The latest response to pressure from the US and the EC was the vast $80 billion package of mainly public works in infrastructure offered in August 1992.[31] It remains to be seen whether construction cartels and the public procurement system will allow any of this money to go to foreign firms.

The recourse to multilateral institutions is seen in Japan's efforts to keep the GATT Uruguay Round moving and in its use of the GATT against the EC's 1987 regulations and its cassette-dumping tariff (*Japan Economic Journal*, 26 October 1992). A GATT review in 1991 stated that the EC favours sector-specific viewpoints against the overall economic or trade climate, citing coal, steel, automobiles, semi-conductors and agriculture as examples of the EC tendency to pursue individual industries' interests separately. The GATT was an ally in Japan's concern over the EC's use of targeted bilateral solutions, such as anti-dumping or voluntary export restrictions (*Japan Times*, 9 May 1991). The GATT remained critical of Japanese import barriers.

Apart from its continued support of global financial activities such as debt recycling, Official Development Assistance (ODA) and exchange-rate stabilization, Japan seems to have moved from a rather passive position to one of being very interested in international regimes, particularly for trade, payment and investment, with the objective of maintaining a system of open and stable markets.[32] It has been important for Tokyo to support the free-trade direction of the Community, and also to make clear that the perspective of the ECU replacing the Deutschmark is welcome. Seen from Japan, the currency world is already trilateral.[33]

Diplomatically, the government of Japan has shifted its attention from bilateral relations to accepting the primary importance of Brussels. There are good commercial and political reasons to do so. Recognition of Brussels priority in itself strengthens EC integration, though Japan does not of course abstain from playing member states against each other. On another front, it has been extremely cautious in avoiding support for proposals for a bloc-like regionalization in East Asia 'in retaliation' to the Single Market.[34] On the other hand, such initiatives have not been amiss, as a reminder of the strong economic area supporting Japan's regional role. However, the main picture – for government as for business – has been one of great caution being exercised, thus minimizing the feedback on European integration or attempting to channel it in preferred directions.

An element of uncertainty has been introduced by the economic and political situation of Japan in 1991-1992. The end of Japan's economic and financial boom, and the return to ordinary growth rates, superficially at least, reduces the perceived challenge of Japan. Together with some current pessimistic appraisals of long-term developments for the country, the slowdown also raises the question of whether Japan will indeed have the capital and technology Europe wants, in the medium to long term (Emmott, 1989). The political situation of very weak prime ministers and a ruling party threatened by division increases the uncertainty and decreases the likelihood that Japan will resolve the dilemma of its place in the world. The net effect of this on European integration is difficult to fathom, particularly in view of the time lag in European perception of developments in Japan.

Perception is the key to any *conclusion about the effects* of Japanese responses on European integration. A detailed analysis of EC decision making would be necessary for firm conclusions to be made. Yet it is possible to provide some common-sense propositions, based on views expressed by the Commission and by other elites.

The 'response challenge' of Japan has had a number of effects on European integration:

a. It has lessened divisions among member states: by spreading Japanese FDI more evenly, by the Japanese acceptance of the auto deal which caused France to acquiesce in the absence of a common industrial policy (Sadler, 1992: 229), and by treating the EC as a unitary actor in foreign policy.

b. It seems to be dawning on Europeans that the new phase of Japanese investment is both export-increasing and conducive to further restructuring of Japanese industry. It is creating a vertical division of labour, both *vis-à-vis* the developing countries and with Europe. This – if understood – should increase integration.

c. A little more technological cooperation with Japan may lead to greater understanding of Japanese technological superiority, in coming areas like aerospace, biotechnology and perhaps defence, which might well lead to more pooling of European efforts to avoid industrial defeat and to strengthen the competitiveness of EC firms.

d. By furthering transcontinental alliances, like Daimler–Mitsubishi's made in March 1990, or Matsushita–Siemens (made possible in the first place by the Single Market) the Japanese response has perhaps lessened the urgent need of Europe's transnational industry coalition for further European integration, but the need for stability, a common currency, expansion of infrastructure and so forth is still there.

Concluding remarks

Our analysis has found that structural change still promotes European integration, though the precise aims of the transnational industry coalition may have changed. It was found that EC–Japan political relations and cooperation on a world order level is vitiated by trade friction and a mutual lack of knowledge, interest and policy. The main beneficiary of this situation is the US. Finally, it was found that the Japanese responses to integration, though marked by caution, are likely to reinforce the fundamental bargains on integration.

It would be regrettable if Europe were to repeat the American mistake of criticizing Japan instead of modernizing its own production apparatus, management thinking, R&D systems and education. It would be even sadder if, in the process, the global economic tripolarity was mismanaged and Europe missed the chance of bringing into its orbit the first non-Western culture to succeed in becoming an industrial power.

List of interviews – June 1991

Toshiyuki Ueda, Mitsui & Co. Ltd.
Kenjiro Ishikawa, Tokyo International University
Masaru Matsuda, Nihon Keizai Shimbun Inc.
Hisao Mitsuyu, The Asahi Shimbun
Koji Sugiue, Ministry of International Trade and Industry
Hideo Takahashi, International Economic Affairs Department, Keidanren
Hajime Ohta, International Economic Affairs Department, Keidanren
Mitsuo Sugiyama, Matsushita Electric Industrial Co. Ltd.
S. Kataoka, Matsushita Electric Industrial Co. Ltd.
Tomohide Sunagawa, Japan Center for International Finance
Aya Yamazaki, The Overseas Economic Cooperation Fund
Eisuke Sakakibara, International Finance Bureau, Ministry of Finance
Yasuhiro Maehara, The Bank of Japan
Takashi Oyama, The Bank of Japan
Minoru Uezumi, Japan Socialist Party
Makoto Katsura, Ministry of Foreign Affairs of Japan
Fujiwara Masaya, Ministry of Foreign Affairs
Albrecht Rothacher, EC Delegation, Tokyo

Notes

1. I thank Albrecht Rothacher for useful comments on an earlier draft.
2. *Financial Times*, 19 March 1991.
3. *Financial Times*, 10 April, 21 September, 3 December 1992.

4. See for instance Charles Leadbeater: 'Masters of the Interior Universe, *Financial Times*, 3 September 1991, p. 16.

5. Washington Post column, *Japan Times*, 10 November 1990; *Financial Times*, 29 April 1991.

6. Calculation by Kenneth Courtis in 'Japan in the 1990s', Tokyo 1991.

7. For a discussion of the concept of pivot and triangular relations in general see Gerald Segal, *The Great Power Triangle*, London 1982, p. 6.

8. Japan–Europe alignments in the course of annual economic summit meetings are well covered in Shiro Saito: *Japan at the Summit. Japan's Role in the Western Alliance and Asian-Pacific Cooperation*, London 1990.

9. Takazaki Kuriyama, 'New Directions for Japanese Foreign Policy in the Changing World of the 1990s', *Gaiko Forumo*, May 1990, quoted in Brian Bridges, 'Japan and Europe. Rebalancing a Relationship', *Asian Survey*, vol. 32, March 1992, p. 238.

10. "Delors Calls for Team to Strengthen EC-Japan Relations', *Asahi News Service*, 24 May 1991.

11. For the internal structure of The Twelve and remarks on the capacity of the EPC secretariat, see E. Regelsberger, 'The Twelve's Dialogue with Third Countries – Progress towards a Communauté d'action?' in M. Holland (ed.), *The Future of European Political Cooperation. Essays on Theory and Practice*, London 1990.

12. *Agence Europe*, EUROPE/Documents no. 1792, 10 July.

13. A comprehensive account of the ministerial meetings can be found in *Agence Europe*, 20 January 1993.

14. See the excellent article by Jean-Pierre Lehmann, 'France, Japan, Europe and Industrial Competition: the Automotive Case', *International Affairs*, vol. 68, no. 1, 1992, pp. 37–53.

15. *Agence Europe*, EUROPE/Documents no. 1779/80, 6 June 1992.

16. *Agence Europe*, EUROPE/Documents no. 1792, 10 July 1992. The Conclusions in particular stressed:

1. Return to growth led by domestic demand, further structural reform and a reduction in external imbalances. Allowing the Yen to appreciate relative to European currencies.

2. Remove barriers to trade, especially in foodstuffs and services.

3. Remove structural obstacles, enforce competition policy and anti-monopoly legislation. Removing obstacles to free distribution of Community goods and services.

4. Industrial cooperation, facilitating the entry of European parts suppliers, small and medium-sized enterprises newcomers to the Japanese market.

5. Japanese investment must fully contribute to industrial development and renewal *throughout* the Community. The climate for foreign investment in Japan must be improved(Mergers & Acquisitions, tax, careers, liberalizing services).

6. Increased Japanese tourism to member states.

7. Public procurement must be further opened, non-discriminatory and with greater transparency. In information technology and telecommunications Japan must ensure strict application of international standards, making its market accessible to Community suppliers.

17. *Far Eastern Economic Review*, 4 June 1992.

18. Maull (1990) includes an extended discussion of the lack of Japanese–European initiatives.

19. Perceptive analysis of the EC and Japanese banks is found in Thorstein Düser, *International Strategies of Japanese Banks*, London, Macmillan 1990, Chapter 4.

20. Cf. *Japan Times*, 24 June 1991.

21. "One Europe', Editorial *Asahi Shimbun*, 15 January 1991 is just one of many articles and editorials supporting European integration.

22. 'Hope for Stability Rests in European Cooperation – Our View', *Nikkei Weekly*, 28 September 1992.
23. Protectionism was thought a realistic danger: 'Fortress Europe' was foreseen. Theoretical support for this fear can be found in Heitger and Stehn's analysis which concludes that the Single Market would mean an increase in the supply and demand for protection. 'Japanese Direct Investments in the EC – Response to the Internal Market 1993?' *Journal of Common Market Studies*, vol. 29, no. 1, September 1990, p. 13.
24. Stephen Thomsen and Phedon Nicolaides (1991) *The Evolution of Japanese Direct Investment in Europe. Death of a Transistor Salesman*, Hemel Hempstead: Harvester Wheatsheaf, is a detailed review, including a case study on the automotive sector.
25. The Matsushita director interviewed mentioned his problems in explaining to production companies and divisions in Japan why there was need for ninety-three production companies overseas. They were a political necessity, though economically not as viable.
26. For details on local content regulations, anti-dumping and country of origin regulations and on quantitative restrictions, commercial instruments, etc. see Colchester and Buchan, 1990, pp. 191–206.
27. For some examples, see Gunhild Lütge, 'Geiseln des Fortschritts', *Die Zeit*, no. 33, 7 August 1992, p. 17. Fujitsu–Amdahl–Siemens and Hitachi–Olivetti are cooperating too.
28. *Asahi News Service*, 12 September 1991; *JIJI News Service*, 15 May 1992; interview at Matsushita regarding its cooperation with Bosch.
29. *Financial Times*, 30 April 1991 and Gunhild Lütge, *op. cit.*
30. Akio Morita set out his ideas in a speech to the Keidanren meeting and in the February 1992 issue of *Bungei Shunju*.
31. *Financial Times*, 27 August 1992 and Georg Blume, 'Der Mega-Schub', *Die Zeit*, 4 September 1992.
32. Japan has worked through both the OECD and the IMF to oppose EC measures and to attempt to expand Special Drawing Rights. For the view that Japan will play a beneficial role, see Helleiner, 1992.
33. Interview at the Ministry of Finance.
34. Interviews at the Ministry of Foreign Affairs, also Yoichi Funabashi: 'East Asian economic bloc wrong answer to Western regionalism', *Asahi News Service*, 15 March 1991.

References

Bergsten, C. Fred (1992) 'The World Economy after the Cold War', *California Management Review*, vol. 34, pp. 51–65.
Calder, Kent E. (1991) 'Domestic Constraints and Japan Foreign Economic Policy of the 1990s', *International Journal*, vol. 46, Autumn, pp. 607–22.
Colchester, Nicholas and David Buchan (1990) *Europe Relaunched. Truths and Illusions on the Way to 1992*, London.
Courtis, Kenneth (1991) 'Japan in the 1990s', mimeo, Tokyo
Dunning, John and Michelle Gittelman (1992) 'Japanese Multinationals in Europe and the United States: Some Comparisons and Contrasts', in M.W. Klein and P.J.J. Welfens (eds), *Multinationals in the New Europe and Global Trade*, Berlin: Springer Verlag.
Emmott, Bill (1989) *The Sun also Sets*, London: Simon & Schuster.
Freudenstein, Roland (1991) 'Japan and the New Europe', *The World Today*, vol. 47, pp. 11–16.

Fuchita, Yasuyuki (1991) 'The Rising Global Demand for Capital and Japan's Role', *Japan Review of International Affairs*, vol. 5, pp. 201–23.

Funabashi, Yoichi (1992) 'Managed Trade Must End for the Good of All', *Asahi News Service*, 17 January.

Ginsberg, Roy H. (1989) *Foreign Policy Actions of the European Community. The Politics of Scale*, London: Lynne Rienner.

Grewlich, Klaus (1988) 'Positive-Sum Game USA-Japan-Europe', *Aussenpolitik*, vol. 39, pp. 216–33.

Hanabusa, Masamichi (1979) *Trade Problems between Japan and Western Europe*, London: Saxon House.

Helleiner, Eric (1992) 'Japan and the Global Financial Order,' *International Journal*, vol. 47, Spring 1992.

Hughes, Kirsty S. (1992) 'Trade Performance of the Main EC Economies Relative to the USA and Japan in 1992-sensitive Sectors', *Journal of Common Market Studies*, vol. 30, pp. 437–54.

Isaka, Satoshi (1991) 'Delors Seeks Broader, Stronger Japan-EC Bond'. Interview in *Nihon Keizai Shimbun Weekly*, 15 June.

Ishikawa, Kenjiro (1990) *Japan and the Challenge of Europe*, London: Pinter.

Kashiwagi, Yusuke (1990) 'Japan as a Major Creditor Country and Her Relations with Europe', *European Affairs*. vol. 4, pp. 59–63.

Lehmann, Jean-Pierre (1992) 'France, Japan, Europe and Industrial Competition: the Automotive Case', *International Affairs*, vol. 68, pp. 37–53.

Maull, Hans (1990) 'The Unfinished Triangle: European–Japanese Relations in the 1980s', *Contemporary European Affairs*, 3, pp. 51–71.

Murata, Ryohei (1988) 'Political Relations between the United States and Western Europe: Their Implications for Japan', *International Affairs*, vol. 64, pp. 1–9.

Ozawa, Terutomo (1991) 'Japan in a New Phase of Multinationalism and Industrial Upgrading: Functional Integration of Trade, Growth and FDI', *Journal of World Trade*, vol. 25, pp. 43–60.

Ozawa, Terutomo (1992) 'Comments on Dunning and Gittelman', in Klein and Welfens (eds), *Multinationals in the New Europe and Global Trade*, Berlin: Springer Verlag.

Peters, E.H. (1992) 'The Computer Industry and the European Community. Issues and Responses in the 1990s', in S. Young and J. Hamill (eds), *Europe and the Multinationals. Issues and Responses for the 1990s*, Aldershot: Elgar Publishing, pp. 47–79.

Pons, Philippe (1992) 'Tokyo se prépare à un monde tripolaire', *Le Monde*, 13 October.

Rothacher, Albrecht (1985). *Economic Diplomacy between the European Community and Japan 1959–1981*, Aldershot: Gower.

Rothacher, Albrecht (1992) *Europe's Japan Problem. Japanese Corporate Strategies and the Western Response*, mimeo, EC–Japan Conference, Firenze, June 1992.

Sadler, D. (1992) 'Beyond "1992": the Evolution of European Community Policies towards the Automobile Industry', *Environment and Planning*, C: Government and Policy, vol. 10, pp. 229–48.

Saelens, F.H. (1986) 'Japanese FDI in Europe', in M. Schmiegelow (ed.), *Japan's Response to Crisis and Change in the World Economy*, New York: M.E. Sharpe, pp. 85–103.

Sandholtz, Wayne and John Zysman (1989) '1992: Recasting the European Bargain', *World Politics*, vol. 40, pp. 95–128.

Shiraishi, Takashi (1989) *Japan's Trade Policies 1945 to the Present Day*, London: Athlone Press.

Sinha, Radha (1990) 'Are EC–Japan–US Trade Relations at the Crossroads?', *Intereconomics*, vol. 25, pp. 229–37.

Thomsen, Stephen and Phedon Nicolaides (1991) *The Evolution of Japanese Direct Investment in Europe. Death of a Transistor Salesman*, Hemel Hempstead: Harvester Wheatsheaf.

Trevor, Malcolm (1991) 'The Overseas Strategy of Japanese Corporations', *Annals of the American Academy of Political and Social Sciences*, vol. 513, pp. 90–101.

Tsoukalis, L. and M. White (eds) (1982) *Japan and Western Europe*, London: Frances Pinter.

Vernon, Raymond (1990) 'The Japan–US Bilateral Relationship: Its Role in the Global Economy', *The Washington Quarterly*, vol. 13, pp. 57-68.

Wilkinson, Endymion (1983) *Japan versus Europe. A History of Misunderstanding*, Penguin.

Dealing with the Community: The Bush Administration's Response to Western European Integration

MORTEN OUGAARD

Introduction

The revitalization and acceleration of European integration is one of several major changes in the international system which have taken place since the mid-1980s.[1] While the end of the Cold War and the breakdown of the Soviet system are clearly the most decisive events since the Second World War, the European integration process also represents a transformation of great magnitude. Moreover, it is a transformation with global ramifications, especially when considering the prospects of an economically and politically unified European actor on the world scene. This new actor would undoubtedly be a true Great Power with the potential for becoming a superpower, comparable in economic, political and military terms to the United States.

For the United States, then, the European process and the perspectives implied are highly significant, and the American response to them is a major aspect of the overall American effort to shape a new international order in the post-Cold War world. The purpose of this chapter is to discuss how the Bush administration responded to this process.

The focus is on US policy toward the current process of unification and integration centred on the development of the European Community. We will not consider US–EC relations in specific issue areas, nor will we discuss US policy toward the wider European dynamic that includes the transformation of the former Eastern Bloc and its relations to the West. In other words, the subject at hand is the American response to the process of Western European integration itself.

Confusion or consistency

In a recent article in *Foreign Policy*, T.L. Deibel describes the Bush administration's foreign policy as 'tactical mastery set in a larger pattern of strategic indirection' (1991: 3). Another analyst, Michael Smith, specifically addressing US policies towards the EC, paints a picture of differing and even conflicting images of Europe among the American leadership and suggests that 'the adaptation to change has been uneven and fragmentary' (1992: 119). Criticism to the same effect is often heard in the public debate in the US. Indeed, strong disagreements and sharp denouncements of current administration policies for their lack of coherence and strategy seem to be a permanent fixture of the US foreign policy process, especially, perhaps, in election years. In retrospect, however, the basic features of American foreign policy have shown a high degree of continuity and stability over the decades since the beginning of the Cold War (Kegley and Wittkopf, 1987: 4). In the words of the Reagan administration: 'While it is commonplace to hear that US National Security Strategy changes erratically every four to eight years as a result of a new administration taking office, in reality there is a remarkable consistency over time when our policies are viewed in historical perspective' (US President, 1988: 1).

It would be wrong to expect the same kind of continuity in the present stage of rapid transformations of the global system. On the other hand, it takes time to develop adequate responses to new circumstances. As pointed out in 1989 by Walter Russel Mead, since the direction of change in the international system is in basic accord with US interests, there is no need for hasty reactions: 'Bush can look before he leaps, and is no doubt well advised to do so' (1989: 60). In such a situation a cautious and hesitant policy might well be the most adequate response. But consistency and continuity concerning fundamental goals when adapting to changed circumstances are not to be ruled out, and it is not too early to ask whether a consistent pattern is discernible behind the barrage of seemingly contradictory decisions, declarations and actions.

When seeking such a pattern, basic assumptions about foreign policy are in order. Here the assumption is that foreign policy is the pursuit of interests rooted in society. The simple question of 'Cui Bono?' is thus central to any analysis of international political economy (Strange, 1984: 193). Yet it is not enough.

The 'Cui Bono' perspective is located at the state-as-actor level of analysis, leaving aside considerations of policy process, bureaucratic politics, domestic pressure groups, and the behaviour and preferences of individuals. This is not to deny the relevance of these perspectives, only to indicate that this analysis is based on the state-as-actor perspective.

Moreover, the assumption that foreign policy is to be understood as the pursuit of interests rooted in society leaves room for different modes of interpretation because of different understandings of the interests involved. One can emphasize the role of political culture, which in the case of the US entails the international promotion of liberty, democracy, human rights, and economic liberalism as a fundamental set of interests underlying foreign policy (Hunt, 1987; Huntington, 1981; Schlesinger, 1986). One can also take the realist position and point to the national interest in terms of power as the most fundamental driving force behind policy (Morgenthau, 1973; Waltz, 1979), or one can point to economic interests as the basic underlying principle behind foreign policy (Williams, 1972; Kolko, 1964; Petras and Morley, 1981).

Few analysts would point to only one of these perspectives, and few would rule out any of them completely. The real problem is one of synthesizing them and perhaps ascribing primacy to one or another (Krasner, 1978; Strange, 1988). This analysis, building on previous work (Ougaard, 1990) will attempt to combine the realist and economic interpretations. Such a synthesis has been suggested by Robert Gilpin (1981, 1987), who sees international politics as fundamentally 'a recurring struggle for wealth and power' (1981: 7, see also Keohane, 1984).

The assumption that foreign policy is the pursuit of wealth and power implies that policy seeks to maintain or strengthen the position of the state in the international power structure, and to promote economic interests based in society; i.e. to optimize conditions for domestic economic growth and for domestically based businesses. This perspective also implies a preference for business interests, such that economic interests for employment, welfare or better living conditions only influence policy to the extent necessitated by political pressures, whereas the promotion of economic growth is a permanent feature of policy. Furthermore, bias in favour of business interests does not exclude the pursuit of stability, order and peace in the international system, but sees such goals as derived from the pursuit of wealth and power, inasmuch as a stable international environment is a precondition for the pursuit of these interests (Hamilton, 1989; George and Keohane, 1975; Mead, 1989; US President, 1987–91).

In this perspective, a fundamental fact about US–EC relations is that EC members, individually and as a single entity, are both allies of *and* competitors with the US. Hence, building European unity implies the emergence of a stronger ally, as well as a stronger competitor and a potential rival. If one emphasizes the shared interests between the two sides, one should expect the US to support and perhaps to actively promote the process of integration. If one emphasizes the adversarial aspects of the relationship, one should expect the US to try to slow down or perhaps hinder the process. And if one holds that both aspects are of genuine importance, but that the shared interests are more important than the conflicting ones, which is my position (Ougaard, 1988), it could be argued that the optimal US strategy would be to reap the benefits of a stronger ally while avoiding the risks presented by a powerful competitor and rival.

This is only a first rough characterization of the logic which might lie behind US policy. The European integration process is a complex one, involving economic, political and military dimensions. US policies are thus differentiated accordingly. In the following sections of this chapter I will therefore begin with the overall perspective of European unification. I will then discuss the economic aspects, focusing on the Single Market, and the Economic and Monetary Union (EMU), and finally consider defence and military aspects.

The US and the emerging European actor

The fact that the US has been a supporter of European integration in word and deed since its beginning is well known and well documented. What concerns us here is the American response to the European Community's moves toward Economic, Monetary and Political Union.

The decision to re-initiate the process of integration was made by the Council of Europe in June 1988. In early 1989 the new Bush administration undertook a thorough examination of European developments and a review of American policy, concluding that the new stage in the integration process 'was for real' and that it was something the US had to deal with, according to administration officials interviewed in Washington. When, in April 1989, the committee headed by Jacques Delors submitted its blueprint for an Economic and Monetary Union, the US was prepared. In May 1989, even before the Delors Report was officially adopted by the Council of Europe (this happened in June 1989), President Bush, in a speech in Boston, called for 'developing new mechanisms of consultation and cooperation' with the EC on political and global issues (*USIA PDQ Index & Text Database*, Eur 503, 11/23/90). Bush went to Brussels to meet Delors in May and again in December, the first such visits to the Commission by an American president since Carter went there in 1978. In December 1989, Secretary of State Baker proposed to Delors that the US and the EC work together to 'achieve a significantly strengthened set of institutional and consultative links' (ibid). Baker presented this proposal publicly in his Berlin speech on 'A New Europe and a New Atlanticism' in December 1989 (US Department of State, *American Foreign Policy Documents 1989*, 126). During 1990, the year in which the Council of Europe decided to work towards Political Union, additional top-level meetings took place between the two sides, culminating in the signing of the joint *Declaration on US–EC Relations*, released on 23 November 1990.

The declaration marked a significant change in the formal diplomatic relationship between the two sides (Krenzler and Kaiser, 1991). For the first time US–EC relations were put on a quasi-treaty footing and a pattern of regular summit meetings and top-level consultations was formally established. Such meetings and consultations had taken place before, but now, in addition to giving them a formal framework, the Declaration also provided for the intensification and diplomatic upgrading of contacts. Two of the declaration's provisions demonstrate this point: since 1982 there had been annual meetings between delegations headed by the US Secretary of State and the President of the EC Commission following the regular December NATO ministerial meeting. In December 1989 it was agreed and formalized by the joint Declaration to hold such meetings twice a year and to decouple them from NATO meetings. Furthermore, the Declaration formalizes the agreement reached in February 1990 between Bush and the President of the Council of Europe, Irish Prime Minister Haughey, to the effect that

> biannual consultations [are] to be arranged in the United States and in Europe between, on the one side, the President of the European Council and the President of the Commission, and on the other side, the President of the United States (*Declaration on US–EC Relations*).

Until 1989 meetings at this level had taken place on an *ad hoc* basis, had occurred less frequently, and, with the single Carter exception, were always in the US.

The diplomatic upgrading of the EC is also evidenced by the fact that the US Mission to the EC, although still only a 'mid-sized mission' in the State Department's internal ranking, has in recent years been the only American mission abroad that has been growing.[2] In the last few years a new Section for Commercial Affairs has been established and new attachés added in various fields, including financial affairs and customs. Furthermore, the number of contacts between Washington-based American officials and their EC counterparts is steadily increasing, as is the number of consultations and agreements between the two sides in a growing number of issue areas.

Of course the US maintains a dense diplomatic traffic with the national capitals of EC members, and the bilateral locus is still the most important one, especially in political and military questions, where the EC profile is less developed and where American policy, as we shall see later, is less forthcoming. In the economic sphere, however, the US frequently addresses the EC simultaneously at the Community and the national levels and, according to some US officials, a subtle shift is underway in the balance between the two. Whereas the national level used to be the more important, in some cases the US has now started to operate through the national capitals in order to influence the Community level. This is done in order to prevent the Community from adopting policies with which the US disagrees, or to promote unity at the Community level. In either case it reflects American recognition that the Community level has gained significantly in importance over the last few years, and US willingness to 'deal with it' accordingly.

Parallel with these American steps to elevate the EC's diplomatic ranking, the Americans have been quite willing to endorse the process of unification, and endorse it strongly, in public statements. The Maastricht agreements, for example, the most decisive step taken to date toward monetary, economic and political union, were met with these words from American President George Bush:

> We welcome the historic steps toward economic and political union ... The results of the E.C. summit represents a milestone, which we celebrate along with our European partners ... [A] strong united Europe is very much in America's interest. A more united Europe offers the United States a more effective partner, prepared for larger responsibilities. (*US Department of State Dispatch*, 16 December 1991).

The US, then, has endorsed the prospect of European integration, and the American willingness to deal with this emerging actor on the world scene makes it clear that the US has not tried to hinder the process. One can even argue that American calls for burden-sharing and, especially, the declared wish to see European nations assume greater responsibilities in international affairs indicate an American preference for a stronger, more united Europe, and that the repeated statement of these concerns has contributed to the renewal of the integration process. In this sense, the US can be viewed as having promoted the move toward greater European unity. On the other hand, US support amounts to little more than saying that such a development would be a good idea, which constitutes only a limited attempt to help the process forward.

In sum, American policy toward the general perspective of a more unified EC has been to declare support in principle, accepting the integration process according to its own speed and dynamics, and to treat the EC as an international actor in its own right, in so far as it acts like one. Clearly the US has not worked against the process, and may even have acted to promote it. However, this policy must be seen in conjunction with American claims to a global leadership role. Such claims have been made repeatedly over the last few years and, indeed, have been a major theme in much of the official discourse on 'The New World Order' (US President, 1991: v, 2, 33, 34; Secretary Baker, 'Opportunities to Build a New World Order', *US Department of State Dispatch*, 11 February 1991). These claims have also been followed by actions where the US has taken the lead in establishing basic common principles on which the new order should be based and in securing the consent of all major allies to these. The political and economic declarations from the 1991 G7 London Summit (*USIA Newsfile* 17 and 18 July 1991), and the 'Tokyo Declaration on the US–Japan Global Partnership' from January 1992 (*USIA Newsfile* 13 January 1992) are cases in point. Currently the US accepts and is encouraging a major European role in Western policies toward Eastern and Central Europe, perhaps a leading one in the case of the war in former Yugoslavia. Concerning the Middle East and major economic and strategic aspects of relations with Russia and the CIS, however, a pattern of American leadership and EC support was maintained by the Bush administration (cf. Smith, 1992). In short, the US has not been asking the EC to assume the mantle of global leadership and is not preparing itself to surrender it. The US welcomes a stronger EC as an ally, appreciating its potential to take a leading role on some issues, particularly those relating to Europe and its close vicinity, while upholding the EC's position in a US-led global partnership.

How does this policy fare when measured against the interests assumed to be underlying US foreign policy? The answer is 'quite well', and for several reasons.

First, there exist a wide range of mutual and shared fundamental interests between the two sides of the Atlantic. These include shared interests in the stability and growth of the international economy, in maintaining and promoting the principles of democracy and market economy, and in a stable world order. A united Europe is not a challenge to the US since it is unlikely that a stronger EC would use its power to challenge these interests. Rather, the reasonable expectation is that a stronger European actor on the world scene would make such interests more secure. American power, understood as its capacity to realize its interests, is actually enhanced if it can draw on the support of stronger allies.

Second, the movement toward a unified Europe is mainly – but not solely – driven by forces that are internal to the nations involved, and it would probably be very difficult if not impossible for an outside power to delay the process, let alone to stop it. Such an attempt would also entail high costs in terms of jeopardizing the existing pattern of Atlantic cooperation, so the risks and costs of trying to oppose the process would be greater than those involved in accepting it. Obviously, the better strategy for the US is to come to terms with a unified Europe. And to the extent that the EC acquires authority in areas of importance for American interests, the US simply has to establish relations with Brussels.

Furthermore, it can reasonably be argued that in the foreseeable future Europe will not have the capacity needed to challenge the US at the global level. A full consensus has not been reached in the debate on 'end or decline of hegemony', and the 'declinist' position still has its adherents. Yet even though the American position has weakened, and although American hegemony is under stress due to a relative decline in power combined with domestic economic and social problems, it is still reasonable to conclude that the EC does not present the challenge of a global rival. This is one conclusion in Joseph Nye's *Bound to Lead* (1990), probably, along with Henry Nau's *The Myth of America's Decline* (1990), the most comprehensive and authoritative academic treatments of the question in recent years. The same assessment is reflected in official statements, for instance: 'Despite the emergence of new power centres, the United States remains the only state with truly global strength, reach and influence in every dimension – political, economic and military' (US President, 1991: 2). Neither in terms of interests nor in terms of the overall global power structure has the US reasons to oppose the emergence of a politically stronger European actor, whereas, as we shall see later, a comparable military strengthening of the EC poses different questions.

American power is enhanced to the extent that it can draw on the support of stronger allies, while on the other hand, the American ability to secure its own specific interests is not jeopardized as long as the EC remains in a secondary position to that of the US, and as long as the EC does not adopt policies in specific areas that work against the interests of the US.

The final qualification is, of course, a major one, and it shall be addressed in the next sections. We can conclude this section by emphasizing that US policies toward European integration in general expresses the logical pursuit of basic American interests.

The Single Market and the EMU

The plans for a Single European Market, launched in 1985, initially brought forth warnings about the dangers of a 'Fortress Europe' in the US and elsewhere. At the end of the decade, however, a more positive, and more nuanced policy had evolved (van Well, 1991). The main content of this policy consisted of general support for the internal market combined with warnings about discrimination against American interests in specific areas and a declared intention to oppose such policies.

Part of the background for this evolution was a number of comprehensive studies of the 1992 project and its likely consequences for the United States made by the administration, by Congress, and by diverse think tanks (US Department of Commerce, 1989; US Congress, 1990; Calingaert, 1988, 1990). The tenor of these studies was that the Single Market would generally be good for American businesses, but that it might also lead to the creation of stronger competitors in some industries as well as to protectionism and lack of transparency in some fields. Since Europe is a major importer of American goods, the perspective of stronger growth here (the American analyses agreed that this would be a likely outcome of 1992) would help US exports. Furthermore, since many American companies had long had a Europe-wide perspective to their operations here, they were being seen as being better positioned to take advantage of the internal market than many European competitors who until recently had operated within national frameworks.

Accordingly, the policy has been to endorse the project in principle, while at the same time to warn against possible negative consequences for American interests, and to back this by intensified diplomatic efforts to counter such consequences. The policy, according to US officials, is to closely monitor developments in the EC and to present American concerns as early as possible and before the EC adopts firm positions. This is reflected in the expansion of the diplomatic staff in Brussels and in the increased contacts between Washington-based bureaucrats and the EC Commission mentioned above. This pattern of what an American official calls 'regulators talking to regulators' across the Atlantic, even before decisions are made at the political level, naturally enhances America's influence on evolving EC policies. Pointing in the same direction is the fact that American interest organizations, especially those representing businesses, have augmented their representation in Brussels.[3]

Such contact between both sides of the Atlantic also implies a further prospect for the US, namely the potential for easier transatlantic harmonization of regulations. Efforts to this effect have been pursued in some areas for several years and are included in the present GATT negotiations. But intensified EC–US contacts of this kind represent a new venue for such efforts, and an improved one, since the US can here deal with a single European authority instead of a dozen national governments.

The movement towards an internal European market is, of course, only one aspect of US–EC trade relations. We must also briefly consider the continued pressure on the EC to complete the Uruguay Round, including efforts on long-standing issues such as agricultural policies, Airbus subsidies, and the like. The thrust of American trade strategy is hardly surprising, and its congruence with major American economic interests is not difficult to demonstrate (Ougaard, 1992). The policy underscores the pattern of American resistance to specific policies set in a larger pattern of support for European integration, but it also calls attention to the fact that resistance can be determined and persistent when significant American interests are involved. Pointing in the same direction is the recent American recourse to regionalism in trade matters, including the establishment of the Pacific Basin Economic Council and the Pacific Economic Cooperation Conference initiated in 1989 (*International Herald Tribune*, 7 November 1989), the signing of framework trade agreements with Asian nations (Philippines, Thailand, Singapore) and twenty-nine countries in Latin American and the Caribbean (*International Herald Tribune*, 12–13 October 1991), and the negotiations on a North American Free Trade Agreement officially launched in June 1991 (Overseas Development Council, 1992). An obvious interpretation is that these initiatives are partly countermoves to perceived European recalcitrance in the GATT negotiations and to the regionalism implied in the internal market and establishment of a greater European Economic Area. They are countermoves in the double sense of opening alternative venues for further trade liberalization in accordance with American interests, while at the same time adding to the political pressure on the EC.

In sum, the move towards the internal market has led to a differentiated US policy, welcoming the prospect of a more integrated and dynamic economy while actively countering any possible negative impact on US interests in specific areas. That such a policy is easily explainable as a pursuit of American economic interests should be clear from what has already been said and needs no further elaboration. Instead we shall turn to the plans for an Economic and Monetary Union (EMU).

In this area, American policy is less developed for the simple reason that the US is responding to intentions and plans, not to established facts. The process towards EMU might be beyond the point of no return, but there are still a number of major unsettled questions as to the exact nature of the union. Yet the US response to the Maastricht Agreement was clear enough, and it fits nicely into the pattern already described, being one of strong general endorsement of the perspective of a unified Europe, combined with an expression of concern that Europe pursues responsible economic policies. This position was stated clearly in Bush's declaration on 11 December 1991 (*US Department of State Dispatch*, 16 December 1991), and the same concerns were frequently raised by US officials interviewed. To place this policy in context, we can speculate on the significance of European economic and monetary unification for American power and interests.

When judged in terms of impact on the international political economy, the most wide-ranging possible outcome of the integration process would be the establishment of a single European central bank and policy convergence carried to the point of a common fiscal policy. This would create a new official player in international currency and capital markets comparable in terms of economic resources to the US authorities, and the fiscal policies of such an entity could influence the international economy as much as the US budget does. In other words, the possible outcome is the emergence of an economic power that is truly equal to the US in important respects. At the aggregate level, this would by definition imply a relative decline in US power. This is, however, too simplistic. The possible effects on the US are uncertain and they cut both ways.[4]

On the positive side, if unification carried this far helps to make the European economy stronger, this will also benefit the US as a result of the export and investment linkage. Furthermore, stronger European institutions can contribute to stability and predictability in the international economy because of their enhanced overall capacity to influence markets. If international policy coordination can be agreed upon, it is not unlikely that such coordination will be more effective if Europe acts as a single player. One could also argue that it will be easier to reach agreement on policy coordination if there is only one European player instead of the present situation where, German predominance notwithstanding, several major European nations have their say. In addition, depending on the set-up of the European institutions it might become easier for the US to influence a unified European system than it is today to influence German authorities in fiscal and monetary matters.

On the other hand, though, it is equally likely that a united Europe will pursue monetary and fiscal policies that go against American wishes, and that strong European institutions, modelled on the German central bank, would be rather immune to American pressure. In that case, the negative consequences for the US economy would be worse compared to the present situation, since the impact on world markets would be greater.

The importance of this concern should not be exaggerated, however. Today both sides of the Atlantic are getting along with a limited amount of policy coordination (Nau, 1990: 283; Ougaard 1992: 151ff.) and it is reasonable to assume that negative effects of concerted European policies on the US can be managed. One could, of course, envision a united Europe using its newfound economic might to engage in outright destabilizing or hostile behaviour – for instance, as a sustained major decrease in the dollar preference of European investors (Mead, 1989: 31), or even determined interventions against the dollar in currency markets. However, these possi-bilities must be considered very remote. Rather, experience from recent years indicates that when serious threats to international stability appear, the major players are willing to take remedial steps in concert, as happened, for instance, swiftly after the 1987 stock market crash (*International Herald Tribune*, 29 October 1987). Even in the present climate of limited policy coordination, the summer of 1992 saw strong concerted intervention in currency markets to prevent the excessive fall of the dollar, efforts involving the central banks of the US, Germany, Britain, Switzerland, Belgium, Spain, Italy, and Portugal (*International Herald Tribune*, 21 July 1992). There is no reason to expect that a unified Europe would behave differently in comparable situations, due to the underlying interdependence and the mutual interest in a stable international economy. Treasury and other US officials interviewed in 1991 and 1992 seemed not even to have considered this possibility.

The only certain conclusion, then, is that the consequences for the US are uncertain, and that the EMU may have negative as well as positive effects on American interests. Nevertheless, even if one argued that the negative effects would ultimately outweigh the positive, they still should be measured against the overall positive effects of a stronger Europe, discussed above, as well as against the risks and costs involved in an attempt to oppose or delay European unification. Compared to any such attempt, American interests are much better served by working to create a solid basis for future cooperation, in order to enhance the American ability to influence EC policy in accordance with US preferences.

Hence, in spite of the uncertainties involved, the conclusion is clear: it is in accordance with American interests to endorse the plans for an

Economic and Monetary Union in Europe while at the same time keeping all venues open to oppose specific European policies.

The main American concerns in the economic area – protectionism, subsidies, monetary and fiscal policies – are not generated by the integration process itself, although the process has increased their significance for American interests. This contrasts with the security and military sphere, where European initiatives directly linked to unification have met with strong American resistance. Let us turn to these questions now.

'The height of folly'?

The breakdown of the Warsaw Pact and the re-unification of Germany produced intense diplomatic activity centring around the 'new European architecture'. This process involved such questions as NATO's new strategy, the future of American troops in Europe, the role of the CSCE and, especially after the Gulf War and the outbreak of fighting in former Yugoslavia, the role of the UN. A core issue in this process, and the one pertaining most directly to European integration, is the question of a European security identity and defence role. Since this is an area where transatlantic frictions have been much in evidence it merits further scrutiny.

The basic American concerns were expressed as early as December 1989 in James Baker's Berlin speech on 'A New Europe and a New Atlanticism'. Quoting President Bush, Baker stated that 'the United States is and will remain a European power', and that 'the US will maintain significant military forces in Europe as long as our allies desire our presence.' On Europe's future contribution in the defence and security field Baker remarked:

> The European Community will ... also take on, perhaps in concert with other European institutions, increasingly important political roles ... And as it continues to do so, the link between the United States and the European Community should become stronger, the issues we discuss more diversified, and our common endeavour more important. At the same time, the substantive overlap between NATO and European institutions will grow. This overlap must lead to synergy, not friction (US Department of State, *American Foreign Policy, Current Documents*, 1989, Washington D.C., 1990: 305).

As events unfolded and various European proposals were presented, the debate came to focus on the role of the Western European Union, its relations to both the EC and NATO, the prospect of creating a separate WEU military force, and the related question of whether France should be drawn closer into NATO's military cooperation rather than participate in such a new force.

When Franco-German ideas for a stronger European military identity were aired in autumn 1990, the US declared itself receptive 'on the condition that it did not undercut NATO's role as the pivot of Western security' (*International Herald Tribune*, 22–23 September 1990). In early 1991 several proposals were discussed among EC governments. One of these was a joint German–French proposal which implied a strong WEU role. Although agreement was not reached, the US nevertheless reacted strongly against some of the proposals. What were seen as plans for a separate European decision-making structure and an independent WEU role in Eastern Europe were criticized as 'dangerous and unrealistic', and the criticism was presented in the form of official 'démarches' to all WEU governments (*Frankfurter Allgemeine Zeitung*, 9 April 1991, *Politiken*, 11 April 1991), causing some irritation in European capitals (*Financial Times*, 22 May 1991).

In the following months matters seemed to calm down, and following conciliatory contacts by Secretary Baker to EC foreign ministers in mid-April (*Financial Times*, 22 May 1991) an understanding seemed to have been reached. When German Foreign Minister Genscher visited Baker in May, their joint declaration noted that:

the United States is ready to support arrangements the European allies decide are needed for the expression of a common European foreign, security and defence policy.

Furthermore:

NATO should be the principal venue for consultation and the forum for agreement on all policies bearing on the security and defence commitments of its members ... ('US–German views on the New European and Trans-Atlantic Architecture' *US Department of State Dispatch*, May 1991).

These principles were reaffirmed when Kohl visited Washington later in May (*Financial Times*, 22 May 1991), and there were some indications that US–French differences had narrowed (*Le Monde*, 8 June 1991). At the NATO ministerial meeting in Copenhagen in June, language almost identical to the Baker–Genscher declaration was included in the final communiqué, but with a few noticeable alterations. For instance, the Copenhagen document states that the Alliance should be 'the *essential* forum for consultation' (and not the *principal* venue) and 'the venue for agreement *on policies*', (rather than *on all policies*) ('North Atlantic Council Texts, 7 June 1991, Final Communiqué', *US Department of State Dispatch*, 17 June 1991: 428). Such discrepancies may be symptomatic of the tensions still underlying the alliance, but the declaration still seemed to settle the matter: the US had accepted a European security and defence identity, including a role for the WEU, while the Europeans had affirmed their commitment to the centrality of NATO.

However, tension erupted anew when in October a German–French proposal for a WEU army corps was presented (*International Herald Tribune*, 22 October 1991). Again the American reaction was that this should not, in the words of Defense Secretary Cheney, 'detract from or undermine or erode the basic cohesion of NATO itself' (*International Herald Tribune*, 26–27 October, 1991). The WEU nations did not reach agreement on this proposal at their summit in Bonn in October (*Frankfurter Allgemeine Zeitung*, 30 and 31 October, 1991), and at NATO's Rome summit in November President Bush sent a strong signal to the Europeans urging them to end their ambiguity about NATO. Speaking outside his official script the President said: 'if your ultimate aim is to provide independently for your own defence, the time to tell us is today', and stated that 'the US could not abandon its place in Europe ... [It] was going to retain a sufficient force in Europe to defend its obligations and its national security interests' (*Financial Times*, 11 November 1991, *Nouvelles Atlantiques/Atlantic News* No. 2368, 9 November 1991). According to Baker, Bush' statement was not an ultimatum (*Financial Times*, 8 November 1991), but it clearly expressed serious American concerns.

The declaration adopted in Rome repeated the key sentences from the Copenhagen meeting, implying American acceptance of a WEU role and European support for continued American military presence in Europe and a commitment that NATO should remain essential ('Rome Declaration on Peace and Cooperation' Section 6, in *Nato Review*, 39, (6) December, 1991). When the EC leaders finally reached agreement on the plans for Economic and Political Union at Maastricht in December, the result was in accordance with American views: WEU would be the EC defence entity, and would be linked to NATO and with a common defence postponed into an uncertain future (*Treaty on the European Union*, Article J4; *International Herald Tribune*, 12 December 1991). This result, as we have already seen, met with a strong endorsement from the US.

Again the matter seemed to be settled, and when Bundespräsident Weizsäcker visited Bush in April 1992 the relationship was confirmed in a friendly atmosphere (*Frankfurter Allgemeine Zeitung*, 2 May 1992). On 21 May , however, outgoing NATO Ambassador Taft, addressing the CEPS in Brussels, urged the Europeans to bring France into NATO's military structure before they establish a common European defence (US Mission to NATO, 1992). The following day – perhaps coincidentally – Bonn and Paris, in direct contravention of the US position, made public their plans for the creation of a German–French army corps by 1995. This drew a negative American response, and serious concerns were voiced unofficially while the administration refrained from publicly criticizing an initiative it felt unable to prevent (*International Herald Tribune*, 19 and 23–24 May 1992; *Financial Times*, 27 May 1992). After extensive consultations, however, German Defence Minister Rühe confirmed in Washington that 'NATO is number one. WEU and the Euro-corps are complementary arrangements' (*Frankfurter Allgemeine Zeitung*, 4 July 1992). This seemed to imply US acceptance of the Euro-corps, albeit given reluctantly and in exchange for renewed affirmation of NATO's primacy. Still the issue was not settled. Discussions and negotiations apparently continued during autumn 1992 until the end of November when, arguably, a conclusion was reached, at least for the time being. France had now accepted that the French–German corps could operate under NATO command in accordance with an earlier British compromise proposal for a 'double-hatted' Euro-corps thus seemingly 'drawing France closer to the U.S.-led alliance' rather than developing an embryonic alternative to it (*International Herald Tribune*, 1 December 1992).

This development is not the result of American diplomatic efforts alone. The double-hatted solution also had support from Britain, Germany, and other European nations, but it seems clear that strong American pressure played a major role in bringing it about. Thus, a clear and consistent American policy is very much in evidence: the US has firmly expressed its intention to maintain a military presence in Europe, it has opposed the establishment of a separate military entity outside NATO's command structure, and has, on occasion, used diplomatic arm-twisting to block initiatives in that direction. The US welcomes a greater European contribution to the common defence, and it is not opposed to closer military cooperation among EC nations. Nevertheless, it strongly resists moves towards the creation of an integrated military command structure, backed up by regular training, joint exercises, etc. In other words, the US cannot accept an integrated European army that is not under NATO command.

How does one explain this? After all, elsewhere we have argued, as do the Americans, that a stronger Europe is good for the US. Why not here? Why would the US Ambassador to NATO insist that 'undermining the alliance's integrated military structure in the uncertain process of developing a European security identity would be the height of folly'? (US Mission to NATO, 1992). American behaviour may be interpreted in terms of the interests governing foreign policy.

We are dealing with a phenomenon that is strictly within the realm of power politics, what Morgenthau called 'political policy' (1973: 32). It pertains directly to the distribution of military capabilities in the international system. Consequently the obvious path is to interpret behaviour in this area in terms of realism. Military power has perhaps become less relevant, but to the extent that it still is relevant, and to the extent that we can treat this sphere as a specific one with some degree of autonomy, we must apply realist logic to activities within this sphere. According to Morgenthau: 'Whatever the ultimate aims of international politics, power is always the immediate aim' (1973: 27). The national interest aims for as strong a standing as possible in the global military power structure, and seeks to maintain international stability through a balance of power that is favourable to the nation's interests in a wider sense.

In this light, European stability is in America's interest for economic reasons and for political reasons, imprinted by the experience from two world wars. However, it is also in the American interest to maintain an international balance in which the US has the strongest possible standing.

One could argue that a new system based on a separate European military structure could also provide for international stability. Yet the transition period to such a system would be both prolonged and unpredictable, and therefore more uncertain than the status quo. After all, the Americans seem to have a valid point when they argue that it might take quite a while for the Europeans to develop the foreign policy consensus required to underpin a major international role (see also Well, 1991). A prolonged period of uncertainty entails the risk of instability. A crisis situation could emerge in which the EC, acting independently, became involved in a war which the Americans eventually would have to enter, without having had the option of trying to prevent the war.

An independent European system could also easily entail a reduction in US power globally. This is not because the modest European proposals would in themselves change much in America's standing, but because they open up a long-term perspective that could lead to profound changes. The proposals could be the beginning of a process that might result in the establishment of a military power on the European continent, equal to, but independent from, the US. The establishment of such a European power-bloc would fundamentally change the international correlation of forces and would mean the end of America's global military supremacy. Furthermore, according to the realist logic, the mere existence of separate powerful actors in the international system implies the possibility of competition and rivalry in the military sphere, i.e. the danger that an otherwise cooperative relationship could turn into a conflictual one. Hence, despite a solid base of shared interests and values and a wide range of cooperative relationships, in the narrow sphere of power politics it is in the national interest to prevent even the preconditions for such a possibility to emerge. Even if the US has now had to accept, reluctantly, the establishment of an embryonic independent Euro-army, the US interest remains with the preservation of NATO as the primary defence structure for as long as possible.

According to this logic, then, a militarily divided Europe and a Western Europe firmly located within military structures under strong American influence is a better basis for US policy. Such an anchoring ensures a balance of power favourable to the US in terms of stability and in terms of US global power. Seen in this light, American resistance to a European military structure and serious concerns about the future of NATO are neither irrational nor inconsistent.

In support of this interpretation, we can point to several indications of the presence of realist thinking in the US foreign policy establishment. In 1987 the Reagan administration declared that one of the 'major objectives' of US national security strategy was 'to prevent the domination of the Eurasian landmass by the USSR (*or any other hostile power or coalition of powers)*' (US President, 1987, quoted from *USIS Newsfile* 01/28/87, my emphasis). A year later the argument ran: '... the United States' most basic national security interests would be endangered if a hostile state or group of states were to dominate the Eurasian landmass – that area of the globe often referred to as the world's heartland' (US President, 1988). There is no mistaking of the influence of the geopolitical tradition here. In 1990 a new twist was added: '... for most of this century, the United States has deemed it a vital interest to prevent any hostile power or group of powers from dominating the Eurasian landmass. This interest remains' (US President, 1990: 1). Listen also to James Baker, speaking to the National Committee on American Foreign Policy upon receiving the annual Hans J. Morgenthau Memorial Award in May 1990:

> The visible reduction in the Soviet threat has lead some to assume that our only reason for being in Europe over the last 40 years was to contain that threat. Beyond containment, in their view, lies the end of the American role. ... This would be the most profound and strategic mistake of the generation. We must leave not only the Cold War behind but also the conflicts that preceded the Cold War. The reduction of the Soviet threat need not cause Europe to revert to an unsteady balance of power or a fresh outbreak of national rivalries and ethnic tension (Secretary Baker, 'The

Common European Interest: America and the New Politics Among Nations', *US Department of State Dispatch*, 3 September 1990).

Finally, in early 1992 a furore was created when a draft Pentagon Defense Planning Guide was leaked to the press. According to this document, the US should 'convince potential competitors that they need not aspire to a greater role or pursue a more aggressive posture to protect their legitimate interests', and the US 'must sufficiently account for the interests of the advanced industrial nations to discourage them from challenging our leadership or seeking to overturn the established political and economic order' (*International Herald Tribune*, 9 March 1992). Although the draft was quickly withdrawn for revision, it is still evidence that thinking along realist lines is present in the American foreign policy establishment.

Such indications lend added support to the realist interpretation of this aspect of US foreign policy. In the present context, however, the main argument is that it makes sense theoretically (for a similar interpretation of US interests see Mead, 1989: 56). The pattern observed in US policy behaviour towards European integration in the military and defence fields is clearly explainable as a consistent pursuit of national interests.

Conclusion

We have argued that the Bush administration's policy toward European integration has been a fairly consistent pursuit of national interests in terms of wealth and power.

The main features of American policy were to endorse European unification; to elevate the EC's diplomatic ranking and to deal with it as an international actor in so far as it behaves like one; to influence EC policy making as effectively as possible when American interests are touched; to accept the internal market and the prospects of EMU while opposing protectionism and those macro-economic policies considered contrary to American interests; and to support the development of a European defence identity while firmly opposing (but not quite successfully) steps towards a separate European military structure outside the NATO framework.

These actions were interpreted as a rational pursuit of American interests. The internal market is good for the US economy as long as it does not turn protectionist; the possible effects of EMU are uncertain, but even if the negative outweighed the positive, the risks and costs involved in opposing it would be of much greater magnitude. US economic interests are better served by developing a cooperative relationship with the emerging European actor. In the defence field it was argued, along realist lines, that a stronger, more unified Europe is in accordance with American interests, since the global power of the US depends on the strength of its allies. Yet an independent and separate European military capacity implies serious risks in terms of uncertainty and potential instability and in terms of potential changes in the overall power structure to the detriment of America's international standing.

This difference, between the mainly favourable reaction to economic and political integration and the strongly negative response to some initiatives in the defence area, lies at the core of the apparent contradiction or confusion in US policy. However, these responses are logical components of a differentiated policy relating to separate dimensions of the integration process.

The essence of the argument is that America's interest is to have stronger allies, but that the stress is on *allies* as much as on *stronger*. Furthering integration and preserving the alliance are of equal importance. In the economic field, shared interests in a strongly internationalized and interdependent world economy mean that European unification poses little potential risk to future cooperation. The dynamics of the market help ensure the persistence and ongoing renewal of the cooperative relationship. Only a European adoption of a much more protectionist stance would entail such a risk, and this event is unlikely due to Europe's own interest. In the military sphere, the situation is different. Shared interests are based on a different dynamic and depend much more on their being embodied in organized structures that can be changed by political decisions. Consequently the US must be much more cautious when European nations take steps that might alter the political structure of the Atlantic relationship.

Notes

1. Research for this chapter was supported by the Danish Social Science Research Council. I am indebted to US Government officials in Washington and Brussels and Congressional staffers for providing information and background, and to the US Information Service in Copenhagen and Washington for assistance. An earlier version was presented to the ECPR Standing Group on International Relations, Inaugural Pan-European Conference, 16–20 September 1992, Heidelberg.

2. This and the following remarks are based on interviews with American officials in Washington, April–May 1991 and Brussels, May 1992.

3. I have no exact indication of the magnitude of this increase, but several US officials have stated that it is significant.

4. The following argument is based on my own reasoning, but it is informed by interviews with US officials, who supported my interpretation on many points and said nothing to contradict it.

References

Calingaert, Michael (1990) *The 1992 Challenge from Europe: Development of the European Community's Internal Market* (Revised Edition) Washington D.C.: National Planning Association.

Deibel, Terry L. (1991) 'Bush's Foreign Policy: Mastery and Inaction', *Foreign Policy* 84: 3–23.

George and Keohane (1975) 'The Concept of National Interests: Uses and Limitations', in *Commission on the Organization of Foreign Policy, Appendices*, vol. 2, Washington D.C., GPO, pp. 64–74.

Gilpin, Robert (1981) *War and Change in World Politics*, Cambridge: Cambridge University Press.

Gilpin, Robert (1987) *The Political Economy of International Relations*, Princeton:

Princeton University Press.
Hamilton, Edward K. (ed.) (1989) *America's Global Interests. A New Agenda*, New York: W.W. Norton.
Hunt, Michael H. (1987) *Ideology and U.S. Foreign Policy*, New Haven: Yale University Press.
Huntington, Samuel P. (1981) *American Politics: The Promise of Disharmony*, Cambridge, Mass.: The Belknap Press.
Kegley and Wittkopf (1987) *American Foreign Policy. Pattern and Process* (third edition), Basingstoke: Macmillan.
Keohane, Robert O. (1984) *After Hegemony*, Princeton: Princeton University Press.
Kolko, Gabriel (1964) *The Roots of American Foreign Policy*, Boston: Beacon Press.
Krasner, Stephen D. (1978) *Defending the National Interest*, Princeton: Princeton University Press.
Krenzler, Horst G. and Kaiser, Wolfram (1991) 'Die Transatlantische Erklärung: Neue Grundlage für das Verhältnis von EG und USA', *Aussenpolitik*, IV 1991, pp. 363–72.
Mead, Walter Russel (1989) 'The United States and the New Europe', *World Policy Journal*, VII (1): 35–70.
Morgenthau, Hans J. (1973) *Politics Among Nations* (fifth edition), New York: Alfred A. Knopf.
Nau, Henry (1990) *The Myth of America's Decline. Leading the World Economy into the 1990s*, New York: Oxford University Press.
Nye, Joseph (1990) *Bound to Lead*, New York: Basic Books.
Ougaard, Morten (1990) *Magt of interesser i den globale samfundsformation*, Aarhus: Aarhus University Press.
Ougaard, Morten (1988) 'Dimensions of Hegemony', *Cooperation and Conflict*, 23: 197–214.
Ougaard, Morten (1992) 'The US State in the New Global Context', *Cooperation and Conflict*, 27: 131–62.
Overseas Development Council (1992) *The North American Free Trade Agreement*, Policy Focus 1992, no. 2.
Petras, James and Morris M. Morley (1981) 'The U.S. Imperial State', in Petras *et al.*, *Class, State and Power in the Third World*, London: Zed Books 1981.
Schlesinger, Arthur M. (1986) *The Cycles of American History*, Boston: Houghton Mifflin.
Smith, Michael (1992) 'The Devil You Know': the United States and a Changing European Community', *International Affairs*, 68 (1): 103–120.
Strange, Susan (1984) 'What about International Relations?', in Strange (ed.), *Paths to International Political Economy*, London: Allen & Unwin.
Strange, Susan (1988) *States and Markets*, London: Pinter Publishers.
US Congress, Congressional Budget Office (1990) *How the Economic Transformations in Europe Will Affect the United States*, Washington D.C.
US Department of Commerce, ITA (1989) *EC 1992: A Commerce Department Analysis of European Community Directives*, vols 1–3, Washington D.C.
US Department of State, *American Foreign Policy Documents*.
US Department of State Dispatch.
US Information Agency, *Newsfile*.
US Information Agency, *PDQ Index & Text Database*.
US Mission to NATO, Ambassador William H. Taft, IV, '*The NATO Role in Europe and the U.S. Role in NATO*', presented to the Centre for European Policy Studies, Brussels, 21 May 1992.
US Mission to the EC, Office of Public Affairs (1990) *Declaration on US–EC Relations*.

US President (1987, 1988, 1990, 1991) *National Security Strategy of the United States*, The White House, January 1987, January 1988, March 1990, August 1991.

Waltz, Kenneth (1979) *Theory of International Relations*, Reading Pa: Addison Wesley.

Well, Günther van (1991) 'Die europäische Einigung und die USA', *Europa-Archiv*, 18: 527–36.

Williams, William Appleman (1972) *The Tragedy of American Diplomacy* (2nd revised edition), New York: Dell Publishing Co.

Conclusion: the Community as an International Actor

OLE NØRGAARD, THOMAS PEDERSEN AND NIKOLAJ PETERSEN

The analyses in this book have served to demonstrate the diversity of the external relationships of the European Community. Relationships vary with respect to their closeness, their degree of reciprocity, and their content. Some are highly political in nature, while others are mainly economic. In some relationships the Community is absolutely dominant, while in others it is equal or even inferior. Some relationships are very close, while others are more detached.

Roughly, the EC's external relationships can be divided into three main spheres, each with their own specific characteristics and internal variation: (1) relations with the rest of Europe, (2) relations with the Third World, and (3) relations with the United States and Japan.

European relations are presently organized as an asymmetrical two-tier system which clearly differentiates between members of the Community in the centre and non-members in the periphery. The second tier, however, has different types of affiliation with the EC, as reflected in the notion of a Europe of 'concentric circles'. Since 1985, the Community has moved to the European centre stage, both through its own internal dynamics, and by virtue of the breakdown of its main competitor in Europe, the Soviet Union. In this process, the perceptions and expectations of European non-members have been increasingly focused on the Community, and for most of them their relationship with the EC has become of overriding national concern. Most European countries outside the Community have expressed their determination to become members as soon as possible. What differentiates these states is therefore not so much their ambitions *vis-à-vis* the Community, but rather their chances of being accepted by it.

In this respect, a clear hierarchy has emerged. The inner circle consists of those EFTA countries which have recently signed the EEA Agreement and which will obtain entry to the Community proper in the foreseeable future; next come the Visegrad countries, recent signatories to Europe Agreements with the Community, who will probably become its first Central and East European members; in the third, less ordered layer, are the

Balkan and the Baltic states, with much smaller prospects of joining; finally, the states of the CIS stand in an even less clearly defined relationship to the Community. As Russia cannot realistically be viewed as a possible member of the Community, and as the Community has not seen fit to develop its contacts with other republics, such as Belarus or the Ukraine, for example, any further than its relations with Russia, relations with the CIS republics will probably remain qualitatively different from relations with other European states.

While the present two-tier Europe may develop into a single institutionalized space in which the EFTA and Central and East European countries will find their place, the Community will probably have to find a special formula for its relationships with the CIS republics. Both processes will require a considerable capacity to act on the part of the Community.

With the Third World community, the scope of relations differs among the Maghreb, the Lomé countries (which now include most Third World countries) and non-associated states like India and Brazil. Whatever the specific relationship, the EC is rapidly rising in importance as a trading partner and also as a political interlocutor after the disappearance of the Soviet Union as the major counterweight to the United States. The power vacuum has given rise to a strongly asymmetrical relationship. Except for the Maghreb, which because of geographical proximity and population pressure has some political assets, the developing countries as a whole have very little influence vis-à-vis the Community. On the other hand, with the demise of the Cold War, the Community will certainly have a greater role to play as a global organizer.

Europe's place in the 'strategic triangle' with the United States and Japan is of a different character. First, the United States is still the dominant partner whose links to both Europe and Japan are stronger than the Japanese–European relationship. Second, the United States still dominates the triangle by its superiority in each of the bilateral relations. Europe's ability to control is therefore limited; Europe is clearly inferior to the United States, and in important respects also to Japan. At the same time, the triangle is probably going to change in the future because of the relative decline of the United States. Europe will become more important, and as relations become more adversarial, their maintenance and development will require increasing attention and resources on the part of the Community.

These likely developments in the Community's external relationships raise the question of whether it will have the necessary actor capability to attend to its interests and to live up to increasing expectations to its higher-profiled international role.

There are various ways of coming to grips with this question. One method would be to evaluate the self-professed goals of the Union, a second approach would be to measure the performance of the Union against some ideal concept of an international actor. Within this second approach we may distinguish between a definition of an international actor as a political unit with state-like properties – the approach adopted by federalist theories – and a less demanding definition which posits a number of basic structural prerequisites for actor capability (cf. Sjöstedt, 1976).

Assessing the Community's external dimension by making a comparison with its stated goals raises a major problem: the Community has not formulated its official goals in very specific terms. The term 'European Union' is sufficiently vague to be able to bridge the distance between a federal-style polity and a unique type of confederation. The Maastricht Treaty, while not using the term 'federal', essentially defers the choice between the two goals. The Maastricht Treaty is therefore not incompatible with a subsequent development of the Union into a more explicitly federal direction (Laursen and Vanhoonacker, 1992). In fact, the decision to review the provisions in the second pillar in 1996 was made precisely with a view to deepening integration in the foreign policy area. When reflecting on the history of European unification, one observes a remarkable continuity in the plans for closer supranational integration which have been tabled over the years by forces in the six original member states. A recurring theme in these plans has been a wish to create a 'political Europe' possessing a common currency and a common foreign and security policy. These actions suggest that it may be pertinent to use federalist theory in assessing the evolving EC system, especially since Bulmer has pointed out that there exists a wide spectrum of federal-type systems with a range of possible power balances between levels (Bulmer, 1991).

Duchacek (1970) is one of the few analysts of federalism to have formulated systematic criteria for a federal system. According to Duchacek, exclusive control of foreign policy is a typical feature of a federation. Does the Community after Maastricht have exclusive control of foreign policy? It clearly does not. Especially in terms of the control of the central institutions, the Union in the making is not federal. However, as Nikolaj Petersen has stressed, the scope of the Community's foreign policy competence has been significantly extended with the inclusion of all aspects of foreign and security policy. Nor should it be overlooked that the provisions in the Maastricht Treaty on foreign policy impose new and more binding obligations on member states. The concept of 'common action' is particularly important: in the designated common action areas, the Union will in fact have control of foreign policy formulation, though without being able to impose sanctions on governments violating the new obligations.

Federalist literature contains another proposition which may help to elucidate the functioning of the Community's Common Foreign and Security Policy. Alexander Hamilton argued in The Federalist Papers (1987 [1788]) that federal states are more democratic and stable than small unitary states, his argument being that extremist 'factions' may more easily gain control of single states than of a huge multi-state federation, in which there will be extensive balancing of interests and ideological views. Now, given the fact that state autonomy is always likely to be high in a European federal-style polity, it is reasonable to assume that decision making within such a Union will involve a high degree of unanimity and a high degree of internal balancing. A common European foreign policy may well entail a rather inactive external policy stance, but inaction should not be viewed solely in negative terms. It would also imply a degree of neutralization of extremes. A similar point is made by Wessels and Weiler (1988), who argue that '... the vice of inaction may in fact be seen as a virtue'.

A different perspective on the Community's external role is provided by Sjöstedt's concept of actor capability. Sjöstedt (1976) argues that the decisive criterion when trying to assess whether or not a unit is an international actor is its possession of actor capability. Actor capability is a measure of a unit's capacity to behave actively and deliberately in relation to other actors in the international system. The structural prerequisites of actor capability are: a) a community of interests, b) a decision-making system, c) a system for crisis management, d) a system for the management of interdependence, e) a system of implementation, f) external communication channels and external representation, and g) resources and a mobilization system.

Now, how does the post-Maastricht Community measure up to this standard? The community of interests is not directly and immediately affected by the Treaty, but the new common policies, notably the EMU and the regional redistribution scheme, will serve to tie member states closer together thus creating new common interests. Geographical widening may increase heterogeneity and pave the way for a more variable integration model. Nevertheless, Thomas Pedersen argues that the difficulties may not be as great as often assumed, at least not in the case of the EFTA countries. The decision-making system of the Community has generally been made more efficient by the Maastricht Treaty, although majority voting will probably only be used very rarely in the foreign policy field. As far as crisis management and the management of interdependence are concerned, the Community presently has a rather weak capability, a state of affairs not likely to be changed by institutional reforms. However, two decisions made in Maastricht could prove significant. The first is the decision to give the Commission a non-exclusive right to initiate foreign and security policy; this will most likely improve joint analysis and planning. Second, the decision to create a single administrative structure for both external economic and political affairs will undoubtedly improve policy coordination. Implementation in external relations remains weak, but the possibility of imposing sanctions on member governments who, for instance, violate external trade policy decisions, could prove important. As already mentioned, compliance with common foreign policy positions also appears set to improve in the future. The chapters in this volume document the expansion in the Community's external channels of communication, and third countries have responded to 'Europe 1992' by upgrading the diplomatic status of the Community. Apart from that, enlargement inevitably adds to the Community's diplomatic network. External representation remains, on the other hand, a sore point. There is still no common EC representation in the UN Security Council, and the institution of the Presidency, already imperfect because of the lack of continuity, will come under growing stress in the coming years as the Union's membership increases. Community resources in external relations are not directly affected by the Maastricht Treaty. However, in justifying its demand for a doubling of the EC's financial resources for external relations, the Commission has referred to the new obligations following from the Maastricht Treaty. Moreover, one of the potential benefits of EMU is that it will place at the Community's disposal the powerful weapon of exchange rate policy. Additional resources will thus be mobilized behind the Community's external policy. Indeed, as pointed out by Morten Ougaard, the external implications of EMU provide one reason why sections of the American elite are anxious about the emerging European Union.

As the analyses in this volume demonstrate, the growth of the Community's external relations is due mainly to three processes: spill-over, externalization and response to external changes.

Spill-over processes have mainly been active in the grand policy sequence from the Internal Market via the Economic and Monetary Union (EMU) to the Political Union, an important aspect of which is the formation of the Common Foreign and Security Policy (CFSP). This is not to be conceived as an automatic process, as the early neo-functionalists believed, but rather, as a political or cultivated kind of spill-over in the form of governments' explicit linkage between economic and political integration. Concretely, the German demand for a *quid pro quo* for the EMU created the foundation for the CFSP and hence helped spawn efforts to give the Community a larger international role.

Externalization, as conceived by Schmitter (1969), speficies a more direct link between the internal and external aspects of European integration by stipulating a mutually reinforcing relationship between internal reforms and external responses. The formation of the Internal Market has raised expectations (and fears) outside the Community which have led the Community to formulate a more coordinated economic and political posture towards its environment. Likewise, the future formulation of common actions towards individual countries and regions is likely to lead to responses which may reinforce (but in certain instances also weaken) the original policy.

The simplest explanation of the evolving relationship between the Community and its external environment, though, is a stimulus-response model. The external environment of the Community has changed dramatically during the last decade and has forced the Community to come up with relevant responses. Again, not all changes are equally conducive to the growth of the Community's actor capability. More than anything else, the unification of Germany provoked the Political Union and the creation of the CFSP. On the other hand, Yugoslavia is a vivid illustration of the difficulties involved, as Knud Erik Jørgensen's analysis shows. The main impact of external change, however, has been to strengthen the Community's actor capability. As the Community's external environment shows every sign of remaining dynamic, if not volatile, in the foreseeable future, we should expect to see strong stimuli for policy concertation to emanate from it, as well as numerous impediments and obstacles.

Developments in the Community's actor capability also depend on general trends in international relations. To the extent that economic and diplomatic power has in recent years achieved a greater role in determining policy outcomes, this adds to Europe's capacity to influence international affairs. Besides, in order to influence world affairs, an actor does not necessarily have to possess tangible instruments of leverage. Allen and

Smith have argued convincingly that the Community has an important role to play by example rather than by leadership (Allen and Smith, 1992: 27), a point substantiated by Ole Nørgaard in this volume. Another example of the Community's normative 'model effect' is the emulation of the EC by, for example, the *Mercosur* countries in Latin America and the Community's attempt to foster regional cooperation in various parts of the Third World (see Regelsberger and Edwards, 1990 and J.D. Pedersen in this volume).

A final important consideration is how a European Union, if successfully developed, will affect international relations and international stability. As shown by Peter Nedergaard, Clemens Stubbe Østergaard and Jørgen Dige Pedersen, economic tripolarity is already a reality. In the post-Cold War era, economic rivalry is not contained by security dependence. Transcontinental linkages at micro-level serve to counterbalance pressures for the formation of political blocs to underpin trade rivalry, as shown by Morten Ougaard in the case of the US–EC relationship, but TNCs appear to be increasingly regionalist in their investment strategies. Geographical enlargement and the internal restructuring in the Union in the wake of the modernization of Central and Eastern Europe and of Russia will provide new incentives for protectionism, while at the same time lowering the costs of adopting such a posture. The global political context in which a strong political Europe would have to find its place remains unclear. Japan is still not a global political actor but may well become one in the years ahead, whereas China seems to be economically as well as politically ascendant, though its international role will hardly change quickly. Russia will probably recover as a political power of the first order despite its serious economic problems. In the immediate future, however, Russia will remain absorbed by internal modernization. This suggests that in the short term the global power structure will be mainly unipolar, with the US playing a central role in a reinforced UN. In the medium term, a European–American condominium or a new tripolarity look more likely. Europe may well become the second pillar in the international system, but it is unclear whether a stronger Europe will be compatible with a continuing harmonious relationship across the Atlantic, especially in view of the negative externalization effects of the economic expansion of the Union. Given the continuing introversion of China, the primary candidate for the role of third pole is probably Japan. It would be unwise to discount Russia. A crucial factor will be whether the new Russia is included in a partnership with the European Union or opts for a more independent assertive role. Fortunately, the Community is at present regarded more as a model than as a threat by the leadership in Moscow.

References

Allen, D. and M. Smith (1990) 'Western Europe's Presence in the Contemporary International Arena', *Review of International Studies*, 16: 19–37.

Bulmer, Simon (1991) 'Analysing European Political Cooperation: the Case for Two-tier Analysis', in Martin Holland (ed.) *The Future of European Political Cooperation*, London: Macmillan.

Duchacek, Ivo (1970) *Comparative Federalism*, New York: Holt, Rinehart and Winston.

Madison, James, Alexander Hamilton and John Jay (1987 [1788]) *The Federalist Papers*, London: Penguin Books.

Laursen, F. and S. Vanhoonacker (1992) *The Intergovernmental Conference on Political Union*, Maastricht: EIPA.

Regelsberger, E. and G. Edwards (eds) (1990) *Europe's Global Links*, London: Pinter.

Schmitter, Philippe (1969) 'Three Neo-Functional Hypotheses about International Integration', *International Organization*, 23: 161–6.

Sjöstedt, Gunnar (1976) *The External Role of the European Community*, London: Saxon House.

Wessels, W. and J. Weiler (1988) 'EPC and the Challenge of Theory', in A. Pijpers, E. Regelsberger and W. Wessels (1988) *European Political Cooperation in the 1980s*, Dordrecht and London: Martinus Nijhoff Publishers.

Index

Page numbers in **bold** type refer to **figures**, page numbers in *italic* type refer to *tables*, page numbers followed by 'n' refer to notes e.g. 49[n2] refers to page 49, note 2. Abbreviations are used as in the text